THE GREAT WAR
1914–1918

MARC FERRO
THE GREAT WAR
1914-1918

MILITARY HERITAGE PRESS

New York

MARC FERRO
THE GREAT WAR 1914-1918

MILITARY HERITAGE PRESS

New York

This edition published by Military Heritage Press,
a division of Marboro Books Corporation,
by arrangement with Routledge
1989 Military Heritage Press

ISBN 0-88029-449-3

Printed in the United States of America

M 9 8 7 6 5 4 3 2 1

For Éric and Isabelle

Contents

Contents

Maps

Tables

Translator's note

I have tried to convey in this translation the individual flavour of Marc Ferro's original French, sometimes clarifying phrases which make sound sense in French, but less in English. This edition incorporates corrections to the French and Italian editions, as well as some new material produced by M. Ferro for this English version, and the bibliography notes English translations of books he cited in French translation or their original language.

N.S.

Introduction

The Great War was long, painful and murderous. Millions of men, who on its eve had been swearing 'war on war', slaughtered each other. They became brothers-in-arms of men they had accused of militarism, chauvinism and war-mongering: millions more went to war simply because it was their duty, without ever quite knowing why. After 1918 ex-servicemen of both types had no doubts about why they had fought: they had sacrificed themselves for their country in a just war, and they hold that view to this day. But during the war, some of them had doubts. What did the war mean? Was the horrible slaughter necessary? Governments assured them that it was; but were governments sincere?

In 1914 there were no doubts. They marched off to war, their faces a picture of delight. Film is of course deceptive and a more searching examination would show other images – the anguish of a father, a fiancé, or a husband. But these were fleeting impressions and these painful reactions did not last, in striking contrast to the mobilization of 1939, when, except perhaps in Germany, the soldiers' faces showed shock and despair. In 1914 they had no doubts that the war would be short, that they would be home by Christmas crowned with victory. In Paris, London and Berlin they left singing and exuberant, 'with flowers on their rifles'. This elation is a factor in the origins of the war and of its after-taste, and deserves as much stress as the more strictly economic or political causes. There are many such unanswered questions. What were people's aspirations before the war? How could societies both want peace and leave light-heartedly for war? What was the nature of patriotism? What economic or political forces governed states and nations? How did those people who opposed war suddenly find themselves without the means to resist it?

Part I

Chapter 1

War, the liberator

In the two generations before the war, to an extent greater than ever before, distances had shrunk and the world in effect had become smaller. Since 1840 commerce had grown apace and the growth of empires had strengthened the mutual ties which bound east and west. European society did not understand the process but soon felt its effects. Other changes were also becoming apparent. For example, the recognized, traditional authorities of monarch, priest, law, family, boss or officer now had added to them new, uncontrolled and anonymous masters, those forces responsible for the brutal depression of European agriculture and the ruin of the European countryside, and for the vagaries of the business cycle. It was these same hidden powers which made and unmade fashions and manipulated public opinion. In this strange, changing world traditional patterns of life no longer had any meaning. Skills were developed and made redundant in the space of a generation. Patents and inventions were created, had a brief flowering, and were superseded by the next technical advance. Some business enterprises grew and prospered, others went to the wall. Everything was done in the name of law, progress or liberty.

There was one clear link between the traditional pattern of oppression and this new form: the growing army of bureaucrats. It provided for the new secular states the strong support which the Church had given to the old system; it protected the holders of property from the poor. Sometimes, indeed, it acted together with the clergy, a development regarded with little affection by the masses. In Germany in 1870 there were 825 inhabitants to every bureaucrat: in 1905, there were 216. Everywhere, as in Chekhov's Russia, the bureaucrats waxed and multiplied. Just before the war one in eleven French electors was a functionary of the state. The link with the old oppressors was reinforced by the fact that the top rank of this new class was composed almost entirely of nobles in Germany, and even in the French republic, the praefectoral corps included eighty-eight former peers; a similar proportion occurred among the councillors of state and ambassadors of the republic.

This had a twofold effect. On the one hand, the old ruling class, thus metamorphosed, managed to maintain itself in power. More and more citizens lower down the social scale were employed by the state, each with his small share of authority. Still others, their futures assured by a pension, swelled the ranks of the conservatives, particularly in the large and growing cities. On the other hand discontent grew among all those whose future was uncertain, those groups which had no part in managing collective affairs. These were particularly numerous in those same cities where they congregated following the depression in agriculture. They counted as inferiors in the cities; they gathered in the suburban belts of Paris or Milan, Berlin or St Petersburg.

The mass of twentieth-century men were outside public affairs. They were prisoners in a universe whose mechanism was a mystery, despite the schools' propagation of science and progress. Democratization of institutions in the previous years had been largely illusory and reform did little to alter this. Reform did result in an overall improvement in living conditions, of material objects, education, and sanitation. Reform also occupied and stimulated the educated classes, as well as enriching them and strengthening their grip on society. But in itself reform did not enable the lower classes to take control of their own affairs. The cheering that greeted the newly elected *zemstvo* members in Russia meant much the same as the *hoch* or *hurrah* to representatives of the people further west: it marked the end of the electors' political activity for years to come, until the next election.

Town and country were now in the same situation. Previously towns had been 'free' and the country 'imprisoned'. In the early twentieth century the townsman no longer took any real part in the affairs of state, province, or community. He had rejoined the peasant in a common impotence. But a peasant could at least spend his time as he liked, a remnant of liberty that left him more initiative than the worker; although when economic crisis struck the countryside had a diminishing area of autonomy and increasingly depended on the town, where decisions were made. There the countryman could see, disguised as senior bureaucrat and acting in the name of the law, the face, at once loved, feared and hated, of his old master. Here was a tyranny harder to bear than that of previous times – *the good old days*. Some of its victims, recognizing the evil for what it was, sought escape. Among intellectuals there were some who sought help in religion, a movement seen in some countries as the century opened – the names Péguy, Solovev, Bergson showing the rebirth of mysticism. As Georges Sorel wrote, in *L'Evolution créatrice* (1907), 'men rejoice at the idea of an omnipotent deity'.

But some people were not so fortunate: their desire to escape was exploited by the press, and between the years 1880 and 1913 every country saw a significant emergence of 'non-political' newspapers – the *Daily Mail* in England, *Tägliche Rundschau* in Germany, *Le Petit Parisien* in France, *Novoe Vremya* in Russia. However, religion, drink, card-playing or reading titbits was not everybody's answer, and beyond such solutions they had two choices – flight or revolt, revolution or emigration. From the Urals to the Abruzzi and Land's End discontent, poverty, racial or political persecution drove thirty million Europeans over the Atlantic. There they discovered that if they were ready for any effort, they could break away from their past and go forward to a new life. British, Germans and Scandinavians set the example; Slavs and Italians followed. Not many returned – it would have been a sign of failure, a confession of bankruptcy.

The revolutionary way was chosen by other men, also optimists, but having a different perspective. Some of them, resenting all forms of oppression, sought anarchy, the abolition of all authority; others dreamt of a world without fear, where men could safely build their own futures. Socialism or communism was advocated, rigorous explanations offered of the way capitalist economies functioned. Marxists were sure they had discovered the 'laws', convinced that their way alone had a scientific value.

The revolutionaries were a minority in this sleeping world; they hoped to awaken the working classes and the oppressed in general. But none of them, except the anarchists, appreciated that in establishing trade unions and political parties, in founding the International, they were perpetuating the governing–governed relationship in a different form. Besides, even in the revolutionary groups and parties, the relationship kept its class character. The anarchist, Kropotkin, was a prince and was treated as such; Lenin, son of a high civil servant, had very respectful treatment from the Tsarist police. Of 110 social democrat deputies in the Reichstag, only two were former workers, and even this symbolic representation was lacking in the French Chamber in 1914 – a step back from February 1848. There was not a single workman among the leaders of Russian social democracy. It was a command-structure: sympathizers obeyed members, members militants, militants their 'leaders'. In 1902

Lenin, appreciating that the revolutionary movement was bankrupt, decided to set up his future party on army lines, with a highly centralized staff – and, for revolution to succeed, workers must be used as troops. They might be educated, lucid, politically free; just the same they were to go on obeying the men who did their thinking for them. The success of *What is to be done?* shows an outlook and a style; leaders of other political groups, particularly social democrats, were indignant, but in Russia, as elsewhere, they too manipulated militants and electors just as staffs manipulated troops or churches their faithful; and they did not even have the excuse of wanting to carry out a total proletarian revolution.

Above all, leaders of the extremist parties did not see that if their support grew it was because society was in the process of transformation, of evolving, into a new and different form – which lessened the chances of a real revolutionary situation. Between 1890 and 1914 it was not England, France or Germany, the first countries to undergo capitalist development, that saw rising possibilities of violent social upheaval, but Russia. Her economic backwardness was reflected in the political sphere by the weakness of her middle class, incapable of neutralizing the activities of the lower classes who wanted a total transformation of society. Italy too was a strong possibility in 1914; but here the American mirage was more powerful than elsewhere, and deprived the revolutionary movement of its future soldiers, the most dynamic, active and enterprising elements; and there was a link between the two, emigration and revolution. The choice once made had to be adhered to, and there was no one more conformist, in the United States as elsewhere, than new immigrants who, with the exception of anarchists, regarded any criticism of their adopted country as sacrilege. For them America was liberty, justice, virtue; everything predisposed the newest elements of American society to become conservatives and rabid patriots. It was in America that anarchists were first executed in 1886. By a similar process any criticism became sacrilege, after 1917, in the motherland of revolution. Soviet Russia forbade emigration, seeing in it a sign of dissatisfaction.

In pre-war Europe social tensions had been slowly weakening for many years. The unemployed found work, and the security of the individual appeared certain. This was so in France, where there was never much emigration, and where the chances of social revolution declined after the experience of the Commune. England was the same, since the failure of Chartism. Early in the twentieth century there were increasingly powerful strikes, but few violent demonstrations; from then on it was mainly Irish and Scots who crossed the seas. The only open revolt in England was that of the suffragettes. In Germany, early in this century, men supposed that if social transformation came, it would do so peacefully, controlled by the social democrat command that would soon have a Reichstag majority. Emigration to America also dwindled once men could benefit from German prosperity. 1837 in England, 1871 in France and 1910 in Germany marked the zenith of these three countries' chances óf effective transformation of the social structure – all dates that shadow, though at some distance, the period of maximum economic development. It seems that the earlier industrial development comes, the less the chance of social revolution, the more aggressive imperialism becomes, and the more internal social antagonism abates. As a counter-proof, social tensions were strong in Russia and Italy, both last in the race to industrialize and both barely enriched by imperialism. Increasing departures for Siberia or America and increasing signs of revolt in both town and village show how men were refusing to submit. Here was the land of anarchism, of Bakunin and Malatesta. It was here, too, that opposition to the war touched society as a whole. Even before they had created communism and fascism, these two countries left their mark on the early twentieth century, the Russians by signing the peace of Brest-Litovsk, the Italians by crying 'farewell to arms' at Caporetto. It was only later that the two peoples were unanimous in fighting – when they saw the homeland in danger, invaded by foreign enemies: then war meant something. There was no equivocation for the British, French or Germans: for them, the war was waged to protect the national interest.

But there was more to it. The workers of 1914, going off to war, had found a substitute for revolutionary hopes. The most miserable, least conscious of them emerged from their social ghetto, reintegrated owing to the war, demobilized as far as revolution was concerned. Their very existence would be changed, as they had always secretly hoped. Conditions had been improving throughout Europe for them, but only slowly and not at equal speed for all classes. The business world in France underwent a virtual resurrection between 1900 and 1914 – the *Belle époque*. The real wages of workers almost doubled, for the most part, between 1900 and the war. At the same time, while the number of users of pawn-shops fell, the number of registered pledges had never been so high as on the eve of war. The diffusion of the press, the development of education, the growth of advertising created new material needs: for more varied food, a town suit, better crockery, or a bicycle. They opened up the possibility of a richer and more interesting, more worthwhile existence; to rise on the social ladder seemed an inalienable right. Already the Paris worker of the Faubourg Saint-Antoine or Belleville crossed the Bastille canal on Sundays; on the Grands Boulevards, respectably dressed, he would go to a café-concert, then the Opéra-Comique. From the Porte Saint-Martin to the Bourse was now no further than from the Bourse to the rue de la Paix, where financial speculators rubbed shoulders with the old notables. At all levels men were anxious to climb, and this was equally true in Berlin or London. Young men went off adventurously, glad to change their lives, to travel. They were successfully answering the call of duty, and were sure they would soon be back as victors.

Far from being an ordeal, the war liberated men's energies. It was enthusiastically received by most men of military age: in England, and later in the United States, where there was no conscription, there were a million volunteers. The behaviour of reservists going to the front is evidence enough: French, Germans, British – all on their mettle. The Russians, being older, were rather less spirited, the Italians were slower off the mark; their dreams were different – hopes of revolution, visions of America. But even in Russia there were few absentees on call-up; and in France, where the military authorities counted on 5–13 per cent refusal to attend, there was only 1·5 per cent. The international spirit is said to have gone bankrupt, socialists to have failed to stop the war, to have betrayed their oath. Contemporaries were struck by this. But men were sure this was false: in answering their country's call they carried out a patriotic and revolutionary duty. They felt their country had been wantonly attacked, that in going to war revolutionary-minded soldiers and their brothers-in-arms would be creating eternal peace. The utopian ideal of fighting a 'war to end war' inspired French soldiers. Pacifism and internationalism were fused with individualism and patriotism, a decidedly exceptional occurrence to be explained only by the peculiar nature of the war which, for all combatants, was a just one, a war for national defence – and in any case, one that was inevitable.

Chapter 2

Patriotic war

The French genius, a historian might morosely conclude, is not so much for arms as for civil war. Save for 1914, France had never known a long and truly patriotic war. She of all nations might most glorify arms, but history, recent and distant, shows that she fought no war that was not, sooner or later, cross-bred with civil war. 1939–45 is an obvious case in point, as are the Revolution and the Empire, Joan of Arc and the Burgundians, Henri IV, the League and the Richelieu epoch. Even in 1870 there was a group that, openly or secretly, wanted the government to be defeated. This was not true of 1914–18: then there was no 'Foreigner Party'.

There were of course opponents of war, but they did not advocate the enemy cause: they were rather pacifists, enemies of all governments if not of all wars. Jaurès for instance condemned only 'imperialist' wars, but felt national defence was legitimate; most people felt the same, even in Russia, where hatred of the autocracy was virtually universal. There was no element of 'defeatism', which, in 1914–18, meant not that discouraging pessimism that weakens national morale and thus leads to defeat, but rather an active will that the country should be defeated and thereby regenerated. In France, and later on in Italy, some clericals, detesting the régime and its secular tendency, hoped that 'divine retribution' would fall on their 'errant fatherland'. But there were not many such. On the other hand, extreme socialists such as Lenin felt in 1914 that nothing would be more calamitous for proletarian revolution than a military victory of the Tsar's or the Kaiser's armies; they must therefore work for their own country's defeat. This stand was universally disliked, and they had to give it up for an international, pacifist one that meant changing European war into civil war. The fragile barrier of the International collapsed on the first sound of the trumpet – in Russia, France and throughout Europe. Frenchmen and Germans alike saw the war as a clear struggle for right, as self-evidently justified as a crusade, defence of family, or faith, or class. No argument could overcome this collective instinct. The two

9

coalitions' world-wide conflict had its origins, of course, in imperialist rivalry. But the particular conflicts of one nation with another obeyed other imperatives, a tradition that had its roots in the depths of collective consciousness. Each people felt its very existence threatened by the hereditary enemy. The war thus became for all a kind of fatal rite, and hence its deadly character, a feature that reference to imperialism alone does not explain.

The peoples derived these passions from a long history. But patriotic unity was of more recent origin. For half a century increasing geographical concentration of industry, of capitalist development, had created general economic conditions that the pre-industrial era had not known. The laws of 1846 affected the whole of British agriculture, the agreements of 1860 the whole of French industry. In the preceding three decades French economic growth had been badly affected by the European agricultural crisis, caused in part by imports from the newly exploited overseas countries, Canada or Australia. In Europe each people felt victimized, surrounded by enemies who were after its goods, its growth, even its existence. Patriotism was one way in which society reacted to the world's economic unification. Nationality movements were one variant of this tendency, and not exclusively linked to racial or religious persecution. The connection is still more apparent when patriotism is associated with the revival of regionalism. In Russia economic development resulted in colonists' penetration throughout the Empire, whose presence, as a foreign body, was all the more noteworthy beyond old Russia as the resources of the Ukraine, or the Trans-Siberian, were exploited. They increased in number – populating and administering peripheral areas they had once merely supervised. Their presence, and the russification policy associated with it, were taken as a hostile act and national movements grew up in vigorous reaction to it: not only among peoples such as Balts or Finns who had never felt Russian, but also among Ukrainians, Little Russians, Mordvinians, Mari and others.

Between forcing Ukrainians to talk Russian and forbidding French schoolchildren to talk dialects there was only a difference of degree, as was the case between the russification of St Petersburg bureaucrats and the centralization of those in Berlin or Paris. The Provençal or Breton revival – the first Inter-Celtic conference was held in 1877 – the survival of 'the southern question' and still more the Sicilian problem in Italy all showed the same tendency: patriotism, but patriotism dissociated from the present. Yet national unity was more strengthened than disrupted by these functionaries from Paris or Berlin or St Petersburg; centralization meant also attack on feudal survivals, defence against the foreigner. The means at their disposal were greater than before, and this led men to suppose that institutions were being democratized. The state became more powerful, but people in 1914 felt that they were now irreversibly free, that democracy could be guaranteed by legal modification and improvement of the social and political order. Men did not appreciate that the ruling classes had merely perfected their religion. The original catechism was now supplemented by another, taught in schools and repeated in the press; for thirty years the rise of education, the rebirth of sport, the dominance of the press produced increasing national faith.

After 1880 education, already widely extended in England and Germany, made great strides in France and Russia. Knowledge of the past now went right through society. The way this was taught was revealing. Frenchmen learnt that the invader came from the east; since the days of Frederick the Great, an anti-Prussian tradition developed into the history of conflict between the two peoples. Popular imagery, from Alfred de Musset to Hansi, substituted Germans for British as national enemies. The war of 1870, the loss of Alsace-Lorraine, the revanchist appeals of Maurice Barrès and the clarion-call of Déroulède daily reminded Frenchmen that they had 'lost two children', that there should be no mercy shown to the murderer. Schoolchildren learnt this from their earliest years – their first textbooks showed the Prussian eagle swooping down on the Gallic cock, ripping out its finest plumage; the people of Paris, starved by blockade, bombardment and war, waiting in icy streets to be fed, reduced, in their misery, to eating rats. These images were fixed in national consciousness, patriotism and education being filled with them. From Bouvines to Sedan, defeat and death came from the Prussian.

In German schools the national territory was portrayed as a graveyard of Slavs, and there would always be a haunting danger in Slav revival. The German nation, once conquering and colonizing, was now regarded as a bulwark of western civilization against Slav hordes: Germans were worried at the western Slavs' growing population and national character. In Saxony, Pomerania and Prussia all trace of Lusatians and Kachuks, former inhabitants of these lands, had been effaced; like the French, Germans felt the danger in the east. There was a revival of the *Drang nach Osten* ideal, to fill

Germany's economic requirements and to assert the permanency of German economic hegemony throughout Central Europe. But children were also told that the Germans, while vigilant in the east, must also be on the watch in the west. Goethe had written in his memoirs that the worst catastrophe of his youth had been occupation of Coblentz by French troops. Now 'English mercantilism and French hatred are joined with Russian ambition against poor Germany'; 'The fatherland is surrounded . . . but God has always struck down our enemies – He struck down Napoleon in 1812 . . . and we Germans fear God and nothing else in the world.' A strong and vigorous Germany need have no fear of the west: every September, Sedan was celebrated – France, henceforth reckoned 'frivolous', had been defeated and diminished. The war, when it came, 'had not been willed by Germany' – the Kaiser had tried to avoid it; it was Edward VII, jealous of commercial prosperity, who had tried to arrange the stifling of Germany. His death reduced British bellicosity, but French bellicosity increased with the election of Poincaré. 'A close-meshed net is stretched round our country, and she can rely only on Austria-Hungary and Turkey, states that are rotting within. A new edition of this textbook added in 1916 that 'the Kaiser was devoted to improving the workers' lot when his pacific activity was brutally interrupted by war.'

In Russia Kovalevski's *History* was as familiar as was Lavisse in France. It taught that a thousand years before, the area of Russia was covered with forest and marsh and its inhabitants called 'Slavs', who were tall, brown-haired, and with piercing eyes. They lived in great families, the father-elder with his brothers, sons, nephews and grandsons, who together worked the land and hunted. A group of families was called a clan, and sometimes a group of these clans would come together, the *veche*, to settle an important matter. They would be summoned by a bell known as the *veche*-bell. Sometimes the Slavs fought off invaders; they would hide in the tall grass and fall on the enemy by surprise, would lie beneath the river surfaces breathing through a reed in their mouths. They were a hospitable people who did not like making war. When a Slav left his house he would leave food on the table and the door open so that any stranger could go in, eat and rest. Invaders came incessantly from all corners. First there were Scandinavian warriors, then Poles and Germans – the Teutonic Knights stopped by Alexander Nevski in 1242 in the battle of the ice. From the Steppe came Tatars who imposed their yoke on the Russian people, and even linked up with the Poles. Russians learned of the scourges they had suffered throughout their history: on the one hand, Tatars, later confused with Mongols and Turks, and on the other, Poles and Germans. In 1905 the eastern enemy was Japan; the 'yellow peril' rose again, and the Mongol theme inspired Merezhkovski's and Bely's poetry, 'recreating nightmare in the Russian soul'. Russia had fought off these phantom figures for centuries and in this century they were still there – Germans attacking in the west, orientals in the south, and now linked.

The history of each people had been marked by a defensive struggle against the hereditary enemy – French against Germans, Germans against Slavs and French, Russians against Asiatics and Germans, Italians, soon to be at deadly odds with the traditional enemy, Austria, or with the Turks, themselves enemies of the Slavs. Austria was the exception: her traditional enemy was the Infidel. But, for a century, the Ottoman Empire had been disintegrating; it lacked a substantial common frontier and had not even a pretext for hatred. In all countries schoolmasters propagated these myths. They were perhaps pacific themselves by conviction; their lessons did not have this effect. When they glorified Joan of Arc or Alexander Nevski, they automatically glorified war. They were to follow in 1914–18 the logic of their lessons, to become the finest example of patriotism.

A further innovation, the revival of sport, had similar results. At the first Olympiad in 1896 there was much talk as to the peaceful character of the games – in Greek times, war had been stopped for them. Organizers and promoters had a different view: Henri Massis wrote in 1913, under the pseudonym *Agathon*, 'Sport calls for endurance and sangfroid, the military virtues, and it keeps youth in a warlike frame of mind.' He was one of the champions of *Revanche*. Charles Maurras said much the same in *Anthinéa*; in France, at least, it was the military who glorified sport. In 1912 the International Olympic Committee contained twenty-eight aristocrats or soldiers in a total of forty-four members. Sport revived provincial loyalties, but before doing so it stimulated nationalism – as its champions stressed. It 'takes men away from politics, gives them an innate taste for discipline'. In western Europe the advance of education, the press, sport and mysticism led to a re-creation, in national terms, of duty, of obedience to constituted authority. Girardet has clearly shown this for France, where the process was well marked in 1914. Patriotism borrowed from both Jacobinism and the Right, influencing society from top to bottom. In Belleville sons of the *Communards* petitioned for the July 14th procession to parade through their *faubourg*. Jaurès never meant to deny that military service might be necessary – he did not condemn just war, war for national defence.

By 1914 the anti-militarism of the post Dreyfus period had lost its vigour. Twenty years before, Lucien Descaves had written, 'For these forgotten lands – Alsace-Lorraine – I'd not give even a little finger. I need the right-hand one to hold my paper when I write, and the left-hand one to shake off the cigarette ash.' 1912 saw a different generation. It had not known the humiliation of defeat and despised the weakness of its elders and their timidity towards life. The change is shown by Péguy's life: Péguy was a Catholic Dreyfusard, a pacifist, and then wrote *Notre patrie*, where socialists are described as agents of German imperialism. There was more nationalism than patriotism in the language of Charles Maurras or Maurice Barrès, whose newspaper, *Action Française*, swept youth in the *Grandes Ecoles*. The new generation was inflamed at every Franco-German incident – an English suffragette, passing through Paris, recorded that the same people she had known as pacifists, anti-militarist, anti-nationalist, Goetheans or Wagnerians or Nietzscheans had been remarkably changed; they still mouthed the old slogans of peace and progress, but showed in each of their words or inflection of the voice and in each look a wish for war, which they could hardly suppress. Outside France there was not the same warlike atmosphere, but German militarism and Pan-Slavism served as much, if not more, to heighten nationalism, to accelerate the arms-race and precipitate war. 'France is a bellicose country, Germany a militarist one', wrote Guglielmo Ferrero in 1899 – in Germany the public were not intoxicated with 1870, which they remembered only on the commemoration-day, whereas in France 'loss of Alsace-Lorraine and memory of defeat became a sort of national obsession'. Press-censorship on the subject of officers' treatment of their men was, on the other hand, nowhere stricter than in Germany, where mistrust of 'Prussianism' was strong.

But, fifteen years later, it was in Germany that soldiers had the greatest influence on public affairs. In England army and navy served civilian society. In France and particularly in Russia the military were a group apart, having no direct connection with the economic factors in control of society, whereas in Germany the soldiers were themselves involved in business, taking precedence as directors of companies or banks. Their share of public affairs was greater than elsewhere; they, more than their equivalents abroad, could decide on peace or war. They, bound up with the economic leaders, were the vanguard of a nationalism that, in P. Renouvin's words, 'reflected a conviction that Germany, through her success in military, economic, even cultural affairs, had displayed her invincible superiority . . . by virtue of the vigorous patriotism of her people'; she 'showed a genius for organization'. This nationalism found expression in the Krupp-financed Navy League, and then through the Pan-German League (*Alldeutscher Verband*) which was particularly active on the eve of war, and whose constitution proclaimed its aim 'to stimulate German nationalism . . . and propagate everywhere a vigorous policy of furthering German interests'. Such sentiments were shared by a small but active and influential minority of military and economic leaders and of university teachers. Their annexationism was given free rein, and they demanded expansion far beyond the German linguistic area, over the seas. This programme influenced the Bethmann Hollweg government's war aims as soon as war broke out. Bellicosity increased from 1900 to 1914 for lack of gains in Morocco and elsewhere. It was willingly kept going by leaders: 'The people must not ask, if war breaks out, what we are fighting for. They must be accustomed to war.' The press repeated school-lessons – Germany encircled by enemies that would emerge from the Vosges, the Niemen, the Isonzo. The danger was continental, all-embracing. Revival of French war mania, reinforcement of the Franco-Russian alliance, rising Pan-Slavism and Slav nationality movements in Central Europe contributed to make it even more pressing. The Pan-Germans' and soldiers' offensive spirit came from a quite legitimate ambition to secure defence of German interests and the national territory.

The Tsarist Empire and the Dual Monarchy were multinational states, where the dominant peoples – Great-Russian, German or Magyar – sought to repress awakening nationalities and consolidate their rule by extending it over their borders. Russians and Austrians glorified their own nationality, and denied their minorities' rights to national status. They ended by terrorizing these nationalities, by browbeating their possible protectors – Serbia and the Russian Empire for Austria-Hungary's Slavs, Turkey, Prussia and Austria-Hungary for the Moslems and other Russian minorities. The Tsar faced many threats – from non-Slavs like the Finns or the Tatars, Azeris, and Crimean Moslems, who indulged in Pan-Turanian dreams; from Slavs such as Poles, Ukrainians, desiring autonomy or independence. Official Pan-Slavism was an offensive weapon for use abroad, where it might gain greater success than russification, and it became quite soon a nationalist ideology. Its prophet, Danilevski, dreamt since 1869, in *Russia and Europe*, of an age soon to come when Slav civilization would rule Europe, finally supplanting the old Latin-German one. His ideas influenced government policy, which was always as ready to russify at home as to defend abroad the rights of 'oppressed' Slavs: Czechs, Bosnians, Ruthenes in particular, and Slavs such as 'our little Serbian brothers' whose independence was threatened.

Paradoxically, the revolutionary organizations' attitudes followed this pattern. Previously they had supported the right of peoples to independence: now they disapproved, where aspirations of this kind came through socialist parties, 'since purely national objectives divide the working class instead of uniting it'. Tactical necessity made them join up with 'national' organizations, to recognize the aims of these as legitimate, but their attitude was always suspicious where the revolution was concerned. On the eve of war Lenin was virtually alone in recognizing that nations had an absolute right to declare independence from the oppressor-state – although he added the rider that right to split off did not imply *necessity* of splitting off. Before the war, the nationality movements of the Tsarist Empire were in an ambiguous position: they were hostile to the Tsarist régime, and misunderstood by the revolutionaries; they were anxious to go their own way. Meanwhile, they went on obeying the traditional authorities: they were integrated with Russian troops, and were to fight as comrades-in-arms of Russians. In fact the war had a liberating effect – Jews, Balts, Ukrainians shared with Russians in defence of their country.

In Austria-Hungary, nationality leaders went further. The Czech, Masaryk, escaped to London to direct the fight against the Habsburg Monarchy. But the peoples themselves behaved like the Russian nationalities: despite peacetime turbulence, they were scarcely troublesome in 1908 and not at first troublesome in the army, either during mobilization or at the front. The High Command was careful to avoid putting Slav troops against the Russians, a sensible precaution, since Czech troops tended to fall prisoner more easily than other ones; but they were essentially loyal, and the Russians did not attempt, for some time, to use them against their oppressors. Governments avoided using this kind of weapon, even when they fought each other. The minorities' attitude can be easily explained – in wartime they changed status. They served the Empire in the same was as all citizens: in uniform, they shared in the adventure, a promotion that delighted them. Šveik in uniform was a soldier like the rest. The Serb minority was different: it could hardly resist the Great-Serb appeal from Belgrade. The Austro-Hungarian annexation of Bosnia in 1908 had made another Alsace-Lorraine, frustrating the ambitions and ideals of Pan-Slavism. The Serb secret societies that fought the Habsburgs were financed by St Petersburg, and since 1908 they had kept up terrorist activity against Austrian functionaries in the occupied lands, their declared aim being to make the Austrian position impossible. The Serbian government was not ignorant of their activities for the chiefs of the Black Hand, the main terrorist organization, had positions of great responsibility in the Serbian intelligence service. They recruited agents from the Serb minority in Austria-Hungary, and the Serbian government cannot be absolved of responsibility. The Habsburg authorities were not duped and the army and its chief, Conrad von Hötzendorf, demanded action against the real culprits.

These problems were vital: the Empire was by nature multi-national and could not surrender to centrifugal movements. In 1867 there had been a compromise with Hungary, which thereby became effectively autonomous and even took a great part in running the whole Empire. Hungary was less tempted to separatism than Slav or Romanian minorities. Indeed roles were reversed, for the Hungarians were even more opposed than the Austrians to the minorities' particularist claims, which by 1914 were being more shrilly advanced than before. Vienna's attitude was divided – some statesmen and members of the dynasty, notably the heir, Franz Ferdinand, were liberally inclined, but many were uncompromising, especially the army as the last bastion of fidelity to the Germanic past of the Empire. Of the officers 78·7 per cent were of German origin whereas Germans were 24 per cent of the population; for Hungarians and Czechs the figures were respectively 9 per cent and 20 per cent, 4·8 per cent and 13 per cent; only 0·2 per cent of the officers were of Ruthene origin, whereas Ruthenes formed 10 per cent of the population of the Empire. The army, more than any other element, resisted the nationalities' advance. Concessions were made to the Hungarians, an autonomous Hungarian corps, the *Honvéd*, being set up; beside the eighty-word language of command and the hundred-word language of service, any regiment could still use its national tongue. The army would not go beyond this, and the quarrelling at first stopped in wartime – Czechs or Ruthenes might harass the military in time of peace; on the battlefield, they would obey.

For the High Command, war was thus a way of solving the nationality problem, of putting Hungarians in their place. The Hungarians knew this, and made a fuss every time military credits had to be raised. As a result of their obstruction, the army in 1914 was behind its enemies in capacity to wage a long war. Every year it took in only 29 per cent of the young men liable for training – Russia took in 35 per cent, Italy 27 per cent, France 75 per cent and Germany 47 per cent. Mustering only one-third of France's number of trained troops from a population some eleven millions larger, the Austrian army was also less well-equipped than the Russian or Italian. One officer went to war in full dress uniform, for lack of battledress. Conrad himself said he would not be ready until 1920.

But the army leaders had a brainstorm. A domestic conflict with the Ruthenes and an external one with Serbia and Russia were both blamed for the troubles. The idea of 'settling accounts with the Slavs' by striking down Serbia and Russia took hold of soldiers and civilian leaders – they preached war at the very moment they declared they had no hope of winning it. Balkan wars were not European wars: they were a different world, where the ancestral feuds of clans scarcely merited European interference. Bismarck had said they were not worth the bones of a Pomeranian grenadier. Several times, when conflict threatened between Austria and Russia over Serbians or Bulgarians, Berlin restrained Vienna, Paris held back St Petersburg. A war here need not become a European war, let alone a world war – no one reckoned England would intervene. War between England and Germany was not part of historical tradition: it came from more recent events, not yet wholly assimilated into the national subconscious: its causes lay in a more recent development of rivalry, essentially imperialist in character.

Chapter 3

Inevitable war

The imperialist aspect of the war, and some of its causes, emerge in the make-up of rival coalitions. These were not created by chance since they came from a rivalry induced by nations' unequal development. Europe had been traditionally dominated by one or other nation – Spain in the sixteenth century, and subsequently England or France. After the wars of the Revolution and Napoleon a new historical cycle developed, dependent on the nations' industrial development. England was outstanding, her power in mid-Victorian times being equal to the rest combined. The situation differed from what has happened in the later twentieth century, since the technical lead of the United States has not declined, whereas in the nineteenth century the British lead over other industrial powers declined decade by decade. Industry was born, grew and prospered in other countries, which would in future no longer be dominated by England. France and Belgium were the next off the mark in the race to industrialize; they were followed by the United States, Russia, Japan and especially Germany.

Germany was a new nation; she had to adapt herself to a world made without her, where other states had their roles and positions clearly defined, with markets reserved, raw materials set aside and future projects worked out in detail. To withstand and defeat competitors, she had to concentrate her energies, even more than the United States. Between 1880 and 1914, owing to her success in this and in technology, she made unprecedented economic strides – a matter of immense pride, since in some ways she could even challenge England, first of the industrial nations, within the English borders. Following British and French examples, Germany was in turn converted to overseas expansion, either for new markets or cheap sources of raw materials. But the world had already been conquered and partitioned; there was no 'place in the sun' for Germany, and her immense economic power remained highly concentrated on a relatively small national territory, her field of expansion narrowly circumscribed by her rivals' positions. The vast demands of a

Part I

maturing economy could not be met, although the economy was itself fully competitive. Her zone of influence and markets could not be extended, nor did she have a financial base on the same scale as her economic power.

England felt threatened: the challenge touched her pride, the pride of outstanding success. Since 1895 Joseph Chamberlain had remarked on 'the black spots' on the horizon – in China or South Africa, England came up against Germany. The greatest worry was the rise of German naval power after 1900, dictated by nationalists such as Tirpitz. The British intended to maintain their two-power standard, whatever the cost, and built super-ships, the Dreadnoughts, assuming that the Germans could not follow them, since the Kiel canal was too narrow. The Germans were not dismayed at this extravagant auctioneering, but widened the canal and built their own Dreadnoughts. Anglo-German rivalry became a public matter, orchestrated and fomented by press and cinema. Some statesmen in both countries sought accord: but the two countries were pushed by the logic of imperialism and the character of statesmen into hostility. For two decades before the war, Germany behaved with more impatience and aggression than England who, being the possessing power, was necessarily conservative, and compromising, if not outright pacifist – as she showed a few days before entering the war. This attitude only showed that she had too much to lose to want change. But if she were under serious attack and her future threatened she would reconsider the position. Her statesmen considered making concessions to expansionist Germany, but even if this meant territorial gains for Germany in Belgian or Portuguese colonies, the future of Great Britain was not guaranteed thereby. German power was an ever increasing threat.

Since the turn of the century British policy had been one of containment (*Eindämmung*). Once convinced that Germany was threatening her hegemony, Britain abandoned her policy of isolation, tightened her links with France in 1904 and Russia in 1907 and accepted an unprecedented burden of defence. Lloyd George wrote, a few weeks after war broke out:

We have been living in a sheltered valley for generations. We have been too comfortable and too indulgent . . . and the stern hand of fate has scourged us to an elevation where we can see the great everlasting things that matter for a nation – the great peaks we had forgotten, of Honour, Duty, Patriotism, and, clad in glittering white, the great pinnacle of Sacrifice pointing like a rugged finger to Heaven. (Queen's Hall speech, 19 September 1914)

This was what the vicissitudes of international affairs in the previous decade had taught. The Kaiser felt insulted: the same British who had offered a *rapprochement* in his grandmother's day were now, under Edward VII, rejecting his advances. A personal grievance was added and nationalism further promoted. Delbrück's words of 1899 were still true: 'We must become a world power . . . we cannot go back. We can do this with England or against her. With her means peace; against her, war.' German leaders were still misled by the pacific utterances of British statesmen and their taste for negotiation, and felt that only personal disaccord or whims stopped agreement. They were sure, in the July crisis itself, that England would not come in, that they could make some kind of agreement with the British; they reacted with surprise and rage to Great Britain's declaration of war when they invaded Belgium. This sense of spite came through in the immensely successful 'hymn of spurned love', the *Hassgesang* by Ernst Lissauer:

> French and Russian they matter not,
> A blow for a blow and a shot for a shot;
> We love them not, we hate them not,
> We hold the Vistula and the Vosges-gate,
> We have but one and only hate,
> We love as one, we hate as one,
> We have one foe and one alone –
> ENGLAND! . . .

The pattern was taken up by parallel conflicts of the same type, for instance Franco-German rivalry with its ancestral roots. Since 1900 the French economy had undergone rapid growth once more, although compared to Germany or America it displayed too many signs of exhaustion. As their demographic curve declined, the French trembled at the mounting shadow of their hereditary enemy. No longer did Germany, in the old way, encourage French expansion overseas to make up for loss of Alsace-Lorraine. Franco-German rivalry reached into all corners of the globe (Morocco, the Congo and China) and appeared at all levels (colonial, commercial, financial). Over the previous few years further points of contention had come with German penetration of French businesses: now Germany was present even within French borders. France did, of course, still have a great part to play early in the century in financial and economic matters. 'France is a Bank', was Nicholas II's phrase. The French investor speculated in loans, particularly state loans; savings were buried abroad, particularly in Russia where interest was high. Banks and government collaborated and French capital acquired a powerful, even predominant, role. It seldom had to combat the British, who preferred private loans, and then mainly in America, the Dominions or China. It did, increasingly, come into conflict with the Germans, backed, like the French, by their government, in Russia, Romania and Serbia. Germany lacked financial power but she was omnipresent, and the French noted increasing resistance between 1910 and 1914. It was appreciated that French capital permitted the client states to make orders in Germany: French money was going, to some extent, to strengthen its rival's industry – the Serbian case being obvious.

Russia was another 'hereditary enemy' of Germany, and she too felt menaced, both by traditional *Drang nach Osten* and by expanding German exports. Men felt more strongly about invasions of foreign goods than about capital penetration and the Russians did not quite appreciate the danger of the British, Belgian or French financial colonization of their country: on the contrary, they saw in the ubiquity of German goods a threat to their future. In the mid-nineteenth century England had exported to Russia twice as much as Germany; by 1913 she exported three times less than Germany; Germany's share of Russian imports, a mere 16 per cent in 1846, reached 32 per cent in 1896 and 42 per cent for the period 1909–14. A Russian journalist, Kulicher, adopted the ideas of Williams's *Made in Germany* and described in these terms the invasion of Russia by German goods:

Toys, dolls, picture-books read by your children come from Germany; so does the paper on which the most patriotic newspaper is printed. Go home and look about: everywhere, things 'made in Germany', from the piano in your living-room to the cooking-pot in the kitchen. Go downstairs, and you'll see on the pump that waters the flowers in the garden the words 'made in Germany', and you'll see them again on the periodicals stuffed in the wastepaper basket. If you put them in the fire, you'll see the poker was welded in Germany; throw it down, and knock off some ornament from the shelf: on the bits and pieces, you can piece together the words 'made in Germany'.

The journalist felt, writing in 1917, 'This is a good opening for British commerce if England can learn from past mistakes.'

Both past and present lent coherence and system to the alliances: England against Germany, now associated, owing to Delcassé's 'diplomatic triumphs', with France and Russia. It was true of other states as well. Turkey and Austria, both threatened with disruption, necessarily sought German protection. Austria had to contend with south Slavs supported by Russia; Turkey had always had to contend with Russia – Tsar and Pan-Slavs alike aimed at the Straits. England had been protectress in the past, but now she was linked with Russia so that the doubly threatened 'sick man' had to seek German protection. Germany eagerly took over the British role and colonized Turkey in the name of 'protection' – building the Baghdad railway, instructing the Turkish army, but not, like the British in Cyprus, demanding bases: the Germans asked for neither garrison rights nor the right to fly their flag. After the Balkan wars of 1912–13 the weakened Turks began to regard German protection as more and more threatening to their independence; and Jagow did indeed tell the Austrians he regarded partition of Turkey as inevitable. Maps of Asia Minor were drawn up showing in various colours the *Arbeitszonen* – a term preferred to 'spheres of influence' – of Italy, Austria and the rest. But Russia did not want to find Germany a neighbour here and attempted a *rapprochement*, via French diplomacy and finance, with Turkey. Austria and Germany appreciated that they would have to combat this vigorously: 'Punishment of Serbia would at once restore the prestige of Germany and Austria in Constantinople', said the Grand Vizier to the Austrian ambassador. In fact, the very day after the Austrian ultimatum was sent, following Sarajevo, Turkey formally requested adhesion to the Triple Alliance.

In the end Germany, seeing herself without a colonial empire, exploited the fact to proclaim that she alone would respect the rights of peoples overseas to independence. She advocated the colonial peoples' right to freedom; and these words, through the medium of the Turkish Empire, reached the Moslems even of Russia, of the British Empire or North Africa. The effects of this propaganda campaign were first noted among the great nomadic tribes of Tripolitania, then an Italian possession; this success gave a worldwide dimension to the idea of national rights which, created by Europeans, was not intended for export. Germany won much sympathy in the Moslem world.

Italy followed this pattern. Her original alliance with Germany and Austria still conformed to the needs of a few businessmen or expansionists, to some extent controlled by German capital or disappointed at colonial failures; many Italians also felt the alliance was justified because of Anglo-French resistance in Tunisia or Ethiopia. But alliance with Austria, the hereditary enemy, was not popular: 'collusion' between Vatican, clericals and the Catholic, conservative Habsburg Monarchy offended many politicians; and the alliance did not in any case bring much. For the long-serving liberal prime minister, Giolitti, who had German connections, it had a strictly defensive, diplomatic character: it made Italy partner of the Great Powers and was itself a sign that Italy had been promoted into their ranks. Still, it could only be presumptuous for Italy to take on the joint forces of England and France, mistresses of the Mediterranean, who controlled the coal supplies of Italian industry. If they showed 'understanding' for the 'legitimate aspirations' of Italy in colonial matters, Italy could afford a *rapprochement*. The two western powers supported her when she made war on Turkey for possession of Tripolitania, and by 1914 she was tending towards the west: there was even a suggestion of constructing a railway, with British money and Serbo-Russian agreement, from the Adriatic to the Black Sea. The British and French could not do much to help Italy reach her objectives in the Adriatic or Tyrol, but they were better placed than other powers to satisfy Italian ambitions elsewhere – and these were now openly directed towards Asia Minor. Alfredo Oriani wrote, 'Turkey's exhaustion, Greece's futile revival, the Balkan states' slow and late awakening give Mediterranean Italy the essential role. We have never been more Italian than now.' The myth of the fourth Rome was born.

These ambitions brought general negotiations. They caused a veritable diplomatic revolution; as the Kaiser said, 'Italy is dropping off like a rotten pear.' In July 1914 Vienna concealed her intentions from the new Italian leaders, an attitude felt by Salandra and Sonnino, in view of the Triplice's recent renewal, as an affront. They were even ready to intervene – in any event a wonderful answer to social and revolutionary agitation, which, over the past few months, had been lively enough (following 'Red Week'). This was an argument other countries could appreciate, though not in such a direct form. On the other hand, Giolitti and many deputies feared that war, with its inevitable sacrifices, would also create a demand for equal rights. The question of intervention was highly complex, since Italian statesmen, whatever their sympathies, announced that they would accept the highest bid. These annexationist ambitions show the essentially imperialistic character of intervention. But in August 1914 the peoples and their governments felt, rightly or wrongly, that they had gone to war to defend their rights, honour and security. Annexationist aims were not there at the time though they emerged later. In Italy it was different – public opinion had to be tempted before it would support intervention. The nationalists wanted to intervene, but not the other Italians, who through the press had to be diverted from other aspirations. Expansion might solve the problem of emigration; many socialists felt war would be the midwife of revolution.

In the Balkans it was almost a different war altogether. It had begun long before Sarajevo and went on after Versailles. In 1912–13, in the first Balkan war, Bulgaria, Greece and Serbia had defeated Turkey; they shared out parts of Thrace and Macedonia. Bulgaria had borne the main burden and won the greatest victories. Both she and Serbia felt their share was insufficient, and planned war even before peace was signed with Turkey; Serbia received help from Greece and Romania, while Turkey once more attacked Bulgaria, who was thereby attacked on all sides at once. The peace of Bucharest in 1913 allowed defeated Bulgaria only the Strumitsa valley and the Thracian littoral of her former conquests, while her erstwhile allies increased their territory through land that Turkey had originally lost to Bulgaria in the previous year. This was a different world, a different war from the European one, although it took its pattern and means from Europe. The Great War did start in the Balkans, and it is legitimate to trace the causation from Sarajevo to Versailles; but the assassins of Franz Ferdinand and the men behind them had in view at most an Austro-Serb conflict, not European war: they could hardly imagine any connection. In a sense, there was no inevitability about the spread of war after Sarajevo, but by 1914 alliance systems had their own logic, the rivalries were fixed, and the antagonism of nations came from the depths of their past, from part of their collective consciousness. Contemporaries might believe war could be put off a year or two; it would come in the end. War had conquered men's minds before it even broke out.

Chapter 4

Imaginary war

The war men imagined was indeed imaginary. But imagination itself was revealing; the war that failed to happen is as legitimate, historically, as the one that did happen. Since 1880 there had been many articles and books on what war would be like: I. F. Clarke has counted several. Some were fictional, some full of military foresight, but the dividing-line was not clear and many illusions were common to them.

Fictional war rapidly increased in popularity, in England, after *The Battle of Dorking* in the 1880s; weeklies and journals such as *Black and White* were filled with imaginary conflicts. Before 1900 *The Battle of Boulogne* and *How John Bull Lost London* were the echo of Fashoda, a possible war with France. After the *Entente Cordiale* and the naval race, there were imaginary battles with the German navy: *The Great Naval War* and *The Capture of London*. There were ten more to follow. Germany had little literature of this kind, but there was a great deal in France, closely reflecting diplomatic vicissitudes. Up to 1904 British and Germans were linked or alone in war with France and Russia; after 1904 only Germany – *La bataille de la Woëvre, La débâcle de l'Allemagne dans la prochaine guerre,* and *La fin de la Prusse er le démembrement de l'Allemagne* (1913). Over twenty works in England foresaw the British surprised, invaded and defeated – an idea to which cross-Channel tunnel projects lent some actuality. Overall this literature reflected the nagging worries besetting the country. The Germans were more confident, for they had less need of their imaginations, whereas the French always dreamt of the revenge so impatiently awaited. Here, France always won. Military writers hardly concealed themselves – thus Captain 'Danrit' was the anagram of Auguste Driant, Boulanger's son-in-law, later killed at Verdun in 1916. His *La Guerre de demain* was dedicated to his own regiment: 'I have always desired to fight with you the Great War we all hope for. But it is slow in coming; to kill time, I have described in imagination this Holy War we are going to win' (1891). All such works precisely described what battles would be like:

there is virtually no connection with reality. Essayists and military writers thought in Napoleonic terms – infantry charging in serried ranks, cavalry winning the decision, the whole thing lasting no more than a day. It was almost a sporting event between red-trousers, *Feldgrau* and Italian green. The British scrapped bright-coloured uniforms, and, always one ahead in ideas, brought in khaki – though they only made a few thousand uniforms. Illusions were virtually universal – only the 'wild' H. G. Wells, the designer, Albert Robida, the Russian theorist, Ivan Bloch, appreciated that war would be industrialized, with millions of deaths and entire nations mobilized. Works on war became so numerous after 1906 that they provoked a whole subsidiary literature, a great army of critics. When war came, these were still attempting to make something of the phenomenon.

Men were mentally prepared. Still, statesmen were no better than writers of fiction at foreseeing the industrial nature of the war. Delbrück in Germany, towards the end of 1912, could not see much benefit in the idea of an economic staff to regulate the Ruhr factories' output; in July 1914 the secretary of state for finance refused to buy up grain-stocks at Rotterdam since 'civilians have no title to intervene in a situation that might arise through war: that is a military matter'. In France, Germany and elsewhere soldiers thought in terms of numbers or equipment, not of the possible new character of war. It was reckoned absurdly out of date to suppose that war could last more than a season – with conscription (and there was a good chance of it coming even in England) life would be intolerably disrupted. The powers would have to make peace. Hence the idea that modern war would be short. Hence also the soldiers' initial outlook and plans.

Admiral Raeder, commander of the Nazi navy, writing his memoirs in 1960, asserted that there had been no naval plan for war with England in 1914. He also said elsewhere that nothing had been planned to help a German army invade France. Despite appearances this confirms what we supposed. The failure of naval and military commands to co-ordinate their actions is not improbable, but it is odd that no naval operation in the west was planned. Did this mean that the military thought they would win before the British came in? Or that the German navy was never really built for battle with England? Some men thought of 'Copenhagen' – the British would repeat their *coup* of 1802 by preventive strike against the German fleet in the North Sea – but was this a serious belief? The second hypothesis is more fruitful; it confirms that German naval armament was intended to achieve not war but negotiations, forced on the British – and this puts in peculiar focus Bethmann Hollweg's policy in the summer of 1914.

The British for their part had been preparing since 1911 for a possible landing on the coast of Jutland; latterly they had decided to send their expeditionary force to the main armies' chief front – they would set up a strong-point in Antwerp, attach their forces to the French left at Maubeuge. They were prepared to go to war if necessary. Did they ever appreciate that the Germans were unaware of this? Whatever the pacific tone of their words, their offensive plans against Germany had at least as much meaning as writers' dreams and were more realistic than their enemies' plans; for the Germans had many illusions as to the real British attitude. In England the army was subordinate to business interests, whereas in Germany the armed forces inherited a long, purely continental tradition.

French military schools between 1890 and 1914 used a series of textbooks, *Exercices et problèmes*, which evolved in a revealing way: up to 1906 many exercises concerned English landings in the Pays de Caux. These disappeared from the textbooks, as, after 1912, did exercises designed to repel Italian attacks on Bizerta or over the Alps. There was now only one enemy, Germany. Besides, in the days of Bonaparte, at his Brienne school, exercises were done on maps of southern Germany, the Low Countries or Italy; now all tactical problems were posed in Champagne, Burgundy or Franche-Comté. No one supposed the war would be fought on enemy soil, unless possibly in Alsace-Lorraine. The French horizon now stretched only to the Rhine.

There is a further well-known feature. Hearing that the British were going to disembark with metropolitan and colonial contingents, a French strategist remarked, 'They seem to think the war will last for years. There's nothing wrong with that, except it's a century out of date.' Everyone counted on a short war. Kitchener, Galliéni and even Joffre were occasionally sceptical, but to no effect; in general they shared the illusion of allies and enemies alike. Men supposed the war would end in one or two great battles, and strategists were essentially divided as to the ways of winning them: broad or narrow fronts, attack in mass or in columns, heavy or field artillery, usefulness or otherwise of machine-guns. In the end both French and Germans virtually wrote them off and were pledged to open methods of attack.

In *La Revanche* Contamine notes that the French soldiers, unlike the politicians, felt their country's position was more critical after 1906 than before. Links with England gave little military advantage, the Russian alliance lost most of its value after the Manchurian war, and in any case the French army was weaker, relative to the German, than it had been ten years before. By 1911 the soldiers were less optimistic than before, certainly less so than the diplomats. The great problem was how to use reservists, what the counter-offensive should look like – associated matters, which were heatedly discussed when it was planned to attach a reserve regiment to each active regiment. In Joffre's words, 'The emotion aroused by such a project can only be understood with reference to the political situation of the times. Odd as it may seem, reserves became a party-political question. The Right claimed that only the professional army really counted for national defence and objected in principle to the nation in arms, which in their view would mean a mere militia; hence they would use reserves only as a supplement needed to bring the professional army to war strength. They expected the war to be a short one and therefore lavished attention on the professional army, which they considered as the bulwark of the nation: no sacrifice would be too much for them if it fostered the professional army. Reserve formations, by contrast, were reckoned to have no solidity, no ability to wage real war – partly because their *cadres* were weak, partly because, given the need to use all possible material, they contained many relatively older men; they were to be used only for secondary tasks, and that after preliminary training. The Left, by contrast, could only think in terms of the nation in arms. They objected to long-term service and felt that a few months' training would be enough to fashion the citizen-soldier for the coming war. Jaurès's *L'armée nouvelle* provoked lively argument.'

Operational matters also came in, for they depended on the view taken of the Republican soldiers' worth. The military believed for many years that, in the event of war, they must adopt a waiting attitude. Men supposed that a Republic could never be ready as quickly as an Empire; therefore, while Germany undertook an immediate, prepared offensive, France would have to wait and manoeuvre. As Contamine says, 'Planners felt this after 1875, and with the years it was more and more categorically asserted.' The planned counter-offensive was increasingly postponed, and French forces placed increasingly further back from the frontier. In this way they could be more easily distributed according to the line of German attack. In other words the war could be won on the Marne; it would not be carried over the Rhine.

But the lesson of the Russo-Japanese War brought men, after 1906, to think in offensive terms, personified by Colonel de Grandmaison: 'Train others, and prepare yourselves; we must foment the spirit of offensive everywhere, even in the smallest details of training. Go to any excess you like – even then it might not be enough.' The aim was not so much to expose troops to fire, as to draw the initiative from the enemy. Another theorist said, 'We must not rely on reserves, or allies, or slaves to do the work.' In 1913 President Fallières said, 'We shall go straight for the enemy, without hesitation, for the offensive corresponds to our soldiers' temperament.' The socialist Paul-Boncour approved, saying, 'The news that our army has gone back to more offensive ideas in strategy and tactics is welcome. The offensive is an axiom, both military and French.' The 1913 manuals contained no prescription for retreat.

Joffre, commanding since 1911, was not against this. But it all needed greater manpower, and the parliamentary opposition, taking Jaurès's line, was mistrustful, remembering Boulanger and the Dreyfus affair. The Left demanded defensive warfare, fought with large masses and maximum exploitation of reserve formations; they thought in terms of the wars of the Revolution, and overlooked the fact that the French demographic curve was declining, that the French recruit contingent diminished each year, that numbers counted in favour of Germany. In January 1913 there was a Reichstag bill to increase the effective strength and equipment of the army, and this pushed the French General Staff in turn to propose, as it had long wanted, an increase from two to three years of military service. The opposition protested, but gave way. As a result, the French, with a population almost half that of Germany, could field an army only 20 per cent inferior. Their new mobilization plans took this into account. They would not wait for the British or rely on the Belgians' resisting, for their sympathies were far from clear, or even count on Russian help, although the Russians promised to attack by the fourteenth day of mobilization. Instead, they would launch both the victorious counter-offensive and an offensive as well, a variant of Plan XVI. Joffre has ably explained how he foresaw things:

The least likely hypothesis was a German attack on Epinal-Toul, for it would mean neglecting a possible British intervention, and would tie down large masses of troops in the difficult

mountainous country on the upper Moselle. Besides, it did not
square with the great material efforts made north of Trier, and
the extraordinary development of the *Moselstellung*. Other
hypotheses foresaw the debouching of large-scale forces towards
the Eifel, destined to fall on the French left *via* Belgium, and
these were amply justified by the enormous sums put up by
the Germans for the last ten years to the Metz-Thionville
group. In this way, having examined what the role of the
Metz-Thionville fortifications was likely to be, we came to
reckon that the Germans would probably violate Belgian
neutrality.

The problem had often come up. British and French were not sure
of Belgium's attitude. The French High Command were sure the
Germans would not go beyond the Meuse, and therefore expected
only token resistance from Belgium – she 'would join whichever side
was stronger'. Schemes for a preventive offensive over Belgian territory were raised and rejected by the French Cabinet. Plan XVII, which
came next, organized concentration such that the right could attack
Lorraine while the left opposed a German army crossing Belgian
territory. But the size of German forces to be employed here would
not be known till relatively late; up to the last moment Joffre knew
nothing of German deployment or placing of reserves.
  The Germans, for their part, had faced the same problem for
forty years: which of their two enemies to strike at first, how much
to leave as a guard on the other front. There was no question of
making two offensives. After 1871 the great Moltke reckoned France,
not Russia, should be first attacked; then, from 1879 to 1891 the
General Staff preferred attack, first, in the east. From 1891 to 1914
Schlieffen and Bernhardi returned to Moltke's ideas, but the attack
would no longer be through the Epinal defile, but *via* Belgian
territory. Some ten divisions and the Austrian army would keep a
cover in the east – Germans and Austrians alike fearing that, if the
Russians reached Bohemia, the Czechs would rise in their support.
They hoped to defeat France in two months or less, the time needed
for Russia to mobilize and deploy her armies, so that this threat
might be anticipated. As a further innovation Schlieffen decided to
reinforce the right of the army earmarked for Belgium, so that
Antwerp would be occupied, the French outflanked and enveloped.
The younger Moltke adopted this with reservations; but in any case
he and his assistant, Ludendorff, did not give up hope of getting the

Belgian army on their side, although they were not even sure they would succeed in taking even Liège. Moltke said in a report of 13 March 1913:

> The German people must be made to see that we have to attack, because of our enemies' provocation. Things must be so built up that war will be seen as a deliverance from the great armaments, the financial burdens, the political tensions. We must also prepare for war financially, though without awakening financiers' suspicions. Our army needs a high effective strength. If we are attacked, we shall do as our brothers did, a hundred years ago – the eagle will rise in anger, swoop with his talons on the enemy and destroy him. Let us remember that many provinces of the old German Empire, such as the County of Burgundy and much of Lorraine, are still in French hands; that thousands of our German brothers groan under the Slav yoke in the Baltic. Germany must regain what formerly she lost.

The French knew of this document; but they underrated the extreme right wing's importance, supposing – not altogether wrongly – that a threat to Antwerp would stimulate Belgian resistance and, also rightly, that it would bring Britain into the war.

Over the past few years the arms race was accelerated; it increased tension, and produced an obsession with the coming war. Barbara Tuchman quotes, in *The Proud Tower*, an illustration of this:

> When the Barnum and Bailey circus played Germany in 1901, the Kaiser, hearing about the remarkable speed with which trains were loaded, sent officers to observe the method. They learnt that instead of loading heavy equipment on each freight car from the side, the circus people laid connecting treads through the whole length of the train on which all equipment, loaded from one end, could be rolled straight through. By this means three trains of twenty-two cars each could be loaded in an hour. The circus technique promptly went to feed the insatiable appetite for speed of the German mobilization-system. The Kaiser's observers also noted the advantages of the great circus cooking-waggons over stationary field kitchens so that meals could be cooked on the move.

There were few doubts about war – whether it would come or how it would be fought. Men wondered only as to the occasion for it, whether it should be now, or later. In Germany, where government circles felt Great Britain would not intervene, ideas of preventive war against France or Russia spread; and in Austria as well, among the military. In the July crisis, Conrad told Moltke that 'any delay lessens our chances', a view shared by the Germans, who saw the Russian army recovering, on its way to becoming irresistible. Joffre for his part felt that things were better than they had been three years before, and Delcassé, architect of the Triple Entente, that they had never been better. Abel Ferry recorded:

> On 30th July I saw this little man becoming a Bismarck. With implacable logic he revealed the ambitions he had always enter-tained, summed up his impressive achievements, and showed how they had been won – the French Army strongly organized, a system of alliances created. He spoke lovingly of his creations, the Entente with England and the alliance with Russia; here was the extraordinary feat of one man, whose life was com-manded by a single ambition, to make life impossible for Germany, to throttle her. I appreciated that, since Bismarck, no one had shaped European events as Delcassé did. He was no longer foreign minister, but his web had been spun, and now Germany was blundering into it like a great bluebottle.

Chapter 5

'War on war'

Men were obsessed by war. But already it had failed to happen – conflicts were sparked off in the Balkans and then followed a familiar pattern, the Great Powers intervening, not directly, but through their clients. The expected war was in fact far from inevitable; governments also feared that if it broke out there might be revolution, a threat brandished by the socialist International. Its Stuttgart congress of 1907 had sworn 'war on war' and there had been monster demonstrations during the Italo-Turkish War of 1911, which led men to suppose that the peace movement was very strong. The International itself was tireless in fighting for peace once war seemed to threaten. In all countries International leaders accused their own ruling classes: Jaurès more than anyone, but Adler, Kautsky or Lenin taking a similar view. The International hesitated only as regards means. Vaillant and Keir Hardie proposed that mobilization should be the signal for a general strike, but delegates would not accept this, many of them objecting that this could only succeed where there was a large and politically conscious working class: countries such as politically backward Russia would thereby steal a march on advanced ones like Germany, if these were paralysed by the strike.

Following Jaurès's lead, delegates refused to let the International be imprisoned by a formula: war should be opposed 'by any means deemed suitable', a decision pronounced by Kautsky, 'Pope' of scientific socialism, to be 'wise and mature'. But, other than this mere resolution, nothing was done; and when the trumpet called socialists left for war with the rest. Apart from a few, leaders and militants were said to have behaved illogically – the International sank in a few hours without trace. Once the initial surprise was over, opposition to war was again raised by a few men, and by 1917 this simple spark had lit up the whole of Europe. Nor was this accidental, given that revolutionary ideals came, in Russia and Europe as a whole, from the depths of popular consciousness. These ideals had only been in abeyance, militant socialists supposing hitherto

34

that the war was itself a struggle for liberty. They learnt otherwise only later when war, revolution and intervention showed the
realities. But the bankruptcy of the International requires further
explanation.

The speeches and resolutions of the pre-war International led to
a somewhat surprising conclusion: although socialists of the International were fighting to overthrow the existing social and political
order, they acted on the pattern of that order, indeed perpetuating
it. In various congresses, for instance, men divided on national lines,
not on ideological ones into radicals, revisionists, or Marxists and
non-Marxists. The co-ordinating Bureau was no more than a post-
office, with no executive, or even administrative power. Inside the
movement, 'all parties rigidly adhered to the principle of autonomy;
judgment was suspended as to the division between general principle
and particular, national questions.' It was a federation without
federal government. Besides, the differing experiences of socialists
in the various countries had much effect, with socialists opposing
each other in consequence, and a new version of the international
relations game being superimposed on the original. In the International sectional conflicts paradoxically reflected the relations of
the nations themselves. The French, inheritors of 1789, assumed
their ancestors had given them an experience and a virtue in revolution entitling them to lead the International. The Germans, more
successful in asserting socialist unity at home, objected to this, and
in any case had a true hegemony in ideology, owing to the outstanding
quality of their theorists – Bernstein and Kautsky in this century,
Marx and Engels in the previous one. The Poles imagined after 1905
that Russia would never bring off a revolution, a feeling shared by
the French. Russians were regarded with pity; French 'revolutionaries' treated Russians and Germans much as French diplomats did
– revanchist towards Germans, condescending towards Russians.
Besides, the debates of the International followed the pattern of
governments' disputes. French and Germans disagreed about the
likelihood of war – the Germans believing war probable, the French
not. A similar dispute over nationality questions split Russians and
Poles. There were of course minority groups within the national
sections, but even here they reproduced in reverse the alliance
system, with Bolsheviks allied to German radicals, and these radicals
in turn linked to the Poles, adversaries of both Germany and Russia.
The International socialists, though fighting governments, thus
were ranged, and acted, in the pattern of international relations, and

simply according to country. They themselves did not appreciate this: among them, it was only the Russian exiles who lived on the fringes of society. They had failed to reject society *in toto*, could no longer see the distinction between revolutionary purposes and their own behaviour.

Haupt's *Congrès manqué* ably explains the gradual paralysis of anti-war movements before 1914. The paralysis can only be understood, at the outset, with respect to the theoretical quarrels dividing radical socialists in Germany and Russia from reformist ones. These began around 1900, by when it had become clear that society was not going to collapse as previously supposed. There was a motion at the Paris Congress of 1900: 'In a modern democratic state, the proletariat must not conquer power by *coup*, but rather through a long, patient organization of proletarian activity in economic and political spheres, moral and physical regeneration of the working class, gradual conquest of municipal councils and legislative assemblies.' Bernstein, one of the revisionist theorists, said that in any case practice had preceded principle in this. Socialist parties had become electoral machines more or less absorbed in the parliamentary struggle; they had integrated with political society, had become a kind of institutionalized opposition, functioning on much the same lines as the régimes they meant to destroy. The Left disliked this, and wanted to intensify revolutionary struggle: but its radicalism was still only one of words, as Rosa Luxemburg, Kautsky and Lenin alike accepted the parliamentary forum of the International in order to get their way. The Left was a minority in each of the national sections, and in any event the composition of the International could not have much effect either on the real aspirations of the peoples in whose name it claimed to speak or on decisions made, which were national, not international, matters.

The conflict became more heated with every international crisis between 1906 and 1911; Hilferding and then Rosa Luxemburg sought to analyse the nature of imperialism and the mechanism behind the conflicts to which it gave rise. Rosa Luxemburg asserted that the contradictions of capitalism would inevitably bring it down – socialists must take the offensive and hurry this up. She bitterly criticized the pacific illusions she saw about her, the utopian idea of parliamentary action for international arbitrage or arms limitation. Otto Bauer followed Hilferding and believed differently: he concluded, from a closely argued view of price movements and accelerating factors in capitalist development, that the system was not threatened by collapse, at least not in the immediate future – on the contrary, it would tend to get more pacific, particularly in the social field. Vliegen went even further and said this would apply internationally, since a capitalism able to resolve its own economic contradictions would also be able to eliminate factors making for war. Socialists should press this progress to social improvement and international peace.

Early in this century war had almost broken out three times at least; each time, capitalist powers had avoided it. Maybe they could go on doing so. In 1914 Vliegen did not deny a danger, but he was convinced that 'the real and self-evident interests that might justify war have now been ruled out – the world has already been partitioned, war could only ruin things, revolutions would threaten, and so governments must proceed increasingly to mediation of disputes.' Kautsky and Bebel more or less agreed with this – 'Imperialism may contain enough matter to cause war . . . but trusts and cartels have an interest in peace.' The Morocco crisis bore this out since, in the final analysis, French and German cartels had found a way of accord despite the tension of their governments. 'International movement of capital is the biggest single guarantee of world peace', was Jaurès's view. He, like the German radical, Haase, felt that peace would be maintained by three factors: 'The common activity of French, German and British capital; solidarity of the international working class; governments' fear that war will mean revolution.'

When socialist leaders heard of the Sarajevo assassination on 28 June 1914 no one thought war was likely to follow. It was by an accident of timing that the German socialists were first to meet. As regards this crisis, their only fear was that the Austrian government might place obstacles in the way of the International's holding its next congress in Vienna, or that the Serbians would be prevented from attending. Once these fears were settled, they went off on holiday. The Bureau was preoccupied with preparing the congress, and was taken by surprise at the Austrian ultimatum of 23 July. Camille Huysmans then summoned the International Bureau with urgency. Once convoked, it expressed anxiety, but reckoned – apart from Victor Adler – that the conflict would be localized, that the situation should not be dramatized. At home German, French and other socialists did sound the alarm, but at bottom were convinced that a diplomatic solution would be found. There was surprise and anxiety regarding the attitude of the masses, who outside Russia had not been moved by any protest; but again it was only Adler who worried deeply, who saw at once how the crisis would end and how the International would be powerless to prevent war.

At the Brussels meeting of 29–30 July members merely hung on events, discussing them but doing nothing. They were reassured by a telegram from Berlin, saying twenty-seven meetings had been held against war; Haase told Jaurès, 'We will do our duty', though adding that the test would be difficult. Discussion none the less chiefly involved ways and means of convoking the congress – where and when it would take place, what would be on its agenda. Balabanova reminded them of the Vaillant–Keir Hardie resolution to stop war by general strike: 'her suggestion was met with surprise and indifference.' The interminable discussion was resumed. Members left expecting to meet again at the congress. But it had been put off *sine die* and never was to take place. Each one went home hoping to avert disaster; but by 1 August general mobilization and the murder of Jaurès were announced – the great pacifist having been assassinated by a crazed supporter of *Action Française*.

The men of the Second International never saw that they had accepted the idea of war before it even became a reality. 'Hitherto they had been stressing their own ruling class's responsibility for crisis and war; now they were tempted to shift it to the enemy ruling class', said the Romanian Racovski. It was the German government, not his own, which he believed pacific, that Jaurès denounced in Brussels; he wanted his own government to exert pressure on 'our ally, Russia' (sic). Similarly, most German socialists reckoned that their government wanted peace and accused Russia instead, stressing the danger of Tsarist autocracy for future socialism. *Union sacrée* was in the soul before it was even formulated. The national, not the class, enemy was now made out to be seeking war: not the enemy proletariat, but rather Kaiser or Tsar. Even this subtle distinction vanished with the illusions of summer 1914. Victor Adler said, 'For us, hatred of Serbia is almost a natural phenomenon.' In France, Germany or Russia the depths of popular consciousness produced suspicion, anxiety, hatred of the hereditary enemy. Collective instinct spoke louder than idealism, or reason.

Chapter 6

War is declared

On 28 June 1914 Archduke Franz Ferdinand, heir to the Habsburg Monarchy, was murdered by Serb terrorists. They were Austro-Hungarian subjects. Perhaps their victim's political leanings had something to do with it: he was less hostile than others to the rights of Slavs in the Monarchy. Had his ideas been applied, perhaps the Serb problem could have been settled in Bosnia and the revolutionaries' dream of a Greater Serbia dispelled. This does not sufficiently explain the murder, since Serb terrorists had attacked the Austrian occupation authorities whenever possible; the Archduke's visit might seem a provocation, as it occurred on the very anniversary of Kossovo, the Serbian National Day – but for this to be so the Austrians would have needed to think the Serb past belonged to history. There was a further reason to remind them, and young Serbs felt the visit deserved punishment. The terrorist organization, the Black Hand, was in open conflict with the Pašić government. The government accused it of treason or irresponsibility, and feared that it would provoke Austrian intervention, whereas Russian protection might not cover Serbia if she pushed Austria to the limit. Pašić was warned that an attempt would be made on Franz Ferdinand in Sarajevo and sought to forestall it, knowing that it stemmed from members of his own Intelligence in the Black Hand. He had his minister in Vienna warn the Austrians that the journey could have an unfortunate outcome and told Colonel 'Apis' to do all he could to stop the attempt. But the Serb revolutionaries on Austrian territory were no longer controlled by Serbian government departments and the group of Bosnian revolutionaries involved refused to stop. Their act did not occasion much heartbreak in the dynasty: Franz Joseph disliked his heir's liberal ideas and the soldiers were not much affected. The Emperor is said to have declared, 'A Higher Power has restored the order I could not uphold.' Franz Ferdinand got 'a third-class funeral', national mourning being superficial both in Vienna and in Budapest. Vienna was Vienna, and the music went on.

Just the same the military, Conrad at their head, demanded mobilization, seeing in the murder an excuse for preventive war on Serbia. The situation was difficult for the foreign minister, Berchtold, who had already been accused of weakness before, during the Balkan crises. He had doubts, foreseeing that Russia might intervene. The Hungarian prime minister, Count Tisza, was altogether against war. But the hotheads were insistent and would give way only to the idea that Germany should be consulted. The Germans were divided. Military men wanted preventive war against Serbia – it might be quickly accomplished, since Russia was not ready for intervention. Civilians were less sure: maybe Russia would push Serbia to make honourable amends. The Kaiser's view was all-important. Franz Ferdinand had been his friend; he was enraged at the report of his ambassador in Vienna, Tschirschky, who counselled calm to the Austrians, and scribbled on its margin, 'Now or Never!' He did not want it said that Germany had held Austria back, and consulted his soldiers, who felt that the quicker Austria attacked, the better. He did of course consider the possibility of French and Russian intervention, but neglected it – the Tsar would not feel able to support regicides and the French had not enough heavy artillery. Austria was therefore encouraged and, once the Kaiser had made up his mind, he left for his summer cruise – though being careful before leaving to see Krupp, the great arms manufacturer, and tell him to review his stocks.

This German reaction had an immediate effect in Vienna, and the Kaiser's promise to 'cover' Austria dispelled doubts there. The Council of Ministers decided (5–7 July) to send Serbia an ultimatum couched in such a way that it could not be accepted. In these discussions in Berlin and Vienna there was talk of possible intervention by Bulgaria or Romania – seldom of Russia, hardly at all of France. The British scarcely received mention – this was a Balkan crisis, not much more. Berlin and Vienna were both after war with Serbia, but there was an imponderable: how the Great Powers would react. While the Austrians got busy with their ultimatum and prepared to mobilize, the two governments pretended that not much was happening – secrecy had to be observed so that the coming action could go forward in strength and speed. 'It would be good if you and Krobatin could go on leave for a time so as to give an impression nothing is happening', said Berchtold to Conrad. The Germans had the task of localizing the war. Bethmann Hollweg dissuaded the Kaiser from following his impulse to cancel his cruise, 'so as to avoid

calling unnecessary attention', and for the same reason the Kaiser
sent a telegram of congratulations to the old King Peter of Serbia a
few days later. It was known that Poincaré, President of the French
Republic since 1913, would be visiting St Petersburg with the prime
minister, Viviani, and the Austrians decided to put off their ultimatum to Serbia until after Poincaré left Russia, not before 23 July, so
as to forestall any direct co-ordination of French and Russian
activity. Ten days or so went by, with Berlin and Vienna seeking to
lull the diplomats. But a commentary published in the semi-official
Norddeutsche Zeitung caused alarm: 'It would be desirable for the
Austro-Serb conflict to remain localized, since other Powers' intervention could well have incalculable consequences in view of the
numerous alliance obligations.' Sazonov at once told Count Pourtalès, the German ambassador to Russia, that this conflict might
cause European war: he appreciated that Austria had legitimate
grievances, but warned against any attempt to intimidate Serbia,
particularly through an ultimatum. At the time Poincaré was still
in Russia and told Szapáry, the Austrian ambassador, that the
Monarchy must not hold Serbia responsible for the murder so long
as no proof had been shown – 'Otherwise a step of this kind could
only be a pretext . . . and in any case you must not forget that
Serbia has friends, and the step could endanger peace.' The British
Foreign Office announced on its side that Great Britain would influence Serbia to accept Austrian demands, provided they were
moderate and compatible with the independence of the country.

On 23 July Pourtalès's report, stressing Sazonov's oft-repeated
statements that England and France would consider the situation
critical, was received in Germany: if Vienna went on, Sazonov felt
that she would be condemned even in England. Bethmann Hollweg
wrote on the margin, 'This is wrong.' On the 23rd the Austrian
ultimatum was handed over, the Serbians being given forty-eight
hours to accept it. The text stated that, despite the 1909 undertaking
to establish friendly relations with Austria, Serbia had never ceased
to pursue an aggressive policy, even with criminal acts on the life
of the heir to the throne. The Serbian government was required to
publish on the front page of its official newspaper an order condemning Serb propaganda in Austria-Hungary and any participation
in this of Serbian officers and functionaries, to promise to dissolve
societies engaged in political propaganda, and to 'admit collaboration
of Austro-Hungarian officials in suppression of the subversive movement'. This, point 6, put the entire administration of the country

under Austrian control. If the Serbians agreed to all this, Austria-Hungary would provoke war by other means – perhaps including, in execution of these clauses, demands that went even further, the ultimate aim being dissolution of the Serbian state, large parts of which would be offered to Bulgaria and Albania. Direct annexation was not desired, since it would increase the already existing difficulties with the Serb minority. In this way Austrians could claim, for foreigners' benefit, that they were 'disinterested'.

News of the ultimatum brought explosions in France and Russia. With Poincaré absent, the two Powers could not co-ordinate policy as the alliance entailed. The British too were alarmed. Grey, the foreign secretary, feared the repercussions of the ultimatum, particularly in Russia, and suggested mediation between Vienna and St Petersburg. The Germans believed that the British were thereby unwittingly helping them – mediation would allow, in advance, a rapid ending of the Austro-Serb conflict. Jagow pressed Austria to intervene militarily 'as fast as possible' as soon as Serbia replied, for her answer could only be negative. Meanwhile he would try to neutralize the Entente's reaction, hoodwink these Powers and then present them with a *fait accompli*: Austria, after this, should accept English mediation. Jagow happily told the British that their good offices would be usefully employed.

The Serbians, having failed to exact a longer time limit, replied on the 25th to the Austrian Note, saying that they would accept virtually all points save the sixth. This was the signal: Giesl, Austrian minister in Belgrade, broke off relations, and half an hour later the Austrian diplomats left the town. On reaching their own territory, they telegraphed the news to their government; Serbia and Austria mobilized. The Austro-Hungarian General Staff had timed things for a declaration of war on 6 August. Jagow persuaded them to act more quickly, otherwise the Great Powers would come in, and the war could no longer be localized. Conrad gave way, resentfully, and war was declared on 28 July. But everyone blamed the Austrians, the French and British also suspecting German involvement, and believing it, in turn, must involve Russia and thus also France and Great Britain. 'You have your sources of information, we have ours', said Jagow to Jules Cambon, the French ambassador, 'and they are quite different. We are sure of British neutrality.'

The Kaiser returned from his journey, and learnt of the Serbian reply on the 28th, in the morning: 'What an outstanding result, more than ever we hoped for . . . a great moral victory for Austria –

now there is no need for war.' This, addressed to Jagow at 10 a.m., may have escaped Bethmann Hollweg's attention: an hour later Austria declared war on Serbia, and in the evening Bethmann stressed how vital it was for her to act quickly if there was to be a hope of shifting responsibility for war onto Russia. Sazonov was assured of French support by their ambassador, Paléologue, acting without instructions (but he was known to be Poincaré's confidant). Sazonov announced on the 28th that he would even press Serbia to accept humiliation. But when he heard that Austria had declared war, he decided to mobilize against her and asked Grey to state publicly that England would, in the event of war, take the allies' part – in his view the only way of making Germany and Austria retreat. But Grey preferred inviting the Powers to submit the Austro-Serbian conflict to mediation; Serbia was to be pushed, made to agree in advance that she would accept the Powers' decision, whatever it was. Germany refused this, on the grounds that it would reduce Austria to Serbia's level whereas 'the Serbian government must bear responsibility.' The Germans, having rejected the British project for mediation, still felt the conflict had been localized; in fact the Central Powers' attitude merely convinced France and Russia that they wanted war. As soon as war was declared on Serbia, the Russian military demanded the Tsar's permission to speed up preparations for general mobilization. The Tsar gave this on the 29th, but cancelled it following a friendly telegram from the Kaiser, and then returned to the formula of partial mobilization against Austria. He proposed holding a conference of the Powers at The Hague; Sazonov suggested suspending Russian preparations if Austria agreed to remove from her Note the points aimed at Serbian sovereignty. The British once more offered mediation and even accepted the principle of Austria's occupying Belgrade as a pledge, provided she then said what her intentions were. Grey said that if Germany and France were dragged into the conflict Great Britain could not stand aside for long.

Bethmann Hollweg appreciated this danger; but now Moltke intervened, explaining that the threat of war came from Russia – even partial mobilization on her part could endanger Austria, and Germany must not allow this. She would have to mobilize in turn to avoid this weakening of her ally. 'Time is increasingly against us', was his conclusion. On the 30th Bethmann required France to suspend the military preparation she had been making and also asked Russia to cancel even the partial mobilization against Austria.

If Russia gave way she would cease to be a Great Power; if she resisted she would have to take responsibility for the war. Simultaneously, Germany demanded from Belgium free passage of German troops through her territory and tried to obtain a guarantee that England would remain neutral in the event of continental war. Germany could guarantee the integrity of French and Belgian territory and could offer England a neutrality agreement for after the war. Grey replied that in this event England could not be neutral; the entire German plan was thus in collapse.

Meanwhile Moltke invited Conrad to declare general mobilization, which he did early on the 31st, and likewise Bethmann Hollweg was asked for an assurance that decision would not be later than noon on the 31st. Everything depended on Russia, since French diplomacy was relatively passive. Sazonov felt that the latest German demand only showed desire for war and in the circumstances, seeing the slowness of Russian mobilization, did not want to weaken his position by further delay. On 31 July at 11.55 a.m. – five minutes before Moltke's delay ran out – Pourtalès telegraphed to Berlin that Russia had proclaimed general mobilization. The Germans replied with an ultimatum to France and Russia, demanding from Russia immediate cessation of mobilization and from France a statement of her intentions. Grey for the last time proposed mediation, refusing to give France the guarantee felt by Paul Cambon, French ambassador, to be the only way of stopping Germany. The British on their side felt that France was doing nothing to stop the slide to catastrophe.

On 1 August, at about the same time, orders for general mobilization were issued in Germany and France. A German declaration of war on Russia followed, since she had failed to back down. The Kaiser hoped to stop there, but the 'necessities' of military planning demanded attack on France and violation of Belgium; the German news agency accordingly announced that French 'planes had bombed Nuremberg, and this false news was used to justify war on France, declared on 2 August. Only Austria had yet to come in, a 'grotesque' situation ended only on the 6th by her declaration of war on Russia – clear evidence of the degree to which Vienna followed Berlin. Grey, despite Cambon's appeals, hesitated and would give no more explicit undertaking to France than a promise to protect the French coast but gave firmer assurances to the Russian, Benckendorff. England's doubts were cleared up by German violation of Belgian territory on 4 August, when an ultimatum was sent to Germany, threatening war if she failed to evacuate the country forthwith. This was rejected, after much discussion between Beth-mann and Jagow. It was then that the phrase, 'scrap of paper', was used with reference to Belgian neutrality. The chancellor told the Reichstag on the 4th, 'Necessity knows no law'; and the Great War began.

'War guilt' is still an open question. Its solution, obscured by national or other bias, really depends on how it is posed. The role of 'evil genius' behind the explosion no doubt goes to the German leaders, who must be submitted to 'the Judgment of History' – they tipped the balance towards radical solution of the Serbian question, carefully stage-managed its course so as to have a kind of 'perfect crime', deliberately rejected attempts at mediation when the conflict threatened to go further, and deliberately risked this when Russia threatened to intervene. On the other hand, England was 'the apostle of peace' – trying not to aggravate the Austro-Serbian conflict and to ensure it would not lead to war. Just the same, her policy of con-ciliation did as much to produce war as the Germans' 'calculated risks' – the Germans, sure that whatever happened England would stay neutral, went further in their adventurous way than they would have done had they known they were wrong.

In comparison with these two contrary attitudes – the effects of which were much the same despite differing intentions – other Powers' roles seem, as time passes, increasingly passive. After Sarajevo the Austrians' singularly artificial rage had more noise than bite – Conrad did want to settle accounts with Serbia, but could be restrained by Germany. In the final analysis Vienna only did what Berlin said – to a degree described, by Fritz Fischer, as 'grotesque'. The Russians declared partial mobilization on Austria and were also first to decide on general mobilization – but they did cancel it. Sazonov and the Tsar were conciliatory; several times they declared Serbia guilty, and deserving 'punishment'. But the Central Powers rejected these offers. Paléologue, acting in France's name without a mandate, approved what they did – but in any case the Central Powers had clearly shown they meant to disrupt the Bal-kan balance, blackmailing France and Russia into hesitation by threat of continental war. In reality, both before and after Poin-caré's visit to Russia, French leaders were simply being dragged into war, more worried about their alliances' solidarity than about the fate of peace. Within the narrow framework of the July crisis they had almost no role at all, neither fomenting nor arresting the ex-plosion.

These conclusions change if the perspective is altered, or if the search for war origins goes further back. Tsarist Russia financed the Serbian intelligence service; Pan-Slavism would in the end have destroyed Austria-Hungary, and she could legitimately make out that she was under permanent threat – the more so as she did not herself feel the Slav minorities *were* being oppressed. In effect, the whole past of Central Europe was in question, Germans, Turks and then Hungarians treating other nationalities as inferior. In 1914 they attacked these nationalities for 'duplicity', asserted that 'they understood only force' – terms familiarly applied to colonial peoples. Even western history might be reinterpreted in this light: first England, then France grew up before Germany; then Germany herself grew up with astounding strength. She displayed an aggressive impatience in a Europe too small to contain her giant ambition. France, Russia and England would not give way to her, as this would mean the end of their position as Great Powers – a point of pride as old as themselves. They feared that concession would mean their own arrest and decline. Governments feared what their peoples would say to surrender; their entire policy was designed to glorify the state and the nation, to keep governments in power, safe from revolutionary pressure. Here was a permanent threat to peace; and so also was the belief on both sides that the sooner war came, the quicker it would be won. They were not of course talking about the same war, local or continental, with or without English participation. They agreed only on one point. Not seeing that this war would kill off twenty million men and three European empires, they reckoned it would be short and victorious.

Part II

The war began much as foreseen. There were many surprises and changes of fortune – France invaded, a sudden Russian offensive, the Marne fought, German victory in the east, Austrian defeat in Serbia and the intervention of Turkey and Japan. By Christmas 1914 all the millions of soldiers were astonished to see themselves immobilized – paradoxically having to bury themselves in order to live. Kitchener, visiting trenches, said that this could not be real war; nor was it the war as foreseen by Guillaume Apollinaire, full of intervals and with much chance of leisure. In a few weeks the nature of the war changed – method, style, character, spirit, aim, size. It became the Great War.

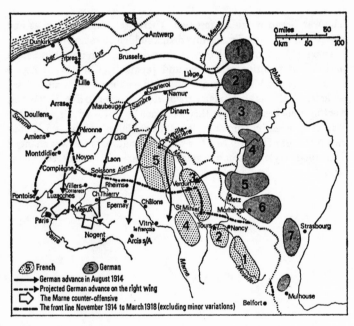

MAP I *Location of armies*

Chapter 7

From movement to stagnation

The July crisis had ended unexpectedly for the Central Powers with Great Britain intervening. For the Allies hostilities also began with a disagreeable surprise. The Germans carried out the Schlieffen Plan boldly, concentrating on their extreme right, and threatening the eastward-leaning French army with massive out-flanking. In less than three weeks they were before Paris. But there were further surprises – the Russian offensive opened much earlier than the Central Powers had expected, and the Allies stopped the invasion of the Marne. By autumn Serbian resistance, Turkish and Japanese intervention, and the stabilization of both eastern and western fronts gave the conflict a wholly unexpected turn.

On 4 August, in the morning, German troops violating Belgian territory went over the border and crossed the Meuse north of Liège. The city held out for thirteen days, during which Joffre was unable to see what Moltke intended: would the Germans go up the Meuse, and encounter the French III and IV armies, or would they go further west, and encounter Lanrezac's V army? The strength of the German right could not yet be appreciated. Just the same, Joffre applied Plan XVII and attacked Alsace-Lorraine. On 8 August the French were at Mulhouse, astonished to find so little resistance. The German VII army was in fact concealed in the Hardt forests, threatening encirclement, so that the French had to retire. The German right continued its deployment in Belgium, much outnumbering the forces opposing them. Kluck's army, on the right, advanced on Brussels while Bülow's army on the centre-right advanced on Namur. Joffre expected the Belgian army to resist, but it was submerged by superior numbers, and had to retreat quickly. Much to French disgust, it retired into Antwerp instead of joining the left of Lanrezac's army and the British. In the circumstances, Lanrezac wanted to shift towards the north-west; Joffre agreed and sent reinforcements, but only to the Meuse. He underestimated the scale of the German enveloping manoeuvre, counted Lanrezac's alarms as futile and still believed in the first, and incorrect, of his hypotheses.

He then launched the planned double offensive in Lorraine: yet at Morhange, in the Saar, and in the Ardennes de Castelnau and Langle de Cary were repulsed with heavy losses, despite their numerical advantage. Joffre told Poincaré, 'What happened yesterday confirmed my fears of the last few days – our troops are not good at attacking in flat country.' Senior officers could not manage their units, troops were not properly trained, units advancing in parallel lacked liaison, discoveries that augured badly for the French army.

Thereafter the decisive battles were fought in the north, where Bülow's mass advanced with the regularity of a metronome. They met up with French and Lanrezac on 21 August in the battle of Mons and Charleroi. 'We must recognize the truth,' Joffre once more informed Poincaré, 'for our troops, despite the achieved numerical advantage, have not displayed the offensive capacity we hoped for on the battlefield . . . we have been forced onto the defensive, relying on fortified points and the great natural obstacles . . . Our aim is to hold on . . . to wear down the enemy . . . and resume the offensive when we can.' Joffre himself thus declared that defeat in the double battle of the frontiers had not been the result merely of numerical inferiority or the surprise achieved by Moltke's turning movement. Joffre, of course, interpreted things in his own way – at Charleroi the French, with only nineteen divisions, had faced thirty – and no one had authorized Lanrezac to take on battle in such unfavourable circumstances. It was, none the less, once more patent that the French were inferior in manoeuvre. Joffre took these lessons to heart, and with defeat everywhere, withdrew.

The Lorraine offensive and the Belgian counter-offensive had been marked by a series of reverses, each more serious than the last. That the withdrawal succeeded was another surprise. The Germans had failed to envelop the Anglo-French left which fell back towards the centre and thus escaped. In the same way, the German right advanced into a void. Throughout, Joffre kept absolute control of the situation, a miracle quite as astounding as the one that was to come. He succeeded in mastering all these reverses with astonishing calm, and remained imperturbable. In less than two weeks all his plans had been dashed, northern France occupied, Paris threatened, and there was not a single success to mark up elsewhere. Yet Joffre was as even-tempered as on manoeuvres – eating and sleeping well, displaying a firmness of character that showed in his daily reports to the President, in the middle of action. As de Gaulle said, 'It was France's good fortune that, after the bad beginning, he managed to keep balance.' Joffre knew why he had been beaten; he could judge his own errors; now he expected the worst so as not to be deceived again. He courageously went on with retreat until he could meet the conditions for victory, if need be south of the Seine.

Galliéni, now appointed governor of Paris, had already been thought of as Joffre's possible successor. He had conquered Tonkin and Madagascar, had even been Joffre's instructor, and displayed towards him a patronizing esteem. His health was precarious, he was nearing the age of retirement (and died in 1916), so he had not been given the overall command. But at least he could take on defence of Paris. He acted with energy from the start and brought a new style to the conduct of the war: stopping the spreading of false news, by which the French had been deluded into believing that Mulhouse was still occupied and Antwerp still resisting – the town itself was holding out, but the rest of the country was in German hands. On the morning of 25 August France learnt from a brutal three-line communiqué that the armies were retiring 'from the Somme to the Vosges'. Newspapers the next day revealed the threat to Paris; a day later, the government's departure for Bordeaux was announced, along with Galliéni's undertaking to defend the capital – 'He will carry out this mission to the end.' At once, people of means fled over the Loire. Nothing had been prepared for defence of Paris, which was guarded only by two divisions and a few territorials. Once he got troops, Galliéni had them cross the city to give heart to the populace, and, at last in charge of an army, he hurried to make use of it, harshly criticizing the activity of his old subordinate, Joffre, whom he thought clumsy and incapable of boldness.

The Germans saw their offensive succeed beyond all expectations. Moltke said at the end of August, 'In six weeks all this will be over.' But there was an alarm in the east, which forced him to alter things – the Russians had attacked earlier than expected, and had shaken the Germans at the battle of Gumbinnen. This unexpected offensive might seriously affect operations in the west; success there might even be turned into catastrophe. Moltke – fussy, unimaginative, terrified at the boldness of the plan he was supposed to carry out – called two corps from the west to face this threat. He took them from his right, thus weakening the decisive army.

Joffre, in a directive of 24 August, set the line Amiens–Verdun for the retreat. But it was the heavily engaged British army that would have to carry out the most difficult movement; it might well be unable to reassemble on the Somme. It went back south of the Aisne, and the new French army (VI) that had been intended to assemble by Amiens now had to do so further back. Lanrezac's V army carried out a normal retreat, but the withdrawal of the British and of Langle de Cary's forces on its right forced it to make for the Oise. There it won a rearguard action, the battle of Guise, permitting general retreat in good conditions (29 August). By early September the German right, under Kluck, carried on its advance over the Aisne and then the Vesle. Joffre decided to give more ground, and on 1 September ordered, 'Despite the tactical successes won by III, IV and V armies between Guise and the Meuse, the enemy turning movement on the left of V army has been insufficiently held up by the British and by VI army, so that our armies must pivot on the right. Once V army has escaped the threat of envelopment from its left, the forces of III, IV and V armies will resume the offensive.' Thereby he prescribed abandonment of strong points on the Argonne and Verdun, and retreat to a line Pont-sur-Yonne, Nogent-sur-Seine, Arcis-sur-Aube, Brienne, Joinville. Cavalry would hold the Seine between Montereau and Melun, the British would assist as far as Juvisy. Troops from the now fortified capital would attack due east, towards Meaux.

But Kluck devoted himself to pursuing the French left, and gave up his initial objective, Pontoise. He turned in, not as Joffre had assumed towards Paris, but towards Meaux, where the French were regrouping. He meant not to take Paris from the west so much as to encircle and destroy the French armies, a plan involving risks that the Germans, in the euphoria of victory, did not take properly into account. In his ardour Kluck went beyond Bülow's line to his left instead of staying level. If he went on, his flank could be taken by surprise by the armies being regrouped around Paris; and if, simultaneously, the retreating French left counter-attacked with the British, Kluck would be taken in a trap. This was indeed the situation Galliéni hoped for on 4 September when, on his initiative, an operation was launched that started the battle of the Marne. Now, Joffre – sensibly using the railways – had managed to group his troops such that the twenty divisions of the German right were faced by thirty. To avoid a Charleroi in reverse Moltke told Kluck to fall back and link up with Bülow's army, and thus face the French attack with three rather than one army corps. But Joffre believed the time had come for a general battle. This was a tense moment: the army commanders were prepared for the decisive test, felt they had retreated enough. But French disagreed – it was too early to fight; he must go on retreating, over the Marne, and disliked engaging all his forces at once in this battle. Joffre, spoiling for a finish, was all set for decision: he went to see French and, his emotions barely under control, said, 'In the name of France, Marshal, I must ask your help . . . this time, the honour of England is at stake.' The mood was tense – Murray, French's chief-of-staff, was known to oppose the offensive. There was a heavy silence until French said, in a weak and hardly comprehensible voice, 'I'll do my best.' Joffre, suffused with gratitude, sent a message to the troops: 'Let us stop looking back; let us be killed on the spot rather than go back again.'

The operation conceived by Galliéni on the evening of the 4th was carried out on the 5th and went as planned. Maunoury attacked east, towards the Ourcq, to envelop Kluck; but Kluck had already retired, a retreat covered against the British by Marwitz's cavalry, such that the British made no progress. Further east battle was joined: Bülow and Foch both attacked in the area of the Saint Gond marshes, and this battle raged for several days as both sides sought to manoeuvre with their wings; Bülow, threateneed on the left, had to appeal to Hausen to help him close the breach. Further east the French also attacked, but it was the Germans who made the running, although without breaking through.

By the evening of the 6th, in view of these results, Moltke was worried and hesitated, while Joffre, always even-tempered, could afford some satisfaction, given that for the first time the French had stood up to the Germans in a general engagement. Joffre's forces had been successfully regrouped and numbers would now count in their favour. The next day was marked by Kluck's withdrawal north of the Marne, Bülow following so as to preserve a level line – a retreat caused by the previous day's operations, and one of vital importance – the more so as on that day Maunoury had almost been submerged by an attack on Kluck's part and Galliéni had had to requisition the taxis of Paris to send him reinforcements. On 8 September the British and Franchet d'Esperey – who had replaced Lanrezac – exploited their discovery that the German retreat had been badly conducted, leaving a gap between Kluck and Bülow, and probed the gap: cavalry made a breakthrough that could have immense results. The Germans, by 9 September, were reckoning that their defeat on the Ourcq marked a turning-point. Before the reverse could become fatal, Lieutenant-Colonel Hentsch, who had been given full powers by Moltke in his Luxembourg headquarters, intervened to tell Kluck and Bülow to fall back if the British, who had been thrown back over the Marne some days before, managed to recross it. The British did so, and Hausen in the centre was also forced to retire.

Moltke noted that things were going badly on the right, and now tried to succeed with his left – V and VI armies, under the German and Bavarian Crown Princes. But he made the same mistake as a week or so before – withdrawing four corps from here to help the extreme right, now threatened by Maunoury. In the end the German Crown Prince could not exploit his initial successes against Sarrail, despite his superiority in guns. On the 8th the situation was none the less so far to the Germans' advantage that Joffre told Sarrail he should give up Verdun and keep a link to the centre. On the 9th and 10th, just as the British and French were breaking through to the west, the Germans made a last effort, but failed, for lack of reserves, to take Verdun. At this, Moltke ordered general withdrawal from Nancy to the Vesle, and the battle of the Marne came to an end.

The Marne was an indubitable French victory – a victory, as Pierre Renouvin has said, for command. The armies, both inspired by the greatest patriotism, had fought equally well, and had lost heavily. But the commands had not been equal. On the Allied side, Joffre's mastery, Galliéni's perspicacity, Foch's impetuousness, Sarrail's resolution and French's loyalty gave the chance to plan and carry out a manoeuvre that gave the Allies the initiative, restored their morale and their will to win. On the German side there was by contrast unceasing discord between Kluck and Bülow, each of them anxious to grab victory for himself. Their movements were all the more independent as the commander stayed in Luxembourg, leaving a lieutenant-colonel to take such decisions on the spot and in his name as were felt suitable. This was at the root of innumerable pieces of clumsiness – as innumerable as historians who assert that the battle was won mainly through chance.

After this battle the German plan was in ruins. France had not been knocked out; Russia could still strike. The Schlieffen Plan had not taken into account the possibility of a British Expeditionary Force joining the French left. This 'contemptible little army' was hard-hit during the retreat, as almost the main object of German attacks; its continued existence showed how far the Germans had been wrong in neglecting the likelihood of England's intervening. French had wanted to save what was left of his army – he thought the French would be unable to recover, and several times desired to re-embark for England. Kitchener and Wilson stopped him, and, through their intervention, the British army took an increasing share of the battle. 100,000 men were lost in four weeks, and their role should not be underestimated. Kluck himself subsequently declared that he would have taken Paris but for the British.

The victory of the Marne appears to be as much a result of Joffre's strategic intelligence as of German blunders. The Germans' initial success with their enveloping manoeuvre was certain, because the manoeuvre took place at a great distance from Paris. The railways were laid out in the form of a wheel, and transfer of troops was more difficult the further off they were from the centre. Once the Germans advanced and crossed the Somme, this same factor counted in reverse: and that twice over, towards the centre in the French army's favour, on the periphery against the German army. Joffre soon came to see that, in the Paris region, the German plan would turn against Germany, and elected to fight there. From the beginning, he had demanded control of the railways: trained in technique, he had foreseen that his victory, the Marne, would be won on the French railways.

After the battle accounts were drawn up: on both sides there had been huge losses, although Joffre himself was more perturbed at lack of munitions. Jean Ratinaud writes: 'When war began, there had been 1,390 rounds for each 75mm. cannon. This fell to 695, and only 10,000 rounds were manufactured daily, for over 3,500 cannon. This worried Joffre so much that he carried about him permanently a little notebook where an exact record of munitions was entered.' On 28 September he ordered, 'Any munitions in excess of 300 rounds per gun will constitute a reserve which army commands will keep exclusively for themselves, and will use only on express authorization of the commander-in-chief', and went on, 'every evening, or every night before 6 a.m. armies will inform the Director of Supply how many rounds they have used that day.' On the German side Moltke was removed and replaced by Falkenhayn. Losses had been 40 per cent in places; and since lack of munitions was almost as serious as in the French case, stabilization of the front can be understood. The armies were bled white, lacking munitions, and immobilized.

The two sides tried a last movement to outflank each other. In the east the German Crown Prince once more sought to take Verdun and invested three-quarters of the citadel: he threatened its lifeline by setting up a great salient around St Mihiel. In October the French managed to give the fortress breathing-space by recapturing heights near by – at a price that became understandable in February 1916. In the west Joffre failed to exploit the breakthrough of the second week of September, and tried to envelop Kluck's army. In turn the Germans tried to outflank him, and as a result the fighting shifted further north, both sides seeking the Channel. This 'race to the sea' caused furious fighting from 14 September to 17 November; both sides saw its importance, and sent there all the reserves they had: British troops in ever-increasing number, Belgian toops falling back along the coast after losing Antwerp; Marines under Admiral Ronarch; Royal Fusiliers covering the Belgian retreat. There were reinforcements also on the German side – troops freed by the surrender of Antwerp and Maubeuge, and recent conscripts, with young volunteers. Unlike the pre-Marne operations, these out-flanking attempts were marked by reinforcement of lines in depth, with networks of barbed wire: immobile fronts were implicit in this.

The 'race to the sea' was a series of bloody actions ending in Flanders, where Falkenhayn was first to attack, throwing in fresh troops, most of them volunteers. They moved along the coast and on 20 October a battle opened on a front of 100 kilometres. The Belgians lost the Yser and flooded the entire region; there were furious combats in the marshy area of Ramscapelle and Langemarck. On the 29th the Germans carried their efforts to Messines and Ypres and the battle here was among the bloodiest of the war – the London-Scottish losing in a day one-third of its effectives. Belgians, French and British held on, launching attacks and counter-attacks of their own, and some of these actions had an epic quality, such as the Bois des Nonnes fighting, where British and German Guards met in battle. Neither won, the efforts of both turning out to be futile. Falkenhayn called a halt in these actions, where Admiral Ronarch's 'red-tasselled ladies', the Royal Fusiliers and the Imperial Guard had distinguished themselves; the flower of German youth had been cut down in return for an insignificant piece of ground, at Langemarck.

The eastern and southern fronts also went through extraordinary reverses of fortune and were then stabilized. Towards the middle of August the Austrian 'punitive expedition' against Serbia began; Russian intervention had forced them to reduce considerably the forces they had intended for this, but they went on, mainly for psychological reasons. They took Belgrade, but their success did not last long – a fortnight later, the Serbians retook their capital and threw the Austrians over the Save, with losses of over 200,000: the 'punitive expedition' ended in disaster. In Galicia, likewise, the

Austrians were beaten, though the Germans did better. In 1913 Joffre and Zhilinsky had arranged basic plans for strategic co-operation – a joint offensive against Germany, with the Russians attacking on the fifteenth day of mobilization. But the Russian army required sixty days to mobilize and deploy fully; Grand Duke Nicholas was thus obliged to take the offensive before his troops could be ready. If he did not do this, he would be unable to stop the Schlieffen Plan, and the Germans, after beating France, would be able to turn against Russia at will. The Russians began their offensive as agreed on the fifteenth day, although this army could not be ready until the thirty-sixth day. It launched the attack almost without reserves.

The Germans under Prittwitz were surprised and shaken at Gumbinnen in mid-August and the East Prussian population underwent the horrors of evacuation. Moltke was shocked at the extent of the reverse and called two corps from the west – making the mistake of taking them from his decisive right-wing, which had reached Charleroi. The turning movement planned by Schlieffen was thus weakened, and it was claimed, though mainly for abusive purposes, that 'without Gumbinnen there could have been no Marne.' Whatever the case, the Russians had gained their objective. However, the troops, prematurely launched, were vulnerable and a turning movement planned by Hindenburg, Prittwitz's successor, allowed the Germans, with 13 divisions and 150 batteries, to attack the 10 divisions and 70 batteries of Samsonov's army. By 31 August this had been decisively beaten at Tannenberg; Samsonov killed himself, and the Germans took 92,000 prisoners. They went on to further success at the Masurian Lakes, the Russians having to retreat to avoid wholesale destruction although they were still highly dangerous. The Hindenburg myth had been born: and it was cleverly exploited by this saviour of the fatherland.

Further south the Russians had also attacked the Austrians to save Serbia. In Galicia, with the battle of Lemberg, the Austrians were forced to withdraw to the San and beyond, the Russians occupying a large part of Galicia and its capital. The fortress of Przemyśl was besieged, 120,000 Austrians being shut in, and Russian foreposts reaching the Uzsok Pass to threaten the Hungarian plains. But high losses prevented sufficient exploitation of the success, although General Belyaev reckoned that the Austrians had been 'annihilated', and proposed that the 'débris' should be pursued into the Carpathians (8 November). Grand Duke Nicholas wanted to send twelve cavalry

divisions towards Budapest, since 'Hungary would be vastly intimidated if we threatened her with the Savage Brigade.' But this dream
was dispelled by the threat extended in the north by the Central
Powers. The Russians were keeping the initiative in the east, but at
a great price – over 1,200,000 soldiers. This had been caused by their
weakness in firepower: since August, Rennenkampf had been asking
the war ministry for 108,000 shrapnels, 17,000 bombs and 56,000,000
rounds of small-arms ammunition, and was given 9,000, 2,000 and
seven million respectively. 'The action of the Russian III army was
a massacre, the Russians having to attack without artillery support.'
But in general, as Pierre Renouvin puts it, 'When the fronts were
stabilized, the Russian army had, in the final analysis, done what
was expected of it.' It had forced the Germans to take troops from
the west, and this contributed to victory on the Marne. On 14
September General Laguiche, French military attaché, telegraphed
to Sukhomlinov, the war minister: 'The way the Russian High
Command directs operations, and the way its troops stand up under
fire, give us all an impression that can be summed up in two words,
which we all say again and again – bravo, and thanks.' By the end
of November 1914 neither side – despite adhesion of Turkey to the
Central Powers – could see how victory would come. The collapse of
the Germans' plan had been spectacular, but they were still occupying all of northern France, their lines reaching Arras, Noyon,
Soissons and Reims. The war settled on France for four years and
gave her deep wounds. Her existence was threatened and she was
paralysed for generations.

Chapter 8

Strong points and weak points

At the beginning of the war, it was the Central Powers who took the strategic initiative. The Russians had upset this, though at the cost of a heavy defeat. Tannenberg had been largely compensated on the Marne: but the Germans were still only a hundred kilometres from Paris. When the front stabilized, the Central Powers again took the initiative, this time in the east; operations followed a previous pattern, with spectacular successes and no overall decision. In the west the Allies managed to shake the Germans but to little effect and with high loss. Attacks like this, which concentrated on the strong point of the German line, turned out to be costly and ineffective and ended not in victory but in paralysis. In the circumstances combatants, not surprisingly, reached about for different strategies, seeking to attack a weak point instead. Operations in an area where the enemy's main strength was not to be found would hardly be decisive, but they would sow disorganization, might knock out an ally and open new paths to victory. Both sides tried this, though both hesitated to weaken their main lines to concentrate on less important ones. Leaders were divided on this – was it wise to divide forces, divert troops, say, to Turkey, when the Germans were at Noyon? Could Serbia be punished, the newly intervening Italians be attacked, when Cossacks stood at the gates of Hungary? These problems disrupted strategic orthodoxies, just as the immobility of fronts disrupted tactical orthodoxies.

France and Britain had won on the Marne, had not been knocked out and had driven the invader back. The Germans now applied the second stage of their plan and switched many divisions to the east between October 1914 and March 1915. With Austrian help they could manage to knock out Russia. Russia had been hard-hit by the reverses of 1914, her fighting capacity seriously impaired for lack of heavy artillery, lack of munitions, absence of *cadres* through casualties, although the Central Powers were always taken aback at her toughness: 'The more you strike the Russian bear, the worse he hits you back.' The Central Powers' forces had a great superiority in heavy artillery, a still greater one in munitions. The Russians – technically handicapped by economic backwardness and closure of the Dardanelles, which prevented foreign imports from reaching them – had only a numerical advantage which in the circumstances was illusory. But, though often defeated, they were not knocked out and several times could threaten the frontiers, particularly the Austro-Hungarian ones.

Failure of their Warsaw offensive in December 1914 convinced the Central Powers that only an operation on the flanks could succeed, and this was tried early in February. From East Prussia Hindenburg managed once more to encircle large Russian forces in the forest of Augustów. To avoid total encirclement the Russians fought a great battle near the Masurian Lakes, lost twice as much as the Germans, but retained Grodno and thereafter forced the Germans back on the defensive. In the Carpathians the Austrians were at first successful, but their garrison in Przemyśl, virtually besieged since the Russian invasion, had to surrender. 120,000 prisoners and over 900 guns were taken. The Tsar was optimistic and planned an attack on Hungary for the summer, but the Grand Duke and his chief-of-staff, Yanushkevitch, thought otherwise. Paléologue told Poincaré in a secret report that Yanushkevitch

> gradually opened up on the present and past shape of the army, and the likely outcome of its operations . . . for lack of munitions and rifles, the offensive cannot be resumed for another two or three months: the Germans can certainly send 400 trains a day to the Russian border, the Russians only 90 to the German border, so there can be no idea of attacking again in Prussia or Poland. Only the Carpathians remain . . . I went to Grand Duke Nicholas's carriage, and found him whiter in the hair, thinner and tense: 'I have serious news for you. Talking not as Grand Duke Nicholas but as Russian commander, I must tell you that Italian and Romanian co-operation are of vital importance to us, of inestimable importance.' That evening, I thought about what he had said, and reckoned the Russian army is a paralysed giant. It can still hit enemies it can reach but can never follow up or even complete the blow.

This judgment was confirmed by the Polish campaign of summer 1915. When it opened the Austrians were hard-hit by Italian intervention and sent troops to the new front, also fearing that Romania would come in. But early in May a breakthrough near

Gorlice overwhelmed Radko-Dmitriev's army, which lost 250,000 men (two-thirds of them were taken prisoner) and retired to the San, relying on a set of strong points from Stryj in the south to Przemyśl and Rozwadów. On 12 June Mackensen attacked again and reached the heights between the San and the Bug, an area in which the pattern of rivers flowing south resembles the eastern Paris basin. The Germans, advancing from the west, had to cross these to reach the centre of the basin, and, after retaking Przemyśl, they had to fight on the Wereszyca, a small river which continued the line of the heights. The Russians evacuated Lemberg, but escaped towards the end of June. At Cholm the High Command resolved to give up Poland so as to save the army.

After a five months' campaign the German advance was stopped east of Vilna, Pinsk, Kovel and Brody. The Germans had once more had the upper hand, but their enemy had not been knocked out. Lack of munitions meant that these battles had a dramatic outcome for the Russians and left them an undying memory: the retreat was described by General Denikin:

> For over twelve days, the Germans swept our lines, and we could not reply, as there was nothing left . . . exhausted regiments had only bayonets to fight with . . . losses were high, the ranks got thinner and thinner. Two regiments were destroyed almost entirely by artillery. When our batteries, silent for three days, finally received fifteen rounds, the news was telephoned to all regiments and companies, and was there received with joy and relief.

The front was broken through again and again; encirclement was avoided, but almost half the army was ruined – 151,000 killed, 683,000 wounded, 895,000 prisoners. It was a disaster and the morale of troops and generals was hard-hit. The rear was blamed – government, institutions, the régime as a whole. The High Command claimed that the retreat of 1915 should follow the same lines as that of 1812 and put into effect a systematic scorched-earth policy. Enemy destruction was matched by General Staff destruction and processions of retreating troops were joined by processions of retreating women and children. Thousands of refugees crowded the rear, where nothing was done for them. Krivoshein, minister of agriculture, complained: 'This vast migration undertaken by the High Command will lead to the abyss, revolution, and perdition.' This was the eleventh hour for the old régime; the economy was unable to sustain the army, and Tsarism could not give the will to win or grant concessions to the public that might have helped the public to sustain new burdens.

The Russian army required help from its allies, as is shown by Falkenhayn's figures. These, though not incontestably accurate, show something of the respective positions:

Western front:	Germans (millions)	Allies (millions)
Mid-October 1914	1·7	2·3
Early May 1915	1·9	2·45
Mid-July 1915	1·88	2·83
Mid-September 1915	1·97	3·25
Early 1916–		
February 1916	2·35	3·47
Early July 1916	2·26	3·84

Eastern front:	Germans/ Austrians	Russians
Mid-September 1914	0·563	0·950
End December 1914	1·155	1·688
End January 1915	1·017	1·843
End April 1915	1·323	1·767

The western commanders launched offensives to keep their troops in a state of alert – they might otherwise be numbed by trench warfare and might despair of victory – to relieve the Russians under attack and repay their *beau geste* of 1914 and to use the numerical advantage they obtained once the Germans, since autumn 1914, transferred troops to the east. These reasons overcame arguments in favour of temporizing, based on lack of munitions, inferior heavy artillery, slower growth of output in *matériel*.

The military were not, however, unanimous. French and Castelnau did not favour attacks at any price and knew that many army commanders agreed, but did not dare oppose the victor of the Marne who at this stage was drawn to the energetic and optimistic Foch, champion of all-out attack, and certain of success. Fayolle has described a discussion with Foch at Saint-Pol on 29 November 1914: 'I've never heard such idiocy. It's easy to say "attack, attack", but you might as well try to knock down a wall with your hands ... the only way they think you can win is by killing everybody off.' In justification of his eternal confidence and of these repeated attacks, Joffre used the phrase, 'we're nibbling at them'. Liddell Hart rightly remarked that such efforts were like mice nibbling at a steel safe: the teeth worn down were in fact the lives of Frenchmen. Trenches were built for the defensive, and caused high losses to an attacker. French offensives failed despite a ratio of six to one, even, in the case of a British attack near Lille, sixteen to one. On 7 April Poincaré noted, 'Always the same story. We take or lose a trench at the Bois Brûlé, the Bois le Prêtre, the edges of Hartmannswiller, and that's all. But men fall, and death takes its dismal toll.' German communiqués were much the same; punctuated with Allied attacks, there was the phrase, 'All quiet on the Western Front.'

The offensives decided upon in December 1914 conformed to the 'General Order' of 8 December, and took the form of two main attacks, one from Arras towards Cambrai and Douai, the other east of Reims towards Attigny and Rethel. The plan followed dictates of geography explained by Henri Bidou – 'to throw the enemy back on his restricted base in the Ardennes, and raid his communications with attack in Lorraine: an idea that came up in August 1914, and destined to be Foch's manoeuvre in 1918.' From December 1914 to Verdun in February 1916 all these attempts failed at a terrible cost. Allied generals counted on numerical superiority, underrated the German defence and indulged the illusion of breakthrough. German counter-attacks were also a failure: in the woods of La Gruer in the Epargnes and on the Argonne attacks were exchanged to no effect. The German attack in the second battle of Ypres failed, although here gas was used in the west for the first time, with 100,000 casualties. This attack had not, in fact, been ambitious; the Franco-British ones in spring, and particularly autumn, were. Each time, the unexpected occurred and hopes were dashed.

The first failure came in Artois on 16 December for lack of artillery, and General de Maud'huy concluded from it that attacks should not be made on a front longer than 1,500 metres; then came, from 20 December to 30 January and again from 16 February to 16 March, a great offensive in Champagne. But the cracks made were too narrow to be extended. Generals appreciated that operations could not be properly co-ordinated, particularly if the enemy withdrew, unless a network of trenches existed. Field-artillery was ill-adapted to trench-warfare, could not accurately follow the infantry's progress, and often fired on its own side. Moreover, plans of attack that looked appealing on staff-maps might well look different on the ground – after heavy rain, the chalk-mud of Souain, Tahure, Massiges became so sticky as to make rapid progress impossible, and attackers struggling forward to the barbed wire without cover were mown down. These lessons were applied in Artois, where a wider front was attacked with powerful artillery, and more varied terrain offered a better chance of cover and attack. The Germans, however, cleverly used the heights available such as the Vimy ridge, and used the varied terrain to maximum advantage. The slightest obstacles were turned into fortified points with subterranean galleries and shelters. On 9 May and 16 June the French, British and Canadians managed to advance from one to four kilometres but, without reserves near at hand, they could not exploit the success.

In September the British and French tried again with simultaneous attacks in Artois and Champagne and large forces. But this time Joffre was less optimistic – 'It might work', he told the Belgian King. Even Foch was none too sure, nor was Haig. Despite this the offensive was decided, and Joffre in an order asked the troops 'not to allow the enemy a moment's rest up to the moment of victory.' At Loos the British set their teeth and used gas in their turn. The wind was uncertain, the engineer working the cylinders refused to release the gas, but, Liddell Hart says, General Horne ordered him to act according to plan, whatever the circumstances. Some British infantrymen were thus poisoned by their own gas. In Artois the Allies failed to cross the Souchez and in Champagne there was a similar failure. The Germans had appreciated the events of spring and now set up second positions on the counter-slope some kilometres behind the first – behind the Tahure heights and invisible to the attacker. The French jumped off on 25 September, seized the first line, but could not break the second. They were ordered to try again, 'whatever the cost', but eleven days later Castelnau said he could not go on, and Joffre instructed him to stop. The Germans here lost 140,000 killed and wounded and 25,000 prisoners – by another account 80,000 and 41,000 respectively. The French lost 135,000 men and 290,000 were wounded in the Artois-Champagne battles, and for 1915 as a whole 400,000 were killed or captured and over a million evacuated to the rear, sick or wounded. British losses were in proportion.

The time had come for other ideas of strategy. The British were less hectic, since their own territory had not been invaded. Early in 1915 Colonel Hankey reported that the fronts would not move for years to come; Kitchener said this was not a war he could understand, and schemes cropped up for expeditions of the colonial type. Churchill, the First Lord of the Admiralty, suggested an attack on the enemy flank, a blow not where the enemy coalition was most threatening, in Flanders or Champagne, since there no progress could be made, but rather at some vulnerable point, even at the expense of a new front. Ideas of landing in Schleswig were raised and dropped; an attack on Austria in the Adriatic was also dropped after recognition that the strength and proximity of Pola would make it dangerous. The idea then arose of attacking Turkey. She was the weakest link in the German chain, and her defeat might bring Italy and Bulgaria in on the Allied side. It would also clear the supply route for munitions, *matériel* and reinforcements to Russia, since the Allies believed that the Central Powers' main effort in 1915 would be against her. Attack would also lighten the Russian load in the Caucasus where Grand Duke Nicholas appealed for Allied help at the end of 1914. The Turks had launched a great offensive which was repulsed in the Sarikamish area, but meanwhile the 'Easterners' in England and France had taken the opportunity to put through their ideas.

Briand, Galliéni, Churchill and Asquith had defeated their own military with difficulty. Lord Fisher felt that the operation would fail if the Greeks did not help; even Kitchener hesitated to withdraw troops from the west, for he was shocked at losses, worried about shortage of munitions, and was personally affected by the scandals surrounding this. The operation was fixed none the less, on condition that the navy took part. Thenceforth, Joffre and French were left out of account, the operation going on for some time behind their backs. The attack was expected to force the Dardanelles, threaten Constantinople, hurry the Greeks into intervention and force Turkey to surrender. The fleet involved bore the name 'Constantinople Expeditionary Force', although at the last moment the name was changed so as not to tempt the fates. British and French alike underrated the Turks' capacity for resistance, and in any case the Turks were forewarned early in November 1914 by a precipitate attack by an English squadron whose commander could not resist the temptation to bombard the Straits. Their defences were at once strengthened by Liman von Sanders, German commander in Constantinople. The British did not know this.

The first attack was made on 19 February and the British navy silenced the more exposed Turkish batteries. It was not only the Allies who thought of a great victory: there was also the Greek prime minister, Venizelos, republican in sympathy and partisan of 'Greater Greece', who felt the time had come to offer an expeditionary force for Constantinople. The Russians reacted strongly: there must be no Greek occupation, and this provoked an old quarrel with Russia,

England and Greece being, quite as in 1824, both rivals and associates. Constantine, King of Greece, was a Germanophile, opposed to Venizelos, who was forced to resign. Finally on 18 March the great attempt was made on the Straits by the Allied fleet; it lost a third of its force. The Turks lost less than 200 men. Admiral Carden thought the decision had hung by a thread, that if troops had been landed to clear the area bombarded by the fleet, the way would have been opened to Constantinople. Kitchener agreed to send a small force, thereby taking responsibility for the project without appreciating that its nature had changed. The fleet had been supposed to open the way for an expeditionary force: now it was the other way round. There was no plan for disembarkation; troops were scraped together, there were no maps and aeroplanes had no way of landing. Supply was poor, and when infectious disease came, there was no hospital-ship to which contagious cases might be evacuated. The troops landing on the Gallipoli peninsula were in a trap – the Turks barred their way, yet there could be no question of retiring. Reinforcements were waited for, but were sent with extreme parsimony; an attempt to break through failed at the battle of Anafarta as before. On this occasion, unlike 18 March, the Allies had been close to succeeding, since Turkish munitions ran out. But they did not know this, and, seeing the strength of German and Turkish resistance, went back to base. All this had been foreseen by Fisher. The Allies now had to prevent their troops being thrown into the sea; but, although new troops were to be sent, already men were thinking of evacuation.

It only remained to save 'face'. The British wanted to land at Alexandretta, in Cilicia, which their presence in Egypt and Cyprus would facilitate, and the Dardanelles affair would be announced as a mere diversion. The French disliked this for they wanted Syria, and the ink of the Sykes–Picot agreement was not yet dry. The British gave up the idea, agreeing to send the troops to Salonica, where the Greeks had been forced to allow the Allies to land. Opinion at home was worried and impatient and the future of the Dardanelles expedition was virtually discussed in public. General Monro was sent to make an on-the-spot inquiry; a day later Kitchener asked him by telegram, 'leaving or staying?' On 31 October evacuation was decided and Kitchener diverted convoys making for the Dardanelles: the first of them contained winter clothing and left unloaded. On 27 November frost descended on the troops, 5,000 of whom had frost-bitten feet and 200 of whom died of cold. Evacuation was undertaken in December, an operation for once properly managed

– the only part of the expedition to be a total success. The expedition as a whole cost in killed and wounded 145,000 men and, in comparison with the hopes attending it, had been a disaster. But as far as ultimate use of these troops was concerned, at Salonica, it was not a complete failure. The expedition had been at least worth trying: it was the incompetence of management that deserved severe condemnation.

This was also displayed elsewhere in the Middle East. In Mesopotamia, Nixon and Townsend intended to take Basra, go up the Euphrates, threaten Baghdad and take over the oil wells. There were no maps, aeroplanes or plans. They had 'forgotten' that at the mouth of the Euphrates there were no port installations as at Bombay or Madras; *matériel* remained on board ship and was taken away, leaving the troops in Basra. The landing was made at the hottest time of the year, sick-lists were huge, yet the only hospital-ship in the Indian Ocean cruised between India and East Africa, for it had not been instructed to go to Basra. Many of the sick died. Nixon and Townsend still meant to go on to Baghdad, 2,000 kilometres away, and, while Nixon waited at Basra for the supplies, Townsend moved off. At each stage he would take a town and go on to the next one, hoping to find supplies; and his exhausted army finally arrived at Kut. In Basra the number of troops increased, but food and supplies still failed to arrive. A few days later the Turks invested Kut, with Townsend inside. Attempts were made to save him, but reality had little in common with the Bengal Lancers: the troops died on the way, and never arrived. The British offered Turkey two million pounds to let the forces out, but the Sultan refused, indeed announced to the world that the British were trying to buy out their troops. In December 1915 12,000 British and Indians, exhausted by sickness and the siege, were carried off to Baghdad in the hot season, covering twenty miles a day. In the Holy City they were made to march round and round for hours, Turkish soldiers whipping and caning them, in a nightmare procession that astounded the crowds. The Kut disaster had much effect on the Moslem world. But Halil Pasha could not exploit this victory, as Turkish troops were taken up with their advance in Syria. Here the war changed only in 1917, with the Arab Revolt and Maude's organizing genius. The British recovered, took Baghdad, and Allenby's Anzacs took Jerusalem.

The Dardanelles expedition hastened Italy towards the Allies, despite her former attachment to the Central Powers. In August 1914 the rulers of Italy were divided, with the extreme Right, the military, or associates of the Vatican sympathizing with Austria, and the rest either pro-western or, on the extreme Left, pacifist. Mussolini wrote, 'Down with war: now is the time for the proletariat of Italy to keep its faith with its watchwords – not a man, not a penny.' But the Salandra government could not resist 'taking a little something' (*parecchio*) out of the European conflict. Neutrality had meant virtual breach with the Central Powers – Cadorna had insisted on mobilizing at the same time as France and Russia and on 21 July had even set out his first directives for war with Austria. Public opinion at the time opposed intervention, but the rulers were not of a mind to stay out. In the first week Salandra set a price for his neutrality – Austria was to cede territory, particularly the Trentino. At the same time he negotiated with Russia to see what he could get from the Allies. For the next ten months the Italian government kept two sets of negotiations going and, in the name of *sacro egoismo*, would close with the highest bidder. The Austrians would not give up the Dalmatian islands or the German areas of South Tyrol, though they would set up a Free City in Trieste and give Italy liberty of action in Albania and the Dodecanese.

The Allies could afford more, since Italy promised to intervene on their side, and the lands she coveted were not theirs. But Italian appetites were on the Allied scale: if Turkey were divided, Italy would want Cilicia, southern Cappadocia, south-eastern Anatolia and the Smyrna region. Italian claims to Dalmatia could only be met at Serbian expense, which the Russians disliked. The Austrians however were, despite German pressure, recalcitrant, and Salandra dealt with the Allies, signing with them on 26 April the Pact of London – first 'secret treaty' of the Great War. In exchange for parts of Dalmatia, Asia Minor and Africa – in the event of a partition of German overseas territory – Italy promised to attack Austria within a month. This had been done mainly by three men: Salandra, Sonnino and King Victor Emmanuel. They knew that most politicians preferred Giolitti and his *parecchio* policy. Giolitti felt that intervention would mean invasion and revolution, and invited all who agreed with him to drop cards at his house. 283 deputies did so. If the socialists are added, this meant a huge majority for neutrality; but the mob was called in, the government launching a huge press campaign for intervention; and Salandra later said, 'without this, intervention would not have been possible.' In fact, as Vigezzi has shown, a first stage in winning the people for intervention had been achieved by the somewhat artificial celebrations of the National Day, 20 September.

Nationalists, Futurists, all who believed Italy must undergo the ordeal of blood, were involved: History must no longer say that Italy owed her existence and territorial increase to diplomatic arts and other peoples' efforts. D'Annunzio in the ceremony of the Quarto, commemorating the Thousand, said, 'Blessed are the Merciful, for they expunge a glistening blood, assuage a refulgent grief.' There was a great echo from the press to demonstrations of patriotic character, such as d'Annunzio's arrival in Rome, early in May. The Nationalists supported war for itself, not much caring whether with or against Austria, and supported the interventionist coalition. This came to include men of all left-wing parties, particularly socialists. At first they had been against war and *Union sacrée*; but Claudio Treves observed that war might after all be legitimate, if for instance defensive, and Mussolini opened the columns of *Avanti!* to Gustave Hervé and announced, 'It was feudal, and backward Germany that began the war, against France, the country of revolution, of liberty.' He did not attend the anti-war socialists' conference in Lugano, and was visited by Marcel Cachin, who brought greetings from French socialists and subsidies from Paris. He was accused of equivocation, and took a decisive step in October: he distinguished between 'absolute neutrality and active neutrality', and said, 'socialists, too, must think in national terms.' There was a rapid increase of interventionism among the socialists, supported by men such as Salvemini, who reckoned the war was directly in the *Risorgimento* tradition, and by young revolutionaries such as Pietro Nenni and even, for a time, Gramsci. The party leaders expelled Mussolini from the editorship of *Avanti!*, but not from the party; Mussolini started a new paper, *Il Popolo d'Italia*, with an inaugural cry for war. The *Fasci*, a socialist, revolutionary group advocating war, were established and soon associated with other interventionist groups.

Opinion was mainly deaf to all this, but the interventionists won the mob, pursuing friends of Giolitti, sacking the offices of anti-war newspapers. When Salandra, with only minority support in the Chamber, resigned, the place was invaded by an interventionist mob; and by a small-scale *coup d'état*, the King used mob-support and refused to accept the parliamentary vote. War followed and parliament gave way.

Yet, as the military chief, Cadorna, said, 'The army was then virtually in disintegration, so much so that, had Austria attacked after our declaration of neutrality, it could be said without exaggeration that she would have found us almost defenceless.' But this did not stop him from being very bellicose. Moreover, since in *Triplice* days the military had often found excuses, no doubt by reason of their clerical sympathies, not to stage manoeuvres near the borders, they knew little of the terrain there; and the frontiers themselves helped Austria, whose troops could dominate Italians' positions in Tyrol and Venetia. Besides, the Austrians had already had several months' military experience against Russia. Despite quadruple inferiority of numbers, they could stand their ground, the Italian High Command revealing its inability to organize and concentrate. There was no co-ordination between army bureaucrats and the troops, who possessed in all 600 machine-guns, 1,800 field-guns and 112 heavy guns; but as Pietro Pieri says, 'The bureaucrats none the less went on regardless with their routines, urgently assembling information, even at the front line under enemy fire, about the height of officers, so that they might be eligible for grenadier regiments. There was minute verification of the points of lances and sabres, and commanders were recalled from the front to sit examinations.' Italian troops did not even know the sound of their own machine-guns. Three times they attacked entrenched positions, each time being repulsed. In a few months they lost over 250,000 men.

Just as the British and French lost illusions in Champagne, the Germans also saw that it would be impossible to overthrow Russia – the stout resistance, with possibilities for unlimited retreat, led Falkenhayn to see that the Central Powers would simply be buried in the huge plains of Russia. He looked elsewhere for the decision, but Hindenburg disagreed and suspected Falkenhayn of envying his own success and of wanting to stop it short of Russian capitulation. Conrad, best strategist among the Central Powers, took Falkenhayn's view as regards the defensive in the east, though only so as to punish 'the Italian thieves', against whom his troops – many, as Slavs, ineffective against Russia or Serbia – would behave well. But defeat in Galicia and dependence on Germany forced Conrad to accept her wishes; and Falkenhayn believed that the Allies should be struck at their weakest point, Serbia. By early September 1915 it looked certain that Bulgaria would intervene: hence victory would be secure, a link could be established to Turkey, the axis Berlin–Baghdad set up and unlimited horizons opened.

Bulgarian intervention against Serbia might involve fulfilment by Greece of her obligations. The King and the army would not however commit themselves until Bulgaria explicitly declared war, and until the Serbians concentrated on the Vardar the 150,000 men they were supposed to. Of course the Greeks knew this was impossible, once Serbia was attacked by Austria in the north, and therefore regarded their own obligations as no longer binding. The Allies suggested instead disembarking their expeditionary force from the Dardanelles at Salonica, and Venizelos, back in power, welcomed the scheme – although, if Bulgaria had not yet declared war by the time the Allies landed, he reserved a right to protest at their violation of Greek territory. But the Allies put him in an impossible position: in order to stop Bulgarian intervention, they publicly proclaimed sympathy with her, and all the while landed troops. Venizelos protested. The Allies reassured him. The Bulgarians, disliking the deception, went to war on 14 October. Venizelos sought parliamentary approval for war with Bulgaria; the King once more disavowed him, and he resigned. The Allies' double game had turned against them, with a Greece, whose neutrality had been trampled upon, becoming hostile and a Bulgaria, whom the Salonica landings had not intimidated, now in alliance with Germany.

The Serbian army had been exhausted by victory in 1914. Its barely 200,000 soldiers were badly equipped and had been recently struck by typhus. They could rely only on a few contingents from Montenegro, and put their hopes in the Salonica forces, however limited these might for the moment be. On the eve of the Austro-German attack, troops had been massed in the north, although Putnik, foreseeing Bulgarian attack, wanted to make a preventive attack against her as well. But the Allies opposed this, seeking up to the last moment to keep Bulgaria neutral. Once this game was lost, there was no hope for Serbia: attacked by better equipped Austro-German forces and threatened in her rear by Bulgaria, she could not hold the Niš road, as she had hoped, with the pass of Bagdran. The Serbians, threatened by encirclement, several times tried to break out towards Salonica, but were prevented by the Bulgarians, who also defeated Sarrail's attempts to help. There was only one way out for the Serbian army, across the mountains towards the sea; the army was accompanied by thousands of refugees as it tried to escape through Prizren into Albania – a veritable exodus or a new Anabasis. Riding on buffalo-carts, old King Peter, the populace, and the soldiers crossed the Chkor plateau from Kraljevo to Scutari, attacked by Albanian irregulars; victims of hunger, cold and thirst, they underwent a Calvary known to few peoples: 'Those who got out came one by one to Scutari . . . Early on they had been giving their weapons for bread, their boots for a slice, their clothes for a few mouthfuls. All looked like walking corpses, at the end of their strength; but they did not complain, and said only *hleba*, "bread". Forty-six corpses were lifted in the night of 16th–17th December.' The group that escaped to the south had a sickening reception, for in Valona the Italian occupiers wanted only to rid themselves of these unfortunates and drive them back into the mountains.

The French, in further violation of Greek territory, occupied Corfu and put what was left of the Serbians under protection of the *chasseurs alpins*. The Serbians, once re-equipped, were sent to Sarrail's army in Salonica, which, for lack of the reinforcements refused by Joffre and the 'Westerners', could not move. Failure at Gallipoli and in the Bulgarian affair lent weight to 'Westerners'' arguments and a systematic campaign was orchestrated by Clemenceau – the 'shirkers of Salonica' being castigated by him as much by conviction as by hatred of Briand. Reinforcements did arrive none the less – British, then Russian and Italian. The Bulgarians violated Greek territory in turn, occupied the Dedeagach region, invested the camp and threatened paralysis. Lack of means, insecurity and misunderstanding led to inter-Allied friction.

The Serbian campaign had ended with a success for the Central Powers and Conrad would have liked to go on to throw the Salonica force into the sea. Falkenhayn refused, fearing that his troops, already threatened by typhus, could no longer be well supplied. Relations were broken off and Conrad alone undertook to conquer Montenegro. For the second time the Germans had carried off a decisive success, and again Falkenhayn would not convert it into absolute victory. Hindenburg levelled this accusation over Russia, Conrad over the Balkans. But Falkenhayn was soon to repeat himself at Verdun, and this time would lose his place.

Falkenhayn was now returning to the earlier strategy, of attacking main fronts, preparing the Verdun offensive. Conrad sought to convince him otherwise and wanted attack on Italy. In a letter of 18 December 1915 he explained that an offensive, in south Tyrol, would 'fatally' strike Italy. It mattered more, Conrad said, to strike France; but this could only be done once Italy had been struck down and troops freed from the Balkans. 'Defeat would oblige Italy to make peace, since her home front would collapse; yet the longer we wait, the stronger the Italian army will become.' All this was true enough; but Falkenhayn knew the arguments were not essentially intellectual, and refused to listen. The Austrians passionately sought to punish the Italians, who laid claim, under a pretext of natural frontiers, to

Germanic areas and towns such as Meran and Bozen – now Merano and Bolzano; and this increased their hatred and contempt. Falkenhayn refused to help, but Conrad went ahead. He knew the Tyrol well, relied on surprise and hoped to have done with it when the Russians and the Salonica forces organized their joint attack.

His attack began on 15 May, but the surprise had passed, since the operation was delayed from 10 April to the 20th, and then to 1 May because of thick snow. The first and second Italian lines were pierced and even the third line reached – more than the Germans at Verdun or the British and French on the Somme. The Austrians took Asiago, with 45,000 prisoners, but a counter-attack revealed the size of assembled reinforcements; at the same time the Russians attacked in Galicia, and the snow melted quicker than expected. Conrad had to withdraw, abandoning to the Italians the land he had taken, and sent what he could to the eastern front he had so imprudently denuded, even without telling Falkenhayn. Victory became a drawn battle – Conrad, twice cheated by weather, did not have the luck that crowns great captains. As he foresaw, the Italians were greatly strengthened throughout 1916; and the terms of strategy changed for both sides, in so far as there were now no weak points or strong points; only 'the indirect approach' could affect the enemy, not – as 1916 showed – frontal attacks. But the weak-point strategy did, in the end, win a striking revenge: in 1918 victory dawned in the east.

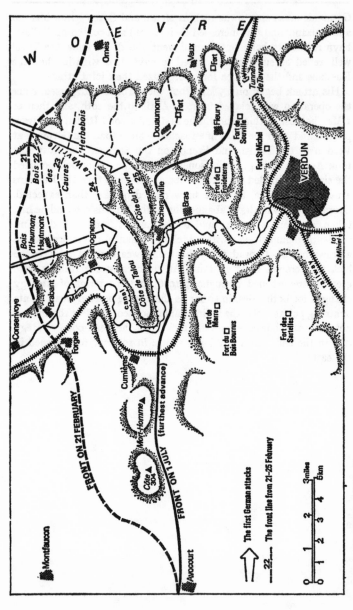

MAP 2 *The battle of Verdun*

Chapter 9

Verdun and the great battles

The Somme killed as many men as Verdun; French losses in 1915 in Artois and Champagne had been heavier still. But it was Verdun that gripped the imagination and veterans specifically of Verdun who were lauded. In 1916 the war began its third year. Twice already the Central Powers had nearly won, only to be dramatically thrown back: in 1914 the French had abandoned Belgium and had gone back as far as the Marne but managed, as if by miracle, to hold there, with of course Russian assistance. In 1915 it was the other way about: while the western front was immobile, from Flanders to the Vosges, Germans, Austrians and Turks stove in the Russian front, but were prevented from completing the triumph partly by Anglo-French attacks in Artois–Champagne. In 1915 the two sides tried to win without undue strain, not only to face the main adversary, but also attack the enemy they judged weakest – Serbia was knocked out in a few weeks, though Allied diversions against Turkey failed at the Dardanelles.

On both sides losses had been high, particularly in 1915. On both sides these were simply written down as costs of victory. Orthodoxies favoured this view: Joffre, who after the Marne was Father of the country, said, 'Let us attack and attack . . . no peace or rest for the enemy.' But if the offensive was supposed to be close, there was little sense in constructing elaborate trenches on German lines with concrete linings. By the end of 1915 doubt gripped the French soldiers, eternally meeting German wire and German guns or gas; they were assured that the next offensive would be decisive, since French armaments would be, this time, more powerful than the Germans'. In the rear uncertainty, anxiety and despair were beginning to gain over the former happy certainty and everywhere there was increasing disappointment, irritation and quarrelling. Governments no longer dared hope for a short war, or even for one with a foreseeable end, and talked of 'attrition' instead. Peoples displayed signs of weariness, and there was already some grumbling for peace. Pacifism was slowest to develop in France, over ten departments being in enemy hands: 'morale is holding out' was the phrase, a sign that morale was under strain, that rulers were anxious about it. The war effort was reaching its limit, and a new miracle was hoped for in the spring. A month before, however, the Germans attacked – at Verdun. Falkenhayn meant to forestall the Allied offensives planned at Chantilly, and felt, 'The essential question is not to take Verdun ... but to pin down the French, pull them towards the battlefield, and since they will have to defend it shoulder to shoulder, we shall bleed them white by virtue of our superiority in guns.' The French would thus be unable to carry out the planned Somme offensive, just as the Italians, attacked in much the same way at Asiago, were unable to do much; the same would be true of the Russians, barely recovering from their ordeal in 1915.

Verdun was high drama. At the outset, just as the defenders of the place began to suspect they would have to face a gigantic assault, the High Command ordered a dismantling of the forts to reorganize defence in depth. The outer parts of the town looked more like an abandoned workshop than a fortress on the watch. General Herr and Colonel Driant, who were responsible for defence, vainly sent appeals: evacuation of the forts was to precede establishment of a new system of defence, for early in 1916 Joffre thought it unlikely that there would be an attack on Verdun, while Castelnau reckoned the first line would hold. Enemy troop-concentration soon confirmed apprehensions on the defenders' part, and Joffre sent reinforcements, but it was too late. The Germans cut the railway to Verdun, and before the road to Bar-le-Duc had been arranged – it became in time the *Voie sacrée* – things had begun. The Germans, under their Crown Prince, had a superiority of five to two; they overcame the first French defences, and took Douaumont (21–25 February 1916). A million shells had been fired by the Germans on the first day alone.

Joffre was taken aback at the scale of this attack; he did not see its purpose until later, and, not wanting to deprive the Somme front of troops it would need for Foch's 'decisive' offensive, told the Verdun garrison to hold out with a minimum of troops and guns – though they were not to give up the right bank of the Meuse, an expedient that both de Langle de Cary and Pétain, appointed to command the front, regarded as admissible only in extreme circumstances. For six months the defenders of Verdun obeyed this. From the beginning they were ill-supplied, lived on starvation-rations and never enjoyed, like the men of the Somme, any feeling of superior strength, of 'victory offensive'. They were the lost children of 1916. This was a battle from the Inferno. It came as a series of improvisations, for, once the front trenches were stove in, there was no network of trenches that could take the strain of a second assault. There was no real front, only an intermingling of separate pieces that soldiers strove to join: Mort-Homme, Côte 304, Côte de l'Oie. Each unit was on its own, often bombarded by its own guns, making do as it could, and told only to 'hold on'. Units knew that on them alone might depend the battle: the inspiration, unanimity, certainty of so many have never been equalled, nor have so many men ever displayed such unflinching spirit of sacrifice. They bore the second shock and permitted their High Command to arrange the defence, to hold on and in the end win the battle.

Orders in the ruined regions of this giant battle were carried by 'runners' through the fire. These men brought something better than life: they brought news. For the soldiers – bombarded, machine-gunned, gassed, knowing neither where to go nor what to do – there was nothing worse than the endless waiting, the obsession with news of other units, or the endlessly repeated answer: hold on, wait till the bombardment lifts, till the Germans attack. That was the time when men were freed from their ruined trenches, though often only to die. There was an extreme promiscuity of life and death on the battle-field – its salients, strong points, parapets and fox-holes often themselves composed of dead flesh. Troops coming up to relieve the soldiers were often overwhelmed at the horror of Verdun: they saw an implacable fate before them, of digging a grave to stay alive, and then supporting its defence with their corpses. The length of the ordeal varied from battalion to battalion, but there would be no relief until part of the unit had been destroyed. The only certainty was death – for one, or other, or all.

Pétain disliked having to keep the same troops and arranged for constant renewal of them: hence the constant turnover that made Verdun almost the entire army's battle. The army at the time counted rather over 330 infantry battalions, not counting *chasseurs*, and 259 of them went through Verdun whereas only 109 underwent the Somme. These scarcely known figures are important, in so far as they show how France saw Verdun as the great test, a purely French affair, since there were only three or four colonial battalions in it and no British. Verdun, fought with unequal material strength, was almost a victory of the race. Here was a great difference from the Somme and 1918, where victory was owing to guns and tanks, or from the Marne, a victory of generalship.

A certain equilibrium came after the great attacks of March and April 1916 had been held; Pétain could say, 'courage, and we'll win'. The battle reached such dimensions that Falkenhayn himself lost sight of his original objectives, was caught up, and determined to take the fortress. But after August more Germans were lost than French, failure was unavoidable, and the Crown Prince took this worse than any other defeat. Falkenhayn lost his command, while the victors rose: Nivelle, who retook Vaux and Douaumont, and above all Pétain, the defensive general who cared for the lives of his men. The soldiers of Verdun had lost the illusions of their youth. They no longer supposed that the war would be won in a single battle; they could at least be sure the Germans would get no further. They all went through the ordeal to save the country, and all France exalted them as no one else, Verdun as no other victory. It was indeed a national one: France paid over 350,000 men for the honour of winning it and fifty years later its memory is alive. In 1916 the soldiers were no longer the happy warriors of 1914; they were 'the men of Verdun', citizens defending the soil of their country.

Just as the battle reached its climax the Allies launched the three offensives planned at their Chantilly conference. Russia attacked first 'responding to Italian appeals' after the menace of Asiago. Russian society, since the disasters of 1915, responded to the incompetence of its government, as displayed in the lack of equipment and munitions. Public opinion wanted to save the country and safeguard its patrimony. Businessmen formed associations – private, though in the public interest – which rationalized production of armaments and munitions, in the 'War Industries Committees' and the 'Union of *Zemstva*'. There was a 'Union of *Zemstva* and Municipalities'; it, in view of the declared incompetence of government, ran supplies in parallel to the bureaucracy. The army was therefore better provisioned in 1916 than in 1915, and on 4 June Brusilov launched his offensive in Galicia. His guns opened up on four fronts at once to disguise from the Central Powers the main direction of attack; this, with a surprise, came in the Lutsk region, and in a few days the Russians had broken through the Austrian front. They embarked on a triumphal march, the greatest success of any Power in the war. But the armies of Evert, on Brusilov's right, did not match this, and the Germans caused high losses: a further attack by Brusilov, alone, in July led to a battle of extermination that knocked out three million men for no result – the 'Kovel massacres'.

The Galician battle brought Russia 416,924 prisoners, a thousand guns and some 25,000 square kilometres of ground: it saved the Italian army from disaster, relieved the western front of eighteen German divisions hastily taken east, and reduced the Central Powers' pressure on Salonica, from where five divisions were removed to Russia. The Brusilov offensive also, in the main, caused Romanian intervention on the Allied side. Russia had never won such remarkable success, and the Central Powers had never, since Gumbinnen, felt so strongly the wind of defeat. But the success had no echo in Russia – war weariness, though not yet expressed in open hostility to the régime, was none the less shown in people's chronic indifference to its greatest successes. Hostility to the autocracy was so great that even its victories became insupportable.

Romania came into the war in the wake of Russian success. This had long been expected, since Romania had her own Alsace-Lorraine in the shape of Transylvania, then under Habsburg rule. She attacked the Hungarians for practising there a kind of compensatory nationalism; with all their grievances against Vienna, they made up for their inferiority by harshly oppressing the Romanian minority on Hungarian territory. Formerly the Romanian royal house's sympathies had gone to Germany, but the old King's death in 1914 removed the illusion. Bratianu's government was free of the mortgage, though it hesitated to intervene on the Entente side in view of German victories against Russia and Allied defeats at the Dardanelles. A few anti-Russian Romanians felt drawn to the idea of substituting Bessarabia for Transylvania; the Brusilov offensive caused a change, and after much tergiversation, Romania declared war on Austria-Hungary at the end of August. She had waited too long. The Russians were already held up in Galicia, and Brusilov had to shorten his front, such that the Romanians received the full weight of large Austro-German forces coming east. They came under Falkenhayn's own command for a punitive expedition against Romania. The country, shaped like an 'L', was vulnerable; the horizontal part was attacked by the Central Powers from the north, and the Bulgarians in the south; within a few weeks the army and most of the country had been 'engulfed', Mackensen entering Bucharest early in December 1916. Henceforth the Romanian role, played out in Moldavia on the Russians' left flank, was largely symbolical, and there was much resentment of the Russians who were alleged to have let the country down. The Russians on their side were openly contemptuous – the Romanians, instead of helping threatened Russia in 1915, intervened only when they could use the Russian army as a shield.

The Italian offensive also began late, on 6 August. This, the sixth Isonzo battle, lasted for ten days or so and was without sizeable result, other than capture of Gorizia. The Italians failed to push the advantage. In September, October and November three new offensives were tried to no effect, and 75,000 men were lost, the Austrians losing a little more. The results were paltry, despite the Italians' numerical superiority. Things went the same way in France, where the British and French, despite enjoying a twofold superiority in weapons, failed to break through on the Somme. Falkenhayn had hoped to bleed the French army white at Verdun, and thus to spoil in advance its forthcoming great offensive, planned for the summer, and on the Somme. Joffre had judged Falkenhayn's intentions correctly, and limited the number of men he sent to Verdun, but his great project had none the less been seriously affected. At first Joffre had hoped to send 42 divisions for it; by March, 34; by the end of April, 30; by 22 May, 22. The front of attack also dwindled from seventy to thirty kilometres, and in the end the British were putting in almost twice as many divisions as the French – 26 to 14.

Haig, in the circumstances, saw no reason to make 'his' offensive dependent on French goodwill, and relations declined again: no count has ever been made of the lives lost as a result of this contest of conceits. The French had learned the lessons of Champagne, and tried 'to prevent the enemy from covering with fresh divisions the breach made in his lines'. As Foch and Pétain reckoned, the troops must 'inflict such losses that we can later attack in depth . . . these losses to be inflicted not by attack, but rather by minor actions prepared by powerful bombardment, supported by all known destructive weapons such as explosive shell, gas, incendiaries, flame-throwers, electric current.' This was attrition: the guns conquered ground which the infantry then occupied, and there would be successive assaults: 'This must be stressed since, after one assault, the troops' losses are so high that they cannot repeat it . . . the infantry are to be relieved, and the artillery given time for its next task; so there will be a pause between attacks.'

The attacker would need crushing superiority in guns and the Allies did in fact have about twice the Germans' number of guns: the Franco-British industrial effort was now to tell. With nearly 2,000 guns the French had one per eighteen metres, the British one per fifty. After a powerful ten-day bombardment conducted on the famous 'rolling' principle, 100,000 men jumped off on 1 July towards Bapaume, Péronne and Nesle. The heat was torrid, the infantry heavily loaded; the British had to go up a slightly inclined plateau. The first and second positions were carried, but the attackers were mown down by machine-guns on the third. Further south, French colonial troops advanced to take eighty square kilometres of German fortified area, almost reaching Péronne. This was the limit; thereafter, despite superiority in men and guns, mastery of the air, the surprise effect of the first tanks, the British and French failed to reach beyond insignificant hamlets: Thiepval, Mametz, Combles, Chaulnes. Although they fought two-to-one, they met the Germans' huge subterranean block-houses, which made a defence in depth impenetrable. Allied attempts on 20 July, 3 September, 20 September all failed in the same way as 1 July – although they were preceded by an immense bombardment that made the country unrecognizable and wiped out all trace of human or vegetable existence. Haig said he would attack only when the guns had destroyed everything; infantry would then occupy the area. By the second day the British had lost over 50,000 men, but Haig did not stop, and the French behaved with like criminal stubbornness, losing heavily for insignificant results. By the end the British had lost 419,654, the French 194,451; the Germans about 400,000. The Somme thus made well over a million victims.

The British generals said they had failed because of their troops' inexperience, but still sent them again and again to the bloodbath. Haig thought the Germans would be struck by 'the fighting will of the British race', that on the first day they would have lost 30 per cent and, if this went on, 'within six weeks they would not find a single able-bodied man'. The Somme battle was in fact disastrous in the loss it caused, almost useless from the military viewpoint, and merely revealed the vainglory of the generals. Haig's narrow-minded obstinacy was matched by Foch's unflinching confidence, which Joffre still highly approved. Fifteen weeks' exertions came to little result. The British broke off the offensive, Joffre was none the less still ordering Micheler to resume it 'in width and in depth'. Poincaré and Briand recognized he must go.

To replace Joffre – who became Marshal of France – the government selected General Nivelle, victor of Verdun, and less linked than other generals with the failed attempts of 1915 and 1916. Pétain was thought to be lacking in offensive spirit, and the Allies were

thought to need a leader willing to use to the limit the material
advantage they could now be sure of. Nivelle met these conditions.
He spoke well, and managed to win round the politicians by
the clarity of his exposition. He showed that attrition was over – the
breakthrough would now be made. Haig was sceptical, but after the
Somme was ill-placed to object; Lloyd George dismissed his objections
and obliged him to accept Nivelle's orders. Lyautey, the new war
minister, and Pétain were also sceptical, but they would not proclaim their doubts in public or join Haig in his attitude, so as not
to 'disturb this fine victory won by the French High Command over
its allies'. But Nivelle began badly. His appointment caused envy;
although he had won Vaux and Douaumont, he had been promoted
over the heads of several army commanders – Pétain, Castelnau,
Franchet d'Esperey, Sarrail, Foch. Nivelle also caused suspicion
because of his good relations with politicians, particularly Lloyd
George, who had been much surprised to find a general not only
articulate but capable of good English. The generals maintained
their reserve, knowing that Lyautey, and then Painlevé who succeeded him, did not fundamentally approve of these offensive plans:
Nivelle's assurance was doubtful – 'We can break through the German
front at will, provided we avoid the strongest point and attack by
surprise, in 24 or 48 hours, and once we have broken through, we
can do as we want, go to the North Sea coasts or Brussels or the
Meuse or the Rhine.'

The Germans knew what was going on. Since Falkenhayn's dismissal following Verdun, Hindenburg had taken over, and he decided
to forestall the French offensive with a retreat, the 'Alberich' operation, conducted almost with a flourish of trumpets, to prepared
positions twenty to forty kilometres back. Without fighting, he
gave up the salient of the Serre, the towns of Lassigny, Roye, Noyon
and Bapaume. This would force the Allies to think again, for their
offensive would now debouch into an area dominated by German
artillery, partially flooded and made almost totally useless. Besides,
revolution broke out in Russia and, whatever its outcome, the
Russian offensive for 1917 would be put off. Haig, Pétain and Painlevé all felt that the joint Allied offensive would now have to be
postponed. Nivelle disagreed: on the contrary, the possible dropping
out of Russia made the offensive all the more urgent, since the French
must act before the Germans moved troops in mass from east to
west. Hindenburg's manoeuvre, he felt, merely helped this: 'Had I
given Hindenburg orders, that is what I'd have told him to do.' But

he was in fact taken aback at the retreat and did not know how to react to his own reconquest of Lassigny and Noyon.

Poincaré and Painlevé decided to debate the offensive in the War Council – scarcely a gesture of confidence in their commander-in-chief. Franchet d'Esperey and Castelnau were consulted by the government, but dodged the issue. Micheler weakly defended his chief. Only Pétain, who disliked the offensive, clearly opposed a plan that, in his view, could not succeed after the German withdrawal. Nivelle offered to resign, but ministers protested wildly that Nivelle had their confidence, and were desperately anxious to avoid another crisis of command, and indeed their own responsibilities. If Nivelle, on his conscience, could say that victory was possible, he must not hesitate with his offensive. Nivelle formally took note of this, and promised to break off the offensive on the third day if it failed. Thus reassured, Pétain came to support the project; but, as a witness recounted, the offensive had only been approved by 'a unanimity of constraint'. Ministers did not want to look foolish in British eyes.

On 9 April 1917 the Anglo-Canadians launched the preliminary operation arranged by the two commands, and Vimy ridge was carried. Another diversionary attack, in the zone of German withdrawal, failed altogether. On 16 April Nivelle launched an appeal to combatants, said victory was at hand and launched his main attack between the Oise and the Montagne de Reims, with the aim of carrying the line of heights dominating the Ailette valley, above the plain of Laon, crossed by an earth-road known as the Chemin des Dames. Mazel and Mangin of V and VI Armies failed to reach it, despite high losses. In the afternoon tanks were sent in, but they were badly designed, with their petrol-tanks in front, and were easily knocked out by German heavy machine-guns. The same happened again on the third day, and Nivelle, as promised, ordered a halt to the main attack; but he continued subsidiary ones, to 'exploit' the main one, for several weeks more without result. The offensive had been a total failure, costing in the first days alone over 40,000 dead. Painlevé now dismissed Nivelle. This was a turning-point. The mutinies that followed convinced Pétain, Nivelle's successor, that there must be no more futile offensives; France must go over to the defensive, wait for 'tanks and Americans'.

Haig was not surprised either by failure or mutiny and was in fact only surprised the mutinies had not come before. But he did not apply the lesson personally and simply supposed that the French failure marked a glorious moment for himself, since his army would now take the main role in France. He persuaded his own government that the Germans must be pinned down if they were not to exploit the difficulties of the French army, although in fact these were overcome by August – as the Malmaison attack shows. Pétain did, however, approve, and begged Haig not to let up until the French had recovered health and confidence. The British, following a plan drawn up early in 1917, launched a great offensive in Flanders, with the help of a French contingent under General Anthoine. Tanks were used massively for the first time, instead of being employed, as in 1916, in little groups; late in the year, at Cambrai, they even broke through, but there were no reserves to intervene, and German artillery won the upper hand. The Passchendaele fighting of summer and autumn 1917 was among the bloodiest and most futile battles of the war, killing 400,000 men for nothing. In the face of such reverses, the Allies did not draw up any offensive plans for 1918; they meant to stay on the defensive until their superiority in tanks, guns and aircraft was greater. The Germans also gave up any idea of winning by offensives in 1917, for they now counted on different weapons, a more indirect approach to war.

Chapter 10

Cannon fodder and the new art of war

The soldiers' war had its own history, though it had little to do with what appeared in the history books later on. It had its own life, its own dramas and its own pauses. First came the illusions of 1914, then discovery of harsh reality, the period of early trench-warfare, of hopes several times dashed in futile offensives, marked by memories of tragedy: gas, dead soldiers impaled on the wire, mud sticky with blood. Then came the inferno of Europe: Verdun for the French, the Isonzo for the Italians, the Somme or Flanders for the British, the retreat of 1915 for the Russians. Later came divorce from the rear, a hidden despair and anger, the final agony of 1918, and the solidarity of front-soldiers, which, after the war, turned into a veritable ex-serviceman's faith. Parallel to this development, and also not forming part of official history of the traditional sort, came technological development – a war experienced at each stage by the combatants, but one won or lost by an obscure army of inventors. Their works are known, though not their names. Western society, still influenced by notions of chivalric battle, disliked having to recognize that wars were lost by men other than great captains.

The war came to Galtier-Boissière suddenly, on 22 August 1914, as his army corps withdrew as part of the general retreat. It had till then been mere marching about.

Suddenly, bullets screamed; we dropped face-down on to the ground, in terror; there was an explosion just above. The men knelt hunched-up with haversacks on their heads, showed only their backs, and stuck close together. The ones I could see, from under my own haversack, were shaking and twitching, their mouths contracted in a hideous spasm, their teeth chattering. They looked, with their heads down, as if they were offering themselves to an executioner. There was a deathly suspense: a corporal, without his képi, said, 'If this is what it's like, I hope I'll be killed off now.' We were not lead soldiers, and the first

85

contact with war was a terrible surprise. We had laughed and never thought about it before, could see war only through a rosy patriotic haze, and since we had left Paris the *Bulletin des Armées* had been keeping up these silly illusions. Everyone thought the Germans would be surrendering for a piece of bread, that our guns were crushingly superior, that it would be a kind of procession. Nerves had not been prepared for explosions like this; we suddenly knew there would be a frightful ordeal to come – 'Sir, we're for it after all.'

The first attacks were far from being the well ordered charges that men had thought: Max Dauville wrote:

A company went forward across the field in open order. The men were bent double, haversack on their backs, by turns running heavily and dropping, to jump up again with the whistle. One of them ran past me: his peasant face suddenly changed to a tragic grimace, and he ran on, and raised his arms from which the hands were hanging, the fingers half-severed by bullets. The rest dropped to the ground, but he ran on and on, and I can still hear him crying, 'Sir, help me'.

These wandering children would be picked up by a doctor at some first-aid post.

The wounded kept arriving in this tiny café, and straw had been hurriedly laid down over its blue tiles. On the tables, open bags spilled over with bandages, brown phials, nickel-plated instruments . . . Outside, just as I was talking to a stretcher-bearer, a shell severed his right leg – there was a crack like snapping wood, and he fell, screaming. One of the men came hobbling in, his eyes fixed. A bullet had gone through his brain, and he died a few moments later, his blood spreading out through the straw like a great red halo. There were wounded coming and going, moving fast, for as soon as one was bandaged, there were other hollow faces in the doorway waiting their turn. Others were laid out, inert, on stretchers.

From 1914 onwards the grave preserved life. Germany had set an example, with systems of trenches, equipped with parallels, saps, communication-trenches, dug-outs and listening-posts. The British followed the example; the French and Russians less so, since they never imagined they would be buried there for three years or undergo in these fields all the coming battles, Champagne, Verdun, the Somme. The French therefore made provisional constructions, whereas British and Germans accepted the new form of war. Salients and re-entrants were needed to avoid enfilading; once the network was established, parapets and listening-posts had to be constructed. Barbed wire would be laid, a dangerous job if carried out under machine-gun fire; sand-bags would be piled up to give protection from splinters: parapets, for observers, would be constructed. The two lines were often close together, and the slightest rise would be fought over, so that units could dominate the enemy while unseen by him. One novelty of trench-warfare was camouflage. Until 1914 the main lesson was how to concentrate troops, and now camouflage, particularly for guns, counted for as much. Sausage-balloons and air-ships would keep the enemy under observation, although later they were also used to strike. Trench-warfare needed weapons of its own. The Germans, for instance, employed a steel-cored bullet to pierce parapets and sand-bags; against air attack, luminous or incendiary bullets were used, since they could blow up gas-hulls and petrol-tanks. The French were also vulnerable in their trenches to mines and *Minenwerfer* as well as air attack. *Minenwerfer* were better than flat-trajectory guns, vertically throwing projectiles weighing from fifty to a hundred kilogrammes and dropping them very close – within one hundred to five hundred metres if necessary. These mines were particularly dreaded, as they could destroy whole trenches. The French had nothing to oppose them for some time, and felt exposed. Joffre had had an interest in these before the war, and when it broke out a specimen mortar was being worked upon; but it was not completed, because the officer involved left for war the next day. Attempts were made to adapt the 75mm but its range, like that of other calibres, was not short enough. In 1915 an answer was found with a shell fitted with trench-mortar blades, which was effective, and was served by gunners who were much more part of trench life than other artillery men.

Barbed wire was one of the attackers' great problems. There were cutters, but not enough, and men were often killed before they could cut a way. Millerand was told, and imperturbably suggested that files should be used. Italian officers said, 'They could try with their teeth'; 'let them pass over a bridge of corpses'. There was a bomb-cradle, worked by strings and supposed to explode on impact with the wire. It was a failure, as were the armoured barrows or oxyhydric pipes invented by the chemist, Georges Claude. Machine-guns were used in the end; they could, at a fabulous cost in ammunition, cut the wooden staves upholding the wire. The 75 was also used.

Close combat meant a return to grenades. As no proper ones were supplied, the French soldiers made their own out of bottles, though in the end they had grenades of the German type. Trench-warfare brought in other weapons that made war still more atrocious – first, flame-throwers, a German invention applied as early as October 1914. The carrier was very vulnerable if his tank were hit, but these suicide-soldiers were dreaded – the Germans chose the fastest runners, though they did not often return alive. Then came asphyxiating gas, first used by the Germans on the western front at Langemarck on 22 April: on a front of six kilometres, gas was released for five minutes, and formed a cloud of 600 by 900 metres, which moved at a speed of two or three metres per second. The effect was immediate and shattering, though the Germans failed to exploit it, their own infantry fearing to occupy the area and there being no reserve force with gas-masks. The Germans were frightened that they could not control the gas-clouds if the wind turned, and from their point of view the front faced the wrong way, since between Flanders and the Argonne westerly winds are predominant. In any case the attempt had been made only as an experiment, the High Command not supposing they could greatly exploit this mere scientific discovery. Several gas-attacks were made and much condemned by world opinion as a breach of 'the laws of war'; the Germans could answer, though scarcely with justice, that they were an answer to French phosphorus bombs and British picric ones. Whatever the case, the British also used gas-clouds at Loos in September 1915, and the French gas-shells – an example soon followed by British and Germans. In 1916 and 1917 the French used mainly phosgene shell, the Germans green-and-yellow gas; both sides particularly used yperite, which could poison an entire area for days, could contaminate clothing and corrode the skin. Use of gas never gave more than a temporary success, usually through surprise, and this was true also of flame-throwers. Trenches could be stormed and this type of warfare terminated only by a weapon that was yet to come, tanks.

Trench-warfare had its own rules, rhythms and customs. Few soldiers escaped its vicissitudes, although the length of time spent in the trenches varied – the time needed for one section to be killed off or for relief to arrive. At Verdun or the Argonne, notebooks were found on the dead, recording their thoughts and memories; they, like survivors' testimonies, deserve quotation. They illustrate what trench-warfare was like – arrival, settling-in, waiting, attack, the moments of glory, the torment of the wounded, the relief and return to base of the others. Daguenet, adjutant of the 321st infantry regiment, described his arrival at the front:

> We came along the Haumont sap, under flanking shell-fire. The trench filled up with corpses all along – men were dying there in the mud, some already with a death-rattle, others begging for water, others still screaming for us to end their agony. Snow fell all the time, and the shelling cost us many men – when we got to B trench, I had only 17 men left out of 39.

A Champagne trench was described:

> There was a vile stench in the new trenches, to the right of the Epargnes. Rain came down in torrents, and we used bits of canvas we had found stuck in the trench-walls. The next day, at dawn, we saw that the trench had been built in a veritable grave-yard – the bits of canvas had been put there to cover bodies and human remains.

Further on, Raymond Naegelaen saw:

> on the front of the Souain ridge, corpses of soldiers mown down by machine-gun in September 1915; they lay stretched out, face down, lined up as if on manoeuvre. The rain fell on them inexorably, bullets snapped their whitened bones. One night Jacques, on patrol, saw enormous rats running off from under their faded caps, fat with human meat. He crawled towards the corpse, his heart beating loud; the helmet had rolled off, there was a grinning head with no flesh left on it, the skull bare, the eyes eaten up. Part of the false teeth had slipped out onto the rotting shirt and some vile animal jumped out of the gaping mouth.

In the trenches, men waited, but 'from brigade came the order to hold on, not to retreat, to be killed rather than retreat. The men reckoned they were finished, and that was the second night we spent without sleep, for the cold started when night fell, and our feet were blocks of ice.' Soldiers learned that they were to attack:

> The hours went by slowly and inexorably; we could not even swallow for tension; there was always the thought – in a few

hours where shall I be, here, or one of these vile corpses, torn
to bits by shell. The moment comes – thirty, twenty, ten
minutes more, the hand goes round, and I go on counting the
seconds. Gradually I got to my knees, my pockets stuffed with
cartridges and a dead man's rifle in my hand – 5.58, 5.59,
6 o'clock. I shouted, 'Forward!', and then a red explosion
blinded me and threw me to the ground. My right knee was
pierced, and I was wounded in the stomach and the cheek.
Near by were other wounded, and dead.

Captain Delvert of the 101st infantry regiment, in a position at Fort
Vaux with his company, told what he saw:

Today the Vaux slopes could not be seen under the rain of our
shelling since 6 p.m. The shells could be seen, falling on the
white traces of the German saps and trenches. At night, under
a starlit sky, green rockets went up from our foremost lines, at
the bottom of the ravine, telling the guns to lengthen their
range, and the appeal was shouted from all around. Red
rockets went up from the Hardaumont plateau, from Fort
Vaux, from behind Fumin, desperate appeals to the guns
coming out of the dark landscape.

Later the Germans' turn came to attack:

At four o'clock the bombardment lifted and the attack began.
An officer came out of the ground two hundred yards away,
followed by a column-of-four – their rifles were at the slope, and
it looked like a parade. We were all taken aback, which no
doubt the Germans intended, but after a few seconds we began
to fire madly, and the surviving machine-guns came in. The
officer dropped dead fifty yards off, his right arm stretched out
towards us, his men piling up and dropping next to him. It was
not to be believed.

Many soldiers were buried alive. Gustave Heger of the 28th infantry
regiment said:

I first got out a soldier of the 270th, who was easier than the
others. There were still more men buried alive, shouting so
loud that the Germans might hear them and open up with
machine-guns. We couldn't work standing up, and I felt like
running off, but I couldn't leave them there. I tried to dig out
old Mazé, who was still shouting, but the more I dug, the more

the earth fell in. I had him clear to the chest, and he could at least breathe more easily, and then went to help one of the 270th, who was still shouting, though getting weaker. There should have been two more, but there were no shouts; I dug away, and cleared a head – but I saw they were both dead, lay down exhausted for a space, while the bombardment went on.

At Verdun the wounded of a whole section of the field were gathered in a disused tunnel, Tavannes. Lieutenant Benech, who was moved there after being wounded, remembered:

The air in the tunnel was foetid; I'd rather have stayed in the open, even to die. Outside you risked a bullet; here, you could go mad. There was a pile of sand-bags up to the vault, and this was our refuge; outside the storm went on, the hammering of shell of all types. Above our heads, under the thundering vault, there were a few filthy electric bulbs casting a shadowy light, with clouds of flies circling round them. They buzzed on, irritatingly, and landed on you; even if you struck at them they would not get off. Men's faces glistened, and the tepid air was sickening. You lay on muddy sand, fixed to a rail, your eyes on the vault, or you lay face down, rolled into a bundle. These stunned men waited, slept, snored, dreamt, and moved only when someone trod on their feet; water and urine trickled through; and there was an animal stench, mingled with saltpetre, chloroform, sulphur, chloride, of excreta and corpses, of sweat and filth, which made you retch. No one could eat, and at best some tepid and frothy coffee-water from a tin could be used to calm the universal fever. Other first-aid posts could not even offer relative quiet: a very young corporal arrived, with both hands torn off at the wrist, and he looked at the hideous red stumps with wild despair.

When, after ordeals of this kind, men returned from the front, the scene, as described by Lieutenant Gaudy, was strikingly poignant:

The two regiments [57th and 144th] of the brigade marched back along the road all day. The companies were skeletal, sometimes led by a surviving officer, stumbling along with his cane; they trailed on, staggering as if they were drunk – knees bent, bodies bent back. Squads, or even simple sections – you could not tell which – came on, their heads bowed; stricken, sad eyes appearing from beneath field-caps; rusty, muddy rifles were held suspended by the sling. Caps and faces were coloured alike by dry mud, and then covered again by more mud, encrusting clothing and skin. Automobiles drove past in tightly packed columns, scattering to either side the survivors of this hecatomb. The men were now beyond speech; they no longer had strength even to complain; when they looked up at the roofs of the village, you could see in their eyes an abyss of grief, a petrification through dust and strain. These dumb faces proclaimed a martyrdom of hideous proportions. Territorials beside me looked on and wept, silently like women. On the road back there was even some shelling, and these wretches were sometimes killed just when they thought they were safe.

Trench-warfare proved the experts wrong in all countries despite the previous indications of the Russo-Japanese War. From that war experts had assumed that 'in modern war, losses will be caused, to 85 per cent by small-arms, 10 per cent by gunnery, 5 per cent by cold steel' – inappropriate lessons, by which the role of artillery was considerably underestimated, even simply equated with the bayonet. Cavalry was wrongly rated. In the east it did what it was supposed to: the Tannenberg manoeuvre was partly its work, and Cossacks spearheaded all the Russian offensives. In the Balkans and the east, cavalry was even decisive – the Jouinot Brigade began the march to victory. But the western war had a different style, cavalry becoming, as General Pedoya foresaw, anachronistic – generals moved about by car, and the trenches certainly had no need of cavalry. It was none the less kept in reserve, in case of breakthrough – as happened at Champagne, in September 1915, which was, in Jacques Meyer's words, 'the swansong of cavalry'. Cavalry, supposed to charge over trenches, could only dismount, and its task henceforth was either to wait or fight on foot. Like so many others, Captain de Sézille refused to recognize reality, and in a handbook on 'Measures to be taken in preparation for service in the trenches' he laid down in the cavalry section:

> The squadron will arrive on horseback, at dawn, at a fixed point usually three kilometres from the front. Two-thirds of the cavalrymen will dismount, leaving the remainder to take back two horses each – one to the left and one to the right of his own mount. The column will then march towards the trenches . . . each section occupying its portion of the line . . . During

the day-time, men will keep below the parapets, and the troops will be kept from idleness by improvements of the subterranean system . . . In the second line service is similar, rather easier by virtue of the greater distance from the enemy, although shelling will be a greater danger.

This, written in 1915, shows how far the new warfare surprised experts. Soldiers were now forced to reconsider the role of artillery, to fit aircraft into the battle-pattern, and there was a prime need for some supreme weapon that could overcome trenches and barbed wire – the tank.

In 1914 the French had 3,793 75mm. cannon, the all-purpose field-gun. There were no heavy guns at the level of army corps or lower – only at army level; in all, the French had 300 against the Germans' 2,000; and the Germans had about 2,500 77mm. cannon. The French were inferior in this because their preconceptions as to the roles of artillery and infantry were incorrect: 'Artillery will not prepare attack, but will support it and will intervene to help the infantry as soon as the advance has begun.' The 75 was thought equal to any-thing, even a barbed-wire system. This was not the German view, and there was even some feeling that France, in 1914, would not go to war precisely for lack of heavy guns. The Russian army was equal to the Central Powers' forces in quality, but it had two times less their guns, and there was soon to be a shell shortage.

Joffre, when he took over, objected to these notions, but the heavy artillery he needed was not ready by August 1914. A few weeks later, Antwerp – which was supposed to be the strongest fortress in Europe – fell, and this convinced Joffre that there was no sense in imprisoning unused guns in fortresses. He carried out a partial disarming of forts that at least gave the army some old *Pange* guns, as it was meant to have. This explains the partial disarming of the Verdun forts before the German attack of February 1916. The Allies' heavy artillery did not acquire new material till the Somme offensive in July 1916, by which time they caught up with the Germans – an evolution also found in aviation.

Aeroplanes were a new weapon. They had appeared, fleetingly, in the Italo-Turkish war in Tripolitania, and experts had since then examined their future role, along with dirigibles and sausage-balloons. Major Besseyre des Horts and his disciples felt that the aeroplanes, being faster and less vulnerable, would be best suited to observation; dirigibles, carrying a heavy load, could bomb. Aeroplanes were also counted suitable for a war of movement, dirigibles and balloons to siege-warfare. No one foresaw trench-warfare, so in the first months of war aircraft were used on these lines, the Germans preferring Zeppelins, dirigibles, while the Allies preferred balloons and aeroplanes. In 1914 the Allies had 220 aeroplanes, the Central Powers 258, as well as some dozens of dirigibles. In 1914 the Friedrichshafen workshops could construct one dirigible in six weeks, and these, together with *Tauben*, were sent on many bombing missions to London and Paris. On 19 January 1915 six Zeppelins crossed the North Sea, bombed London and returned intact to their base. The exploit was repeated. British raids on Cuxhaven and French raids on Freiburg-im-Breisgau never had this spectacular and effective character.

Air-battles were more and more frequent after December 1914, the German Fokkers enjoying marked superiority. The Frenchman, Roland Garros, was first to have a machine-gun synchronized with the movement of the screw, but he was taken prisoner and the Germans copied the procedure, while for a long time pilots went on using rifles and pistols. Aeroplanes could also strafe troops with the help of steel pellets, each weighing some twenty grammes, and deadly in their speed – 100 metres per second. Early in 1916 the Germans were still maintaining their spectacular lead – the giant Schuckert XVIII aeroplane destroyed the British air-base at Dunkirk, Zeppelins went on bombing London. One of them – the L59 – made a remarkable journey – leaving from Yamboli in Bulgaria, it went as far as Khartoum to bring medicine and relief to the German garrison in Tanganyika; it was told by telegraph that the garrison had had to surrender, turned about, and made altogether a journey of 6,800 kilometres. In 1918 the Germans' Zeppelin fleet contained over 100 giant airships. They travelled at 130 kilometres per hour, as against 90 in 1914, and could each carry 40 tons of explosives at a height of 2,000 metres and more. At the front the Germans still, at Verdun, largely dominated the field, but by summer 1916 the Allies were competing: Bréguet, Nieuport, Spad and British fighters were equal to the German ones. Up to the end of 1917 there were great duels in the air; the 'aces' were heroes, symbolizing the spirit of 1914. Almost all of them were killed: the most heroic were the German, Richthofen (80 clear victories), the Frenchman, Fonck (72), the Englishman, Mannock (73), the Canadian, Bishop (72), the German, Udet (60), with Guynemer and Macfollen (54 each). At the same time, the Italians' Caproni mastered the air of the Alpine front.

The great innovation of 1918 was German – squadrons of covering and fighter-planes which, flying low, could support the infantry. In March 1918 thirty-six squadrons of six biplanes each took part in the Picardy offensive. But the Allies had a sufficient counter-force, and inflicted high losses, and the addition of American air-craft could tip the balance. In 1918 only thirty-seven German aircraft, out of 483 attempts, were able to reach Paris; London was protected by over 200 fighters. After midsummer, Foch had an absolute superiority, with nearly 600 planes in the battle, and on 11 November France had 3,437 aeroplanes in line – many more than in 1940. Under General Duval there had even been combined tank–aircraft operations, a lesson forgotten in 1940.

It was the same with tanks, to which the Allies owed victory more than to aeroplanes. The idea came at the same time in France and Britain: Colonel Estienne and Winston Churchill demanded experimentation of block-houses, moving on caterpillar-tracks, an engine, good for all terrain, that might protect infantry-attacks, destroy barbed wire and machine-gun nests, and move as fast as the troops. The British were first. The secret was kept by announcing that the steel plates were meant for petrol-tanks, hence the name of the new weapon. In September 1916 the 'Willies' took four villages, but there was not enough co-ordination with infantry, and the Germans retook them. Nor was the first French experiment – the great Nivelle offensive of 16 April 1917 – conclusive. The huge Schneider 21-ton tanks were vulnerable, and German heavy machine-guns knocked out 60 of the 132 involved. Crews were grilled to death, and infantry, without protection, was then massacred. The Germans, in a fatal error, reckoned that guns would always win.

These heavy tanks were slow and unwieldy; eventually the light Renault, Berliet and Schneider tanks were preferred, although the Saint-Chamond ones were not abandoned, since they alone could cross a two-metre ditch. Serial production of these little machines revolutionized the art of war, and their first great success came with 11 June at Compiègne, 18 July at Villers-Cotterêts, the decisive act in the second battle of the Marne. They took part in all attacks there-after, despite the heavy losses – 50 per cent – they were liable to suffer. They were an essential part of breakthrough, and since over 500 now arrived at the front monthly, replacement was safe. In August the French were using 1,500 tanks, and the British as many: under Rawlinson, these won a great strategic success on 8 August. By November the French were using over 2,000 tanks, the 'tanks of victory'.

In 1918, with mastery of the seas and American intervention, the Allies managed to overwhelm Germany and produce more and more guns and aircraft. But, tanks apart, the Germans were more lively in 'the art of war'. As Gascouin remarked in the 1920s, in a work on artillery, 'They were one war ahead', systematizing their technical advantage, and adapting their war effort to technological and industrial progress, first with field-fortification, then with heavy artillery and smaller engines of trench-warfare. This praise was excessive, for, although the Germans did well with submarines, they hardly integrated gas or tanks into their overall strategy. The French military simply regarded war as a tournament in which 'the best man wins'; it was an affair of honour, governed by chivalrous principles. The warrior virtues of blood and ancestry were reckoned more important than technology. These ideas scarcely changed, despite the passage of time, as was shown with artillery, which went to war with many wrong ideas, which despite experience were hardly modified, being maintained by 'our great captains'. The directive of 12 July 1918 showed this: it was formulated in the elementary way of a military catechism with almost no connection with the technical age. 'Commanders will learn to make simple, bold, rapid attacks . . . which will succeed by surprise-effect . . . Infantry must be persuaded [sic] that it can exploit its first success on its own, can advance by its own momentum, *and without artillery protection*' (author's italics). Discussion, supposedly learned and theoretical, revolved around the length of artillery preparation – if too short, the bombardment would be insufficient; if too long, there would be no surprise. The formulation could become more complex technically, but the thinking never developed any sophistication. Foch and Pétain declaring, 'artillery conquers, infantry occupies', would provoke a discussion of the formula as if it were one of the great scientific discoveries of modern times. In all countries, experts analysed the war only as regards the respective roles of various arms: reign of infantry, competition with artillery, 'decline' of cavalry.

Gascouin said after the war that, in artillery matters, staffs had simply indulged obsessions 'that were more a fetish than a serious analysis of technique – flat trajectory, the 75, and then heavy and very heavy artillery. In 1916 there was an obsession with massive pounding and utter destruction, with immensely heavy shell. Then came an obsession with the long-range, and abandonment of short-range targets'; he concluded 'This was to sin by omitting technical experience.' Lack of scientific inquiry, ignorance of technical factors, disregard of the relationship existing in any period between the art of war and the state of technical knowledge, unconcern for industrial capacity: such were the characteristic features of the men running the military operations. In 1914–18, chivalry was still virtually the rule, which was a regression even from Greek antiquity, when Hephaestus, god of armour, was at least the equal of Ares, god of war.

Chapter 11

Styles of war: direct and indirect

General Gambiez stressed a fundamental difference in the art of war between the 'direct' and the 'indirect' approach. 'The first involves simple destruction of the enemy forces in a battle deliberately sought out, by virtue of sheer strength and energy; the second means gaining a preliminary advantage through disruption of enemy morale and *matériel*.' The latter was applied several times in the war. A campaign was waged to discourage the enemy, in the hope of weakening his morale; but an indirect strategy was also applied in two ways – to break up the coalition from within, or to stifle it from without. The Central Powers tried to raise the Russian minorities against the Tsarist state, to raise holy war against French, British or Italian overseas possessions. The Allies tried to break up the Habsburg Monarchy by sustaining Czech or south Slav national movements, the Ottoman Empire through Arab revolt.

Inside Europe, the Entente was first to claim it was fighting for the rights of peoples. This meant Alsace-Lorraine and the Habsburg minorities; the Entente did not, it seems, appreciate either the value or the danger involved in using this double-edged weapon. The initiative in breaking up multinational states came in fact from the minorities themselves. This was the case with Austria-Hungary. Early in the war the most active organization was the south Slav committee, which aimed at a united Yugoslavia. Its representative, the Dalmatian, Trumbić, was welcomed in London. But Croats and Slovenes suspected the movement of Serbian nationalism, and the Allies would not commit themselves: one chief difficulty being that south Slav aspirations ran counter to Italian ambitions in the Adriatic. Alliance with Italy counted for more than nationality-aspirations, and, in the Pact of London, these were sacrificed. There-after, Croats and Slovenes looked to the United States, finding in President Wilson an ardent champion, whereas at this time the Allies were more reticent. They gave little more than kind words to the Czechs, despite their numerous supporters in France and England (among them the historians, Denis and Seton Watson, and the foreign

98

editor of *The Times*, H. W. Steed). In Austria itself, the Czech leaders' propaganda was not very effective, although the middle classes have been thought (Bernard Michel) to have sabotaged war-loan operations. 'Don't fight your own people', said one pamphlet distributed to south Slav units in the army. But they fought, none the less, with as much enthusiasm as Germans or Magyars, almost as if trying to show they were equals. There were only one or two spectacular examples of mass desertion – notably that of the 28th infantry regiment, recruited in Prague.

In these circumstances the Allies, who hoped to get Austria-Hungary away from Germany for a separate peace, hesitated to use the indirect weapon. It might act against their own secret policy, to spare the Habsburg Monarchy. The ambiguity of their position came to the fore in the third Congress of Nationalities, held at Lausanne in 1916. The initiative for this had come from some Swiss citizens acting in the name of the 'Nationalities Union', which had been set up before the war to defend the rights of oppressed peoples. It was obviously sympathetic towards the Entente, its organizers – Burnier and Privat – making no secret of this. On sending their invitations, they hoped that the Czechs, the Romanians of Hungary and the rest would contribute. But the representatives of these peoples could not go to Lausanne, and in the end it was French, Belgian and British citizens who in turn took the stage to put their grievances for them, which did not have the same effect. On the contrary, it was the delegates from the minorities oppressed by the Allies who expressed themselves at length, in particular the Irish, Egyptians and Tunisians, but above all the delegates of the minority peoples of Russia, who invaded the conference. Since by this time the Central Powers had gained more territory in the war, they were able to encourage travel to Switzerland by numerous Poles, Lithuanians, Ukrainians and even Georgians and Tatars. Together, these put Allied imperialism on trial, and it was in fact the representatives of minorities oppressed by the Allies that had most effect, particularly the Irish, Egyptians, Algerians, Baltic peoples, Tatars and Kirghiz. The Swiss press published part of the proceedings and thus awoke a badly informed public opinion as to these peoples, some of whom were not even known to exist; a hitherto unsuspected link was shown between colonial and national questions. The debates had some effect: *Le Temps* devoted an editorial to the Lausanne conference, and *L'Eclair* remarked, 'It is a happy coincidence that M. Doisy has proposed increased Algerian representation in the Assemblies.'

In *L'Eclair de Montpellier*, Jacques Bainville summed up arguments heard more fully elsewhere, saying, 'I have been saying for years that the nationality-principle is a menace to France . . . a weapon that could be used against our Allies and ourselves. What has happened at Lausanne confirms this.'

The Allies were circumspect about using this weapon, but Wilson liked it, and his word counted for more and more. When the United States intervened, men returned to the weapon, since it seemed there was little chance of a separate peace with Austria. At the turn of 1917–18 the Allies approved the terms of the Pact of Corfu, the charter of Yugoslavia. Seton Watson, with help from British and Italian governments, mounted a campaign of subversion in the Austrian army. He set up headquarters in Venice, and in time this campaign was shown to be effective. It did indeed help break up the Austrian army in 1918.

Indirect attack on the Turkish Empire also had spectacular results. In the north there was catastrophe – the massacre of Armenians; in the south came a solitary hero, T. E. Lawrence, the godfather of Arab independence. The Armenians were partitioned between Russia and Turkey, and wished to recover the independence they had lost thirteen centuries before. If they had to choose between their two masters, the Armenians, as Christians, would prefer the Tsars, who were less cruel than the Turks. The Tsar also claimed on their behalf the Armenian territory in Turkey, promising to grant Armenians some measure of religious and administrative autonomy. Up to 1914 nothing had been done, and the national movement became anti-Russian, although during the war, anti-Turkish feelings revived, along with hopes of liberating national brothers over the border.

In 1915 the *Dashnaksutium*, the main national party of Armenia, sent a secret mission to the west to plead for Armenian independence. Thenceforth the Russian Armenians encouraged their co-nationals to rebel against Turkey. But they had no means to resist. The Turkish army, beaten at Sarikamish, retired, and the Turkish Armenians thought they would soon be delivered – many deserted the Turkish army, and the beaten troops were openly mocked by the local Armenian population, while sabotage went on in the rear. The punishment was hideous: all Armenian soldiers were taken out of the army, disarmed, rounded up and deported as labour-battalions. As for civilians, villages were burned, men, women, the aged, and children roped together and carried off to the mountains to an unknown destination. Where the Armenian population was a majority, in Van, Bitlis, Sassun, the populace and labour-battalions were massacred in cold blood. Early in summer the sinister convoys staggered towards the south. The weak died en route, the survivors arriving exhausted in Aleppo were then sent into the desert, where most of the rest starved to death. There are no figures: it is only known that at Erzerum, of 20,000 Armenians, 200 survived. Over a million men and women had been deported and at least half died of starvation or torture.

At the other end of the Ottoman Empire an Arab rising was encouraged by the British. Before 1914 Kitchener had considered the possibility of helping tribal chiefs, but had no overall plan – although the British had the satisfaction of noting that the Sherif of Mecca did not proclaim the Holy War. The Arab national movement was still, however, in an elementary stage. Ibn Saud, Sultan of the Nejd, tried to unify the peninsula for his own ends, but the other imams, and he himself, were acting more as feudal princes than as champions of nationalism. The imam of the Yemen was moreover still friendly to the Turks. Here was a clear opening for the British; they could play off one tribe against others, and aimed rather at control of the oil-routes than creation of an Arab state or even vassal states. In Cairo, London or Delhi, British statesmen took the Arabs into account, more as tools to serve their own interests – Arab independence was a way of weakening Turkey, a weapon like any other, not an end in itself. It was Lawrence's genius to invert the terms of this problem, more by idealism than by calculation – though of course it still served his country's best interests. He was a young orientalist, familiar with Islam and the Arabs, appreciative of their civilization. He understood it, spoke the various tribes' dialects, lived their daily life, and wore a *djellaba*. When war came, he had a network of friends, among them Feisal, son of the Sherif, and Auda, the Bedouin Robin Hood. Lawrence reckoned the time had come for a grand design. But there was no point in enrolling Arabs in regular formations, where they could always be defeated by the Turks. Instead Lawrence, collaborating with Allenby, whose confidence he acquired, linked the progress of the British army with an Arab guerrilla movement, leaving the Turks in control of Mecca and leading the Arabs in a series of apparently minor operations that in fact had much strategic importance – the capture of Wadi and Aqaba. 1918 was the triumph: British and Arabs entered Damascus.

The Germans had in 1916 been no better than their enemies at appreciating the benefits and drawbacks of a nationality policy. Germany, threatened with a tightening blockade, saw at this time the rise of Friedrich Naumann's *Mitteleuropa*. The Germans were greatly impressed by their own success in the east, and decided to reshape the area. The possibilities open to active support of Russian minorities became manifest at the Lausanne conference; a few weeks later the Central Powers subsidized publication of a Berne weekly, the *Bulletin des Nationalités de Russie*, and links were tightened between Germany and the nationality movements of Russia. Every week Poles and Ukrainians regularly, and Lithuanians, Finns and Moslems where they could, attacked Tsarist rule, and also the Russian liberals, men of Milyukov's stamp, who were against a *real* emancipation of the nationalities. These nationalities could not in any case count on a France increasingly indifferent to their problems, or on an England 'with interests at stake on the whole of the Baltic littoral'. By contrast, the Austro-Hungarian example could be used to show what 'federalism' was likely to mean in practice. The *Bulletin* therefore talked of the future independent nations of eastern Europe – the Ukraine, Lithuania, Poland and the rest, who, it said, out of gratitude to the Central Powers would 'align' themselves with these Powers the better to preserve their independence, since, on their own, they would be 'impotent'. Germany tightened her links with the nationality organizations of the Russian Empire. A Finnish Legion was set up, the Locksted battalion, to fight on the Russian front. Above all, having got together some representatives of the Polish nationalist parties who remained in the occupied territories, the Central Powers set up the Piotrków conference of September 1916. It was intended to display the 'representative' character of these deputies who had stayed in occupied Poland: an essential preliminary to the establishment of new institutions. On 5 November 1916 the Central Powers spectacularly proclaimed Polish independence, a gesture alarming to the Entente. They meant mainly to set up a Polish army for their own side, and the Poles were not deceived – but this was a blow none the less to the Entente's policy.

A further blow could be still more dangerous: German help to Irish nationalism. From 1914 the Irish had proclaimed in the Commons that they would be loyal, accepting that Home Rule would be postponed for the duration. The extremists disavowed this, and opposed the authorities' recruiting campaign. Falcke, German consul in New York, began a resistance movement, subsidized by the

Irish in America; there was a grandiose plan to invade Ireland, the Germans preparing to send munitions and arms, together with the chief of the rebellion, Sir Roger Casement. Secrecy was lost and when he disembarked from a German submarine he was at once arrested and subsequently executed. The rising broke out in April 1916, 1,200 nationalists occupying part of Dublin for five days: the town was scarred by this Bloody Easter, and two divisions of British troops were tied down.

In occupied Belgium the Germans also weakened the Allies by encouraging Flemish separatism. Before 1914 this had been largely literary in character, based on the university of Ghent. German imperialists were divided in their attitude to the Belgian question: whether to make Belgian Flanders and the Low Countries part of the future Reich, or whether to leave these provinces to their old rivalry, and be content merely with control of ports and commercial arteries. The Flemish national movement was fostered by the German occupiers: there was a spread of Flemish instruction from Ghent, and recalcitrant professors were deported. In 1916 bilingualism in official correspondence was ended, and in 1917 administrative separation of Flanders and Wallonia decreed, Wallonia receiving Namur as its capital. A Flemish Council, made up of activists, supported this, but the move, coming from the occupation authorities, was disliked. In February 1918 there were demonstrations against the separation, although of course by this time the terms of the Belgian question had changed, since it was clear that Germany intended to annex much of the country.

In Asia the British had sought to take Constantinople, raise the Arabs, while Germans and Turks tried to raise India, Central Asia, and the entire Moslem world. They tried to dominate Persia, pass from there to Afghanistan, and from there attack north and south, hoping for resurrection of Pan-Turanianism and a flanking threat to Russia. The exact role they played in the nomads' rebellion in Turkestan is unknown – the immediate question was the Moslems' refusal to enlist in the Russian army and the immediate goal was the recovery of land taken by the government for railway construction. But there was also, at the back of it, a *gazovot*, a Holy War, against Russia. Germans and Turks meanwhile supported the Caucasus peoples – Georgian exiles, who hoped to establish a Caucasus Federation with a Georgian kingdom and an Armeno-Azerbaijani state. In the south there were also hopes of raising Islamic peoples against British rule in India. The Turkish alliance helped the Germans, but it was also a serious embarrassment, since Enver Pasha cared much more for the war with Russia than the war with England; and in any case his allies' *Drang nach Osten* worried him as much as the grandeur of their concepts impressed him. In Persia, for instance, Germans and Turks were as much rivals as partners, and collaboration suffered from this. Churchill wrote that in 1916 the Germans' real aim was the Black Sea and the Caspian. He was exaggerating, but there was some truth in it. The idea of reaching India was old enough and illusory, but the Gallipoli failure had given some new interest to it. In 1914 the German gunboat, *Ecbatana*, had tried to seize Abadan and the refineries, while other attempts were made in the gulf of Kuwait. Persian Gulf oil acted as a fascinating second-best for India. As Colonel Sykes wrote, the British regarded this area as their private hunting-ground: but each stone and each piece of mud showed a German presence.

The Persian situation was highly complex. The dynasty was particularly hostile to Russia and often called on British help from the south. In 1914 a Persian declaration of war on Russia had only just been prevented. Germans and Turks were also involved, although the Turks, dazzled by their own successes in the west, behaved incautiously in the east with Pan-Turanian dreams. They occupied Persian Kurdistan to 'protect' it from Russia and committed horrible atrocities in Persian territory. Enver Pasha occupied Hamadan, which the Cossacks had hurriedly abandoned early in 1917. Under the horrified eyes of the Persian government, the country became a closed area where Turks and Russians settled old scores; the Persians had no desire to join in. In the south German initiative took a different form. A civilian mission under Wassmuss, often called the German Lawrence, went native, and raised southern tribes against the British – which contributed to the Kut disaster in April 1916. On the coast Tangistanis threatened the British forces on the Bushir, and further east German and Turkish agents based on Meshed set off to raise Afghanistan. Allenby's victories in Palestine and Syria ended these attempts just when, in Shiraz, Wassmuss had managed to dominate things to such an extent that the government asked Britain to withdraw her troops.

The indirect approach was also applied in Africa. In Tripolitania the Senussi revolt worried the British, who feared for Egypt. The French also worried, but Algeria, despite Oppenheim's evidence of the widespread hatred for France on the part of Algerian and Tunisian Moslems, was not much affected by the contagion of Holy

War. In Morocco, the Germans sent arms to the Princes of the Siba, by stages arranged through their consul in Barcelona. In Black Africa the British, French and Belgians disposed of German forces in Togoland and the Cameroons in a few weeks. In south-west Africa the Germans encouraged the rebellion of the Boer general, Maritz, who saw in the Anglo–German war the right moment for his country to be resurrected; Botha and Smuts put an end to the revolt, and also to Colonel Seitz's German troops, in July 1915. In East Africa resistance by the Germans and their askaris against the British and Belgians went on up to the armistice. General von Lettow-Vorbeck succeeded in immobilizing as many enemy troops as possible, and aimed to make their situation impossible. He succeeded by virtue of Tanganyika's geographical position, which gave him interior lines and allowed him to attack the Kenya garrison to the north and the Nyasaland one to the south-west.

This 'war of the white tribes', as the natives called it, discredited the colonial powers and poisoned the Allies' successes. There was a revival of millenarism in the British-ruled areas, particularly in Nyasaland where there were rumours of the return of Mzilima, a messianic liberator. Elsewhere war encouraged anti-colonial movements where they had begun, and started them where they had not. In India, as Nehru said, there was, despite noisy demonstrations of loyalty, little real sympathy for the British. German victories caused rejoicing among both moderates and extremists, although Indians, after much discussion, agreed to co-operate if only to give their young men a military training. If they went away to distant fronts, they would return not as old-style servile robots, but as mental adults. Discontent would be fostered; and the same phenomenon occurred in Indo-China and also Morocco where a Senussi pamphlet spread round in 1916 stressed the humiliations imposed on the Moslems of Algeria and Tunisia. The war, in the long term, weakened the colonial powers. In the Far East it allowed the Japanese the unprecedented spectacle of a Great European Power being thrown out of Asia. The myth of European primacy and unity was now decidedly in the past.

From the beginning the Allies tried to destroy German commerce overseas, to undermine the economic foundations of the Central Powers. When they saw the war would not be won overnight, they systematized war economically, so as to dry up the Central Powers' sources of supply: lack of raw materials and manufactured goods would force them to surrender in the end, and before then there might even be 'an economic crisis caused by poverty'. The Napoleonic Wars were still near enough to remind men of the efficacy of blockading Germany and her allies. The Germans, like their enemies, had not seen that war would last long, and failed also to see it would be an economic war. They had supposed Britain would be neutral, and were surprised by the blockade measures adopted, although they were not too worried, at first, since neutral commerce could still be used to guarantee overseas supply. But when the Allies supervised neutral trade, the economic arm became fatal. The Central Powers reacted – first using submarines as a preventive weapon, a menace and little more; when this had no result, they tried to break the Home Fleet's iron ring, boldly fighting the British, sinking more ships than they lost, but still leaving the ring closed, since the German navy would no longer dare to escape into the North Sea. Jutland was a victory for nothing. Everything changed in 1917 when the Kaiser determined upon unrestricted U-Boat warfare – his naval experts showing that thereby the economic method could be turned against its British originators, and force them to surrender within a year. In fact submarine-warfare, far from forcing the British to surrender or terrorizing the neutrals, actually brought the Americans into the war – which, in the end, meant defeat for Germany. But the Germans nearly brought it off.

Maritime commerce had been vital to the German economy, bringing in cotton, manganese, tin, rare metals, vegetal raw materials and other products essential to a modern and highly competitive industry. Three-fifths of this trade had been carried in German ships. In 1914 this amounted to a tonnage of 5,200,000 tons, to which a further million from Austria-Hungary could be added. When war broke out 734 ships took refuge in neutral ports, and Germany was left with some 600 ships – 2,875,000 tons of which 600,000 were captured and several thousand more sunk, by the end of the summer. After a few weeks the Central Powers' trading vessels were no longer on the high seas. Germany at once had recourse to neutral commerce. International law laid down that neutrals could trade with belligerents provided they did not resist inspection, violate blockade or ship contraband. This last might make difficulties for any state trading with the Central Powers, for, despite the absolute British blockade, the Germans could still trade through their neutral neighbours – Holland, Switzerland, Denmark. To stop this the Allies applied the contraband principle laid down a few years before at conferences in London and The Hague. Distinctions were drawn there, given the nature of the goods, between absolute contraband – a list of ten items, including arms and munitions – and conditional contraband, including foodstuffs, clothing and the like. At British initiative – since the British then upheld neutrals' rights – a third list was added of articles that were in no circumstances to be declared contraband. This included rubber, cotton, fertilizer, minerals and paper. The Declaration of London in 1909 specified that articles of absolute contraband could be seized if it could be proved that they were destined for the enemy; conditional contraband could be seized only if the ship were heading for an enemy port, which meant that in 1914 foodstuffs destined for Germany were simply unloaded at Rotterdam and could not be legally seized. The British refused to ratify this, being handicapped by their own insular position, their trading structure and their dependence on foreign supply. They could not allow seizure of an Argentinian ship bringing them foodstuffs, still less any sinking of it. When war came Great Britain was the only country not to have ratified the Declaration.

On 6 August 1914, and later, the Americans asked for a definition of the belligerents' attitude to neutral commerce. Britain and France replied with an Order in Council of 24 August and a *décret* of 25 August, stating that they would adhere to the Declaration of London, but would seize *all* contraband items, whatever their destination, unless positive proof could be shown that they were not destined for the enemy. The Americans at once protested, the more so as the Allies extended the number of articles considered contraband, to include even items the British themselves had declared, a few years before, never to be considered contraband. Moreover, systematic rerouting of mechantmen involved assumptions of fraud that were contrary to the traditions of international law: thus between January and July 1915 of 2,466 ships arriving in neutral North Sea ports, 2,132 had been examined by the British government. Even so, the blockade did not much affect the Central Powers. German exports were relatively stable, owing to Scandinavian intermediaries' delivering overseas. The reduction of imports was also far from reaching the degree desired by the Allies. In December 1914 and January 1915 deliveries from the United States to Germany declined from sixty-eight million dollars to ten million, but deliveries to Germany's neutral neighbours rose from twenty-five million to sixty-five. Just the same, in the long run the improvement of Allied control would be fatal to German war industry and to civilian supply. Of course, constant flouting of neutral rights might equally turn against the

Allies; the Germans even hoped that Sweden would intervene on their side. But the Allies, being richer, could anticipate this by promising to buy *all* goods seized on neutral ships. In the same way, Dutch and Americans saw their trade with England rising considerably, and the blockade cost them merely a reduced profit, the prices offered by the British being lower than what the Germans would have given. In February 1915 the German government sent to neutral states a list of Allied violations of international usage, which increased daily as Britain lengthened the contraband category. 'Usage' rather than 'law' is the term to be used in this context, since the British government had not signed the Convention of London. But its moral position was weakened none the less, since its behaviour was directly in contravention of the principles asserted by its representatives. In the case of her Allies, there was a quite literal violation of law; but their role was so subordinate that no one bothered much about this. She interpreted the law to suit herself, and had no scruples about declaring the entire North Sea a war zone, which meant that neutral coasts could be blockaded.

In response to these violations, Germany declared submarine-warfare for the first time against any enemy merchantman encountered in British waters. It could be sunk without regard to merchandise or passengers, even if it was neutral. The threat was universally condemned, and the neutrals became victims of a particularly cruel violation of human rights. In 1915 the sinking of the *Lusitania*, with a number of American citizens on board, reversed neutral opinion. The British profited by extending still further the contraband list, which came to include all items destined for the Central Powers whatever their means of transport; the Americans again protested vigorously. Commerce with the neutrals had risen remarkably, since the Germans were supplied through re-exports, and the British tried to block the traffic. They controlled their own exports of coal and fuel oil to the neutrals, and introduced a quota-system. From 1914 Germans and neutrals vied in ingenuity in escaping British supervision. The Swedes, for instance, turned copper ingots into little statues, showing Hindenburg: these got through under the heading '*objets d'art*', which were not contraband. The *Kim* brought Denmark twelve times as much lard as the country had imported before the war: it was clearly meant for Germany, where it could be turned into glycerine. The quota-system allowed the Allies to restrict neutral imports to what was really needed, calculated on the basis of average pre-war imports.

By mid-1916 all these measures were finally giving results. Lack of fertilizer reduced the German cereal harvest by over a third, meat consumption by two-thirds; copper imports declined by five-sixths. The progressive decline of cotton imports, later hastened by American intervention, caused a decline in textile output that could not be halted even by production of *Ersatz* cloth from cellulose. In 1918 the crisis of clothing was reckoned even worse than the crisis of food, more serious even than the crisis of explosives, since imports of fodder, cattle and fats from Switzerland, Holland and elsewhere were more difficult to control, and German industry accomplished miracles to turn these into glycerine. The technical achievements of German industry were similar to those of blockaded Napoleonic France, allowing Germany to dispense with western trade, and demonstrating that the eastern countries were economically indispensable, since their production complemented Germany's. This encouraged thoughts of a *Drang nach Osten*, an experience not forgotten after the war.

The economic war on Germany and her Allies certainly disturbed their war-machine, though not, in the ultimate analysis, decisively. The economic weapon was used empirically early in the war and systematically only from 1916 onwards, and even in 1918 had not been perfected: even then, England had to conclude an agreement with Sweden to limit exports of iron ore to Germany. It is also too much to claim that U-Boat warfare was merely a response to the blockade: the German proclamation of unrestricted submarine-warfare was meant to bring England 'to her knees' – it was presented as a response to the blockade only to make its use look more legitimate.

Hitherto submarines had warned ships so as to spare lives, the crews being able to use their lifeboats. But when submarines surfaced to issue their warning they were vulnerable, some of the Allied merchantmen now being armed; or the merchant captains could warn patrolling naval vessels or destroyers in the vicinity. If the Allies organized merchant convoys, submarines could be easily sunk by depth-charge if they gave due warning. There was therefore no hope for successful submarine-warfare in these circumstances and Tirpitz resigned in protest in mid-1916. Different decisions were then made: Admiral Capelle, succeeding Tirpitz, was assured that submarines could, if given the chance, sink up to 600,000 tons a month. In less than a year a good part of the British merchant navy would be sunk, the British economy would be throttled and England

would give in within six months. Bethmann Hollweg opposed tor-
pedoing neutrals, fearing America would intervene on the Allied
side if her interests were at stake. Capelle and Ludendorff persuaded
the Kaiser that this might not happen: the United States would
perhaps be deterred by German power, and in any case American
troop-ships could be sunk before they reached Europe. American
intervention would be unreal. On 9 January the Kaiser gave way:
on the 31st the Central Powers declared unrestricted submarine-
warfare. The German ships were ready to attack: by February
540,000 tons had been sunk, only 10 per cent short of the naval
staff's fatal figure. In March 578,000 tons were sunk, in April
847,000, and the German admiralty could well exult, for if this continued, Great Britain would capitulate in six months or even less.

There was panic in government circles in London and Jellicoe
panicked to such a degree that some politicians seriously began to
advocate peace. Lloyd George and others opposed the defeatism,
feeling that an answer could be found. But the peril was great
enough for them to consider abandoning the Mediterranean to
save tonnage, although the idea was given up – withdrawal from
Salonica and interruption of the march on Baghdad would be too
great a confession of failure. The admirals did not know what to do.
They would not convoy merchantmen, a task 'unworthy' of the navy;
besides, submarine-hunting was disappointing in its results, for of
142 engagements between destroyers and submarines, only six had
a positive outcome. The path designed for convoys would have to
be protected, and British industry launched a prodigious effort to
increase production of mines, of which over 600,000 were sown in
less than six months. Over 8,000 warships were now used as escorts,
a hundred warships for every U-Boat. The need for convoys was
only gradually recognized. The Admiralty tried it as an experiment,
without conviction – sceptical as ever of these civilian schemes. The
results were unmistakable: the number of ships sunk in the war
zone declined – in February 212; in March 297; in April 335; in May
and June 230 each; in July 201; in August 148; in September 141; in
October 118; in November 103; in December 107. Later, still other
methods were found of combating submarines.

In fact the Germans had never had more than 101 submarines in
action. Although she renewed and increased her stock, Germany
had not included in her naval calculations the additional tonnage
that the Allies would receive through lesser states; if these declared
war on Germany, they would throw in even the German ships

impounded in 1914. England pressed Siam, Nicaragua, Peru, Brazil and others to intervene, and thus help the Allies round the stormy cape of 1917. In particular, the German admiralty had never set up a careful plan to repair submarines and they had to wait their turn at the specially equipped arsenals, of which there were few. The British exploited this bottleneck, blocking Ostend and Zeebrugge, and observing submarines as they slipped out. Germany had been within an inch of victory in spring 1917 and once more was struck with a fatal powerlessness at the last moment, just as victory seemed hers. Fear now underscored disappointment: the Germans had supposed they could knock out England and either prevent or make harmless intervention by the United States. But the British had restored their predominance in the North Atlantic and the Americans did enter the war – a decisive addition to Allied strength, which was the determining factor in the Central Powers' defeat.

Propaganda was a further arm of indirect warfare. To demoralize the enemy, all possible means were used, even the spreading of ideas more properly internationalist or pacifist – although the supporters of these were truly opposed to the policy of *all* states. Since 1914 the Germans had exploited their advantage of occupying large parts of enemy territory; they brought out large-circulation newspapers, such as *La Gazette des Ardennes, Antwerpsche Tydingen, Gazet van Brussel, Glos Stolicy* in Warsaw. These propagated the Central Powers' cause widely, and some opinions, with the mobility of the front, reached the enemy home front. In Paris the government knew what was said in the *Gazette des Ardennes*: it provoked political disputes, sought to weaken the *Union sacrée* and inter-Allied solidarity. It stressed, for instance, the sympathies Marcel Sembat, the 'social-patriot', had entertained for Germany before the war – 'the most democratic country in Europe' – and fostered French suspicions of England, showing for instance how France put up with huge losses for England's benefit, while England did little. One pamphlet announced that 'the city of Calais has been delivered to the British for 99 years, at £255,000 a month . . . this shows how far the French have humbled themselves before perfidious Albion.'

The French also circulated newspapers in Alsace and behind the German lines – *die Feldpost,* showing German responsibility for the war, the Kaiser's atrocities in Belgium, the horrors of U-Boat warfare; in Venice Seton Watson proclaimed to Austria that the Kaiser intended, in the end, to restore Greater Germany for his own good. The Americans were best at this. Owing to their lead in social sciences, they were more elaborate in technique than France or Germany. To instil the idea of revolution, their agencies manufactured a 'telegram from Stockholm' to the effect that the German minister in Stockholm had asked the Swedish foreign minister to confiscate the *New York Herald Magazine of the War* of 14 July 1917 because it had, on the first page, a photograph of the Kaiser with the legend: 'What to do with the Kaiser after the War?'; the Swedes were said to have ordered confiscation. American pilots in August 1918 were distributing a sheet highly illustrative of American techniques: it asked, would Germany ever be as strong again as in July 1914, were Germany's enemies becoming more or less powerful, had the terrible losses of 1918 brought victory any closer, as promised by Germany's leaders, did Germans still have faith in ultimate victory, were they still ready to die in a hopeless cause? The text would be accompanied by a postcard exactly similar to those used in the German army, on which would be written: 'Write here the address of your family, and if the Americans take you prisoner, give the card to the officer who first interrogates you. He will send it to your family and reassure them.' On the reverse side was: 'Do not worry. The War is over for me. The American army gives prisoners the same rations as its own men – meat, white bread, potatoes, beans, plums, coffee, butter and tobacco.'

Chapter 12

World war and total war

The European conflict of 1914 gradually turned into a world war, one forcing the warring states to summon the energies of the entire nation. Economic and intellectual mobilization were not new: they had emerged in the French Revolution, and indeed Thomas Mann established a parallel between Robespierre's France and modern Germany, both the most advanced nations of their day, encircled by backward enemies. The connection is worth stressing: in both cases, despite obvious dissimilarities, the effect was to reinforce the totalitarian state.

American intervention was the great moment of drama. No one supposed late in 1916 that the pacifist Wilson would lead his country to war, for since 1914 he had been trying to secure peace; indeed he had played the professor of morals, successively condemning violations by the warring states – German of Belgium, British of neutral rights by blockade, Central Powers of neutral rights by submarine-warfare: 'The torpedo that sank the *Lusitania* also sank Germany in the eyes of world opinion.' Wilson's sympathies went to one or other of the sides, according to his own idea of right. But American interests reinforced this pacifism: Wilson feared that the 'melting-pot' might explode if traditional nationalism arose as an outcome of the war. Many Irish or German Americans hated England, a hatred violently expressed when British troops put down the Easter rising in 1916. The alliance of America and England might compromise American unity. Many American interests were also affected by the blockade installed early in the war – it restricted profits that many traders might have made through extension of commerce with the Central Powers parallel to trade with the Allies. Alliance of America with the Central Powers was more unlikely still, despite the Anglophobia, because there were strong links of sentiment between the Allies and the population. Submarine-warfare also directly threatened the life and interests of American citizens. In the elections of November 1916 Democrats and Republicans had vied with each other in stating these views, the campaign being

waged on both sides for neutrality. The Democrats won by successfully branding Hughes, their opponent, as a warmonger, the only
war contemplated by Democrats being an electoral one. Early in
1917 there was little reason to suppose that America would take the
Allied side: it seemed, on the contrary, that British blacklisting of
American firms trading through neutral states with Germany was
alienating a great part of opinion.

Wilson and his chief adviser, House, were not in fact totally
pacifist – unlike Bryan. They hoped to be artisans of a just peace,
which they might dictate to both sides. In 1915 and 1916 they came
out with offers for 'a peace without victors or vanquished', and even
tried to impose arbitration by threatening to intervene against the
recalcitrant side. Allies and Central Powers alike proved recalcitrant,
since both had annexationist aims they could not reveal. Wilson's
generous suggestions would have been a loaded pistol, forcing them
to show the difference between what their governments said and
what they really meant. The President was personally slighted; his
pacifist inclinations were defeated by his desire to impose his own
peace, and no doubt he felt this could be more easily achieved by
American intervention.

In any case the German military's clumsiness and miscalculation
tipped the balance. Germans thought they could impress the United
States by systematically sinking all ships within the vicinity of the
British Isles. They expected, through unrestricted submarine-
warfare, to knock England out before America could intervene
effectively, even if she did decide to intervene. American farmers and
industrialists, however, had an interest in sending war material and
foodstuffs to the Allies, by far their greatest customer. Samuel
Gompers also gave the trade unions' support, and there could be no
fear of loss from exports prevented from going to Germany, as the
British offered to buy them up on the same terms. Unrestricted
submarine-warfare could do great damage to American commerce,
trade with the Allies having quadrupled since 1914. The press was
obviously pro-Allied, giving increasing coverage to German crimes;
and the Germans heedlessly increased American victims and provoked
deep indignation. The pacifists, with Bryan, resisted, but the *Lac-
onia* and *Algonquin* sinkings, rejection by Germany of Wilson's last
peace-note urging renunciation of annexations, and finally the Zim-
merman telegram pushed government and people to war. Zimmer-
man, German foreign secretary, promised Mexico the three provinces
she had lost in 1848 provided she attacked America, and hinted that

Japan could well change sides. This telegram was intercepted by British naval intelligence, and had been sent to Mexico by the good offices of the United States. The fall of Tsarism could now give Americans a clear conscience, for, if they took part in the war, it would be as part of a fraternity of free peoples, not as allies of absolutism. Wilson, under the play of such emotions, requested from Congress a declaration of war early in April 1917. This was resolved by an immense majority.

The country was unprepared, needing months to equip and train an expeditionary force. The force might not even be able to cross the ocean – a harrowing problem in summer 1917. The climax of submarine-warfare, declining French morale, the slaughter of British troops in Flanders, the failure of Kerensky's offensive, all stimulated fears that the Germans would win before the Americans arrived. But a symbolical contingent of them in July 1917 was a tonic: when it paraded on 4 July there was a tremendous enthusiasm, of a type Paris had never seen. It was then that Colonel Stanton is said to have used the historic words, 'Lafayette, we're here.' The Americans were known not to be ready, but the extent of this was not appreciated; the Allies asked for immediate help in the shape of 16,000 planes for the first quarter of 1918: but the entire United States had only 55 planes in any state to fly, almost all out of date. The armed forces contained 200,000 men, among them 67,000 national guardsmen.

The High Command were against volunteering, since volunteers 'could not keep discipline'. Conscription was demanded, and the Draft Act voted on 29 April. But these soldiers had still to be trained and equipped. The navy, though better prepared, was also worse led. Its chief, Admiral Benson, disliked England and disposed his ships with a view to a possible change of alliances, since he was sure America would go to war first with the Japanese and then with the British. Many months were needed to make him adopt naval deployment more in conformity to his government's policy.

American mobilization was spectacular: 'Wilson the war-leader pushed out Wilson the peace-President' – promulgating the Espionage Act of 15 June, arresting 500 persons including the pacifist leaders, Berger and Debs, Bryan himself being pushed into the background. Creel was given the task of war propaganda, with singers, musicians and actors such as Chaplin or Irving Berlin involved. The excited public boycotted businesses belonging to German or Austrian Americans, there were xenophobic scenes à la 1914, and the same collective enthusiasm, with Americans marching off to war with flower-bedecked rifles just as Frenchmen or Germans had done. Americans did know what war was like, thanks to the Hearst cinemas, but they preferred to ignore it. Propaganda went into reverse overnight, and helped ten million pacifist and pacific Americans to turn into ten million bawling chauvinists. This instance of successful press campaigns also shows how complex was the popular reaction to war. Americans, as citizens of a 'free' continent, had written off the European war as an out-of-date barbarity; now they themselves took part. American citizens were fighting for Justice and Right; Irish or Jewish immigrants were transformed into equal citizens of the country adopted by their parents by the simple carrying out of their civic duty for the first time. This latter factor alone made for much enthusiasm. It was this that explained, not only the weakness of the pacifist movements, but also the way they were put down, more by public opinion than by governments: the 2,000 demonstrators who collected in New York on 15 June 1917 were dispersed by 10,000 counter-demonstrators. In Boston, in July, the police helped the counter-demonstrators, but they already had a numerical advantage that made police help unnecessary. The same happened with the most active movement, the Oklahoma farmers' movement of opposition to conscription which, with the 'Green Corn Rebellion', proposed marching on Washington to overthrow the government. They undertook sabotage of the railways and telegraphs, but were attacked and dispersed by 'patriots'. None the less, the 'People's Council of America for Peace and Democracy' tried to get an anti-war movement going: but it encountered general hostility, one of its leaders was lynched, and the Dean of the University of Minnesota declared that 'war-time is no time to quibble about constitutional rights and guarantees'. The trade-unionists of the IWW, also pacifists, were described as 'German agents' by the *New York Times* which, to end the persecution levelled at it by the Vigilante Leagues and the patriots, suggested dissolving the IWW. The Sedition Act of 16 May 1918, signed by Wilson, was followed by many arrests: it was intended to muzzle the opposition. Peterson and Fite note that this also ended the public's own violent persecution of pacifists.

Under Creel, Baruch and Baker, the American economy managed a gigantic spurt. In a few months four million men were equipped, of whom 1,850,000 left for Europe. In November 1918 there were 3,200 fighter-planes and the merchant navy gave valuable help to the British in the Atlantic. Here stood revealed a giant economy and an extremely flexible society. The feat was made easier through the money invested by Europe in America as a result of the profits shown by the American economy in the previous three years – profits not cut to European measurements. In the short term the Allies profited highly from American intervention: there were many concrete and immediate advantages, both moral and material – economic support, military reinforcements in the shape of the 'Sammies', naval help to strengthen the blockade and the anti-submarine campaign, the addition of fleets from Latin America and even of former German ships that had taken refuge there. Germans were more impressed by all this than France or Britain, where the Americans' help had been underrated on the grounds that they were not 'real soldiers'; as Pierre Renouvin has said, 'United States intervention might guarantee military, economic and financial victory, but it restricted diplomatic liberty of action.' America acted more as associate than as ally, and Wilson's former attitude showed that he did not accept the Entente view of the origins and aims of the war. He was conscious of this, but felt it was not yet time to impose his own views: 'There would be plenty of time when the war was over.'

Intervention altered the picture of the war in Asia as well as in Europe. Japan had gone to war in 1914 as Great Britain's ally, although the treaty did not oblige this. She had two main objectives: to supplant the Germans in the Far East and to exploit the vacuum left by Europe in China for her own benefit. She gained these with military success over German garrisons in Shantung and by imposition on China of the 'twenty-one demands' which foreshadowed a Japanese protectorate. Yuan Chi-Kai's government had hoped to forestall this by declaring war on Germany so as to gain a seat at the peace conference: the Great Powers would thereby protect Chinese integrity. Japan opposed this, and the Entente agreed, since it much needed the Japanese fleet to transport Anzacs, Chinese or Annamite labourers to Europe. France and Britain appreciated that it was dangerous to weaken the defence of territories the Japanese were known to covet, but in 1916 the exigencies of war forced this. Necessity made its own law once more.

This was reversed by American intervention. Washington did not intend to leave Japan a free hand, and supported Chinese intervention in the war to restrain Japan. But China was divided – Yuan's death and the failure of attempts at restoration involved the country in civil war in 1916. Sun Yat-Sen and Young China opposed the war, as it would consolidate the militarists' positions; the military were in favour of it and formed a junta in June 1917. Two months later China declared war on Germany, and at once Sun Yat-Sen formed a rival government in Canton. The Japanese reacted vigorously to this western interference – the 'twenty-one demands' should have made China a Japanese preserve. The Americans feared that Japan would go back on her alliances and link up with Germany and Mexico, and, in the Lansing–Ishi negotiations, themselves retreated, recognizing the 'special interests' of Japan in China. Tokyo thereupon supported the Chinese military, the nature of whose patriotism thereby became clear. Sun Yat-Sen's position was in the end reinforced by the Americans' tactical withdrawal, for the Chinese, betrayed by their allies, turned against America and Europe, and two years later, during the peace negotiations, expressed their resentment with violence.

By 1917 the whole world was involved in the war directly or indirectly. The latecomers were expected to give economic rather than military assistance – a novelty in comparison with the earlier period; in 1914 the Romanian alliance had been measured by the Germans in military terms, whereas by 1916 it was counted in wheat. Manpower became more and more of a problem to states involved in the carnage of 1915 and 1916, but the Russian example was striking evidence that superiority in manpower was an illusory advantage when not linked to economic weight or flexibility of industry. This too was a novelty: in 1914 only two sectors of the economy had been thought important for war, production of war-goods and railways, and war was conceived almost purely in terms of soldiers at the front. Victory would be produced by reserve stocks; the war could not last long because society and economic life would not be able to function for long without the manpower mobilized. When in 1914 the German heavy industrialists suggested to the Kaiser a programme for several years of munitions production, it was rejected by war ministry and General Staff on the grounds that it was merely an attempt by cartels to exploit circumstances for their own excess profits.

The idea of economic mobilization came later, long after men had perceived the need for increasing arms output, which they did only at the end of 1914. Soldiers, in 1915, were still sure they would win before the year ended. Only in 1916 did they see that military success would go hand-in-hand with arms production, and only in 1917 was the connection between arms manufacture and industrial production as a whole truly appreciated. 'War economy' emerged only as a series of different experiences in every country, as necessity dictated. In the first months of the war the states faced little more than a crisis of adaptation, with conscription, disruption of transport and interruption of foreign trade. The crisis then evolved according to the flexibility of the economy or simply the changes of the battle-lines. German occupation of the northern basin hit France hard, that of Poland handicapped Russian industry. The naval blockade para-lysed many sectors of the Central Powers' economic systems; then submarine-warfare imposed a difficult bottleneck on the Allies' pro-duction. American intervention altered the economic terms of the war at the very moment when these were becoming as vital to the outcome of the war as military events or human effort.

These variables crossed constants that occurred in all the states, though not everywhere to the same degree or with the same speed. Everywhere the apparatus of production declined as the battlefields absorbed more and more casualties and their demands for war material rose. The first signs of a starvation economy came up just as a need also emerged to accord priority to certain types of produc-tion 'at all costs'. The reduction of foreign trade by blockade or submarine gave an impulse to autarchy, and this was necessarily faster in Germany, where it came with progress in technology and science, particularly in the chemical field, to overcome lack of oils, fats, rare metals. Since only one central authority could rationalize the exploitation of existing manpower and factory space and ensure equitable distribution of supplies, there came, in all countries, a growth of the state sector over all others. The process varied in countries according to the urgency of the situation, the economic structure and the national tradition. England, never having had to mobilize her manpower, was first to rationalize use of manpower between front, factory and field. Germany set the example for rational co-ordination of activities, setting up a *Kriegsrohstoffabteilung* (KRA) as early as 1914 to combat the interruption by blockade of her foreign trade. The government then proceeded gradually with industrial reorganization on lines leading to a kind of state capital-ism, which was the term employed for it by its originator, Rathenau.

It meant a step towards state socialism, because trade was no longer free, being subject to regulation; it also meant we were trying to encourage industrial autonomy. The *Kriegsamt* system was based on industries' doing the work themselves, although without having full liberty. The KRA gave strict government supervision. The offices served the public interest, distributing neither profits nor dividends . . . their co-ordinating committees were intermediaries between capitalism and the government. All this constituted an innovation that the future may take to.

France and Britain were less squeezed than Russia or Germany because they had an open sea. Economic mobilization was only partial, although France had to improvise means of war production, to exempt or demobilize certain categories of skilled workers who had been heedlessly sent to the front, and in 1917 many farmers as well. Conversion of factories to war work and the renewal of man-power – in particular the introduction of women – went on according to supply and demand. In England the problem was different, the High Command sending to the front more men than it could equip and the government reaffirming its faith in 'business as usual'. It was felt that, German competition being removed, there were infinite possibilities for commercial expansion and that any regula-tion would harm this unchecked expansion. The country would thereby become richer, and would be able to pay whatever price was required for arms. The War Office did, however, set up a section to co-ordinate purchases, and this led in the end to state control.

Economic mobilization concentrated the national industrial effort towards defence industries, and this definition came to include more and more as countries advanced to total war. The change was parti-cularly marked in the two least advanced of the belligerents, Russia and Italy. In Russia war work took in, at first, 24 per cent of the industrial working class, and 76 per cent in the end; in Italy the figure rose from 20 per cent to 64 per cent. In the west the effort of conversion was rather less as the economy had a more powerful base. Germany, with 3,500,000 workers engaged in war work, had more than any other country. But only in Britain and America did war work involve a minority of workers.

Despite the effort of conversion, output declined, slightly in industry but catastrophically in agriculture. Figures for industry (1914–17) show how production varied in coal, iron and steel.

	August 1914		*1915*		*1917*	
	Central Powers	*Allies*	*Central Powers*	*Allies*	*Central Powers*	*Allies*
Coal	331	394	355	346	340	841
Steel	21	19	24	13	16	58
Iron	22	22	25	16	15	50

Only British industry resisted the tendency, while it was American industry, from iron production to the cinema, that offered relief and thereby gained a lasting advantage. Agriculture was hard hit by the withdrawal of labour, and German production declined between 1913 and 1917 by 50 to 70 per cent, depending on the sector. For Russia and France the figures were 50 per cent and 30 to 50 per cent. Rationing came in, with cards for bread, meat and potatoes. Germany was again the first state to organize this systematically, as she was first to encounter the problem: from 1914 onwards, the Cereals Office fixed the extraction rate, introducing 'K' bread, containing potato, and restricting bread consumption. Glycerine demanded fats, and therefore consumption of them was restricted. Other restrictions followed. In 1916 the authorities controlled food-prices, and rationed all the main items of consumption. By contrast, in England rationing affected only the few items coming from overseas, such as coffee and butter. In France meat and sugar were rationed, and the lower classes did not suffer from malnutrition as in Russia or Austria where the system of retailing was inadequate and where bread-cards had to be introduced despite the fact that, in 1913, wheat exporting had been greater than elsewhere. Hungary was in no great embarrassment, although in Austria there were food shortages – particularly in the army, and in the Czech areas. An army communiqué of 1918 said, 'worms in food do not cause stomach-ache'. Typhus emerged among the undernourished populations, and in Turkey, among other countries, the death-rate rose brutally. In the lower classes in German and Austrian towns, who were the most afflicted by lack of food, women were even subjected to cessation of menstruation, in most cases accompanied by temporary sterility.

Total war did not merely affect armies, it destroyed the vital forces of the nation, and this meant insoluble problems. Although every effort was made to produce yet more iron, guns and shell, there was still an insufficiency, and in the end declining production. Thus in 1917 there were at the Chemin des Dames less guns per kilometre than on the Somme in 1916. Friedrich Friedensburg's figures for production of coal, steel, and iron during the war show a history running parallel with the military history. It shows, better than words, the extent to which American intervention was decisive and explains Hindenburg's impatience to finish the war in spring 1918 before the weight of American intervention could tell.

To defeat the enemy, governments not only used economic and military weapons, but also intellectual ones. The techniques of propaganda have been efficiently analysed by Harold Lasswell; they were intended to show that the cause was just, that victory was certain, that defeat for America would mean the triumph of evil. For German consumption, only the second was used.

German responsibility for the war was one of the great themes of Allied propaganda. *Le Petit Journal* from the beginning showed, from the main points of the July crisis, the 'Machiavellian duplicity' of the German government. The Germans had their counterpart: A. O. Meyer's *Zur Geschichte und Verständnis des grossen Krieges*. In 1918 the polemic was revived, during the peace negotiations, and fifty years later it is still alive. For the Germans the spectre of Russian invasion was a sufficient reason for the war, just as for the French was the need to liberate national territory. In England the press likewise stressed the need to liberate Belgium, for the future of England.

With the *Union sacrée*, governments appealed to the class enemy. The Kaiser said he recognized no class battles, that his whole people were united; the Tsar, backed by the Marxist, Plekhanov, said the same. In Paris the anti-militarist Gustave Hervé declared 'the fatherland of revolution is in danger.' There was mass-exuberance, mysticism, patriotic frenzy, appeals to the judgment of history, to divine mercy. 'Gott mit uns' appeared in all languages, although in France, with the writings of Henri Lavedan, this frenzy reached an unrivalled delirium:

> I believe in the courage of our soldiers and the wisdom of their
> leaders . . . in the might of our just cause, the crusade for
> civilization. I believe in the blood of the wounded, the water of
> the benediction; I believe in the prayers of the wives, the
> heroism of the husbands, the calm piety of the mothers, the
> spotless glory of the flag, in our great past and our still greater
> future. I believe in our fellow citizens, living or dead. I believe
> in us, I believe in God, I believe and will believe.

General Fayolle, who was otherwise no doubt sane enough and responsible for the lives of many thousands, wrote, 'Joan of Arc must be looking on us with favour, from heaven.' *La Croix* said, 'The History of France is the Story of God.' Even the great intellectuals were affected: Henri Bergson wrote in the *Bulletin des Armées de la République* on 4 September 1914, 'there is at present a conflict of two forces, one that will be worn down, because it is not based on an ideal, and one that cannot be defeated, because it is based on an ideal of justice and liberty.' England was not spared such effusions any more than France, and in places there were tones not far from Nazi Germany: 'It is now time to draw a veil over those works that recognizably express the spirit of our latter-day Huns; the future is to the young hero who will have the courage to banish the works of Handel, Mendelssohn, Wagner, Brahms and Richard Strauss, who will summon forth from his innermost Being the chords that will resuscitate the spirits of the men who went to their deaths with "Tipperary".' German intellectuals claimed that Germany had to defend *Kultur* against the frivolity of France or the sterility of England: in *Händler und Helden* the economist, Werner Sombart, calmly wrote, 'The world is divided into two camps – the merchants, the British, and the heroes, the Germans. The Germans will necessarily see their cause triumph, since it is the cause of civilization itself.'

Victory for the enemy would mean the triumph of Evil. Félix Sartiaux wrote in *Morale kantienne et morale humaine*, 'One of the most subtle features of the German character is hypocrisy, disguised as naïve sincerity. The Latin historian, Velleius Paterculus, has often been quoted: he regarded the Germans as a race of congenital liars.' This enemy would always be cruel, despite Heine's assertion that the cruelty had been tempered by Christianity; the Germans were ruthless in war, said Ernest Lavisse, whereas 'none of our military writers has ever taught the doctrine of atrocious war'. In fact as Demartial showed after the war, some French officers had indeed preached destruction and terror. *Engineer* of 25 September 1914 suggested razing all German factories to break German competition once and for all. To stress such talk during the war would have been 'doing down the side', and censorship muzzled the 'antipatriots'. There was suppression of the fact that the French and British, bombing Karlsruhe on 26 June 1916, had killed or wounded 26 women and 124 children. To stimulate the nation's will to fight, people's imaginations had to be stirred, and the people must be shown they were fighting for Right. Responsible authorities drew up a list of enemy crimes. In France the government published *Documents relatifs à la guerre 1914–1915. Rapports et procès-verbaux d'enquête de la commission instituée en vue de constater les actes commis par l'ennemi en violation du droit des gens* (1915). The crimes were:

1. Violation of the neutrality of Belgium and Luxemburg;
2. Violation of France before war was declared;
3. Killing and wounding of prisoners;

4. Pillaging, arson, rape, murder;
5. Use of forbidden small-arms ammunition;
6. Use of inflammable liquids and poison-gas;
7. Bombardment of fortresses without warning, and of unfortified towns. Destruction of artistic monuments, religious and charitable foundations;
8. Perfidious methods of warfare;
9. Cruelties on the civilian population.

The Germans were not behind with this. In *Der Weltkrieg und der Zusammenbruch des Völkerrechts* Dr Ernst Müller-Meiningen listed in his turn the crimes of the Allies – not mentioning, of course, German ones in Belgium:

1. Connivance of Belgium with the Allies;
2. Violation of agreements on Congolese neutrality; colonial wars;
3. Use of savage peoples in war against Europeans;
4. Violation of the neutrality of the Suez Canal;
5. Violation of Chinese neutrality by Japan, and British attack on Kiao-Chao;
6. Use of dum-dum bullets and similar ammunition;
7. Non-respect of diplomatic usages regarding German diplomats;
8. Non-respect of, and violation of, the rights of the Red Cross;
9. Use of irregular sharp-shooters and maltreatment of civilians;
10. Inhuman methods of warfare, contrary to international conventions;
11. Russian atrocities in East Prussia;
12. Pogroms against Jews and other Russian atrocities in Poland and the Caucasus;
13. Bombing of towns by aeroplane; use of gas-shells;
14. Violation of the neutrality of the seas; blockade.

The details of such crimes were supposed to show the enemy's ruthlessness and barbarity, and some stories – for instance the Germans' execution of Nurse Edith Cavell – acquired great popularity. The Allies exploited these with greater adroitness than the Germans, as is shown by the neutrals' reaction to these 'crimes'. The German ambassador in Washington thus found his government's propaganda wholly ineffective in the United States. This propaganda stressed too far the subtlety of British political machination, so much so that the German propagandists made a serious error of psychology, for the Americans judged superficially and sentimentally, and propaganda concerning 'the martyrdom of gallant little Belgium' affected them more than any account of violations of neutrals' rights in international law. Bernstorff also complains of the contradictory nature of German propaganda. On the one side, there was an appeal to American generosity on behalf of the 'poor German children' who 'should not, despite the British blockade, be deprived of milk'; on the other, an American mission was invited to Berlin to be shown that the blockade was not affecting German power, and, more precisely, that everything had been done to prevent German children from being deprived of milk.

The final *Leitmotiv* of propaganda was to create an illusion of victory, to vaunt one's own military leaders, weapons, and endurance. Joffre was imperturbable, Hindenburg 'saviour of the fatherland', Kitchener was infallible, 'the organizer of victory' – these were legends and myths, fashioned and disseminated by propaganda, with the aid of hitherto unknown means – the mass press, cinema newsreels, records. At the same time every country heard wild rumours and silly stories, maintaining the obligatory climate of optimism. This 'brain-washing' was more advanced on the Allied side, for at least the Central Powers' press published enemy communiqués. Graux has collected for France the inaccurate pieces of news and the wild rumours spread abroad by the press to inflame public opinion. Censorship and self-censorship rapidly turned journalists into propagandists, either consciously or, as with the politicians, by auto-deception. In 1916 Lloyd George told Vandervelde, the Belgian socialist, that Great Britain had merely declared war in 1914. She had begun it in 1915, extended it in 1916, and would end it in 1917. Lloyd George ended: we shall finish this war when we have got what we want.

In any case the censors controlled the news agencies – Reuter, Havas and the rest – and would not release 'bad news'. The British were not informed of the sinking of the cruiser, *Audacious*, on 27 August 1914, and the French were falsely led to believe they were winning the war in Alsace when they were in fact losing the frontier battles in the north. This went on for years, official verities being spread abroad to maintain soldiers' and civilians' confidence. The censors also forbade publication of anything likely to call in doubt the rightness of the cause, the good faith and competence of leaders. Censorship went on with unrestricted arbitrariness: in the name of patriotism it struck at the traditional enemies of the establishment – anarchists, liberals, free-thinkers.

In 1917 the atmosphere on the Allied side became heavy with menace; governments' nervousness emerged from their instructions to censors. The British government sought to conceal the state of flour stocks, food-rationing and the extension of conscription. The Belgian government, installed in Le Havre, imitated the French example and forbade discussion of strikes that took place in factories under its control. Captain Ribouillet in Paris was unceasingly vigilant, and followed the British in announcing only once a week the list of ships sunk; he forbade any mention of the fact that many factories, for lack of coal, could not work, or discussion of the limiting to certain days of chocolate or coffee consumption. On 13 February the list of items subject to censorship came to include articles published by the *Académie de Médecine*, which were not to mention the fact that mixing of corn and wheat flour could cause pellagra. Besides, 'having regard to the number of pregnant women engaged in employment, they should avoid publishing demoralizing statistics on the diminishing birth-rate and on infant mortality . . . and say nothing of the astonishing increase in syphilis since the war began.' Numerous incidents were provoked by the arrival of massive numbers of Chinese labourers and Annamite soldiers: the labourers were accused of taking the places of 'our sons and brothers' at the factories, so that these could then go to the front, and of being cheap labour that could be used to break the unions. As to the Indo-Chinese, they were accused of 'shooting the workers'; but it was a French government that told them to. The censors forbade mention of conflicts between French and foreigners, since they aroused xenophobia and racism.

The weapon was counter-productive – the increasing number of blank spaces in the newspapers showed France to be no longer 'the land of liberty'. The excesses of self-censorship led the public to doubt official versions, and in the end all information became suspect. The press had failed in its purpose, to inform and discuss. Public opinion, daily anaesthetized by patriotic newspapers, announcements, books, films and songs, became less and less capable of exercising its civic function. Official ceremonies, the celebration of victories, the cult of the glorious dead, the sounding of cymbals and drum, the clicking of medals on chests, turned twentieth-century men into national soldiers, for whom criticism was indiscipline and doubt treason. To serve the country was to believe in its leaders, to be certain of victory. 'We follow you with faithful heart', Nazi crowds would soon be bawling. The mystical revival appearing in these crowds had been started fifteen years before.

Chapter 13

The possible and the impossible

The war had gone on for three years, seventeen million men were dead, wounded or prisoners and no one now hoped for a quick victory. Governments and military leaders no longer inspired the same faith in the peoples, and each nation began to distrust its allies. All the belligerents' plans had proved illusory, and even propaganda became useless. The public debt of the exhausted nations became immense; the national energy and the economy could seemingly be stimulated again only by great gains in the war. War aims therefore grew in direct proportion to the weakening of men's capacity to attain them. They might have been attainable had each coalition been solid: but this was not so. Both sides conducted a silent battle among themselves for hegemony, each nation fighting for itself, keeping secret its huge ambitions, and having, within itself, several lobbies fighting things out and hoping to subject the nation to its own control.

Doubts arose as victory receded, doubts that came up at the front, in the government, in the rear, although the brutal question was not openly posed. Governments drew up their accounts and tried to determine how far the national effort could be raised: 'It is not enough to win, we must also win *and* survive', wrote the historian, Aulard. *L'Heure* said early in 1917, 'Another holocaust like Verdun, and France will fall into coma.' Of the 3,600,000 men under arms in 1914, only 964,000 now survived in the French army – 2,636,000 men had been killed, wounded, made prisoners, or reported missing. The gap was filled by the anticipated call-up of younger classes, but the effective strength of the army – 3,114,000 – was less than in 1914. Italy had lost over 877,000, England over a million, Russia 5,810,000: her infinite manpower made useless for lack of material and equipment. France and Britain had colonial troops – *tirailleurs* from Algeria and Morocco being used in the second phase of the Verdun battle, and being very extensively used, along with Senegalese, on the Somme. Mangin was accused of being too generous with the blood of these soldiers – not that he was any more sparing with his fellow Frenchmen. The military still hesitated to use coloured troops: 'Near Arras, a Senegalese regiment has broken', noted Fayolle. 'It's butchery. These people [sic] can't fight a European War.' Moreover, this new slave trade created difficulties in Black Africa, where people worried at the absence of their men-folk. The censors forbade mention of incidents in Dahomey and Senegal, and in Morocco Lyautey and Gouraud feared that the *tirailleurs'* absence would weaken the *maghzen*, and therefore had Annamite *tirailleurs* used instead. They arrived in 1917 with Chinese labourers, but the military preferred to use them in the rear, thereby relieving workers who could be sent to the front. The workers complained with bitterness and xenophobia – they had to leave their wives working with Orientals 'who've taken our jobs'.

Lack of manpower forced call-up of the 1917 class on 29 December 1915, and soon thereafter the 1918 class. The upper age-limit for military service was pushed up further and further. In 1914 half the men called up were aged between twenty-nine and forty-seven; by 1918, half were aged between thirty-three and fifty-one. At the end of 1916 the government 'permitted' common-law convicts to serve at the front, and in October the *loi Dalbiez* ordained compulsory re-examination of all soldiers in the auxiliary services and all physical exemptees. Paul Morand noted, 'Even the blind are being summoned. Marcel Proust expected it, but he was afraid of being classed as a deserter because if, as was likely, the appointment was during the day he could not go, since it was then that he slept. He asked Lucien Daudet to get his brother Léon to arrange for medical examination at midnight.' The Central Powers faced the same problem in manpower. In 1917 the Germans still had two million soldiers of 1914 in the ranks; but their law on conscription of civilians showed a serious manpower problem, even though there were still ten million men who could be mobilized. Bertolt Brecht noted that in 1918 the High Command even mobilized a corpse. The Austrians were harder-hit and had only 383,000 left of their 1914 soldiers. The reserve was over seven million, but equipment was increasingly poor. Together with Turks and Bulgarians, the Central Powers could throw in another ten million soldiers, three million less than the Allies: and the disproportion would increase with American intervention, and systematic use of British Commonwealth forces, particularly Anzacs, Canadians and Indians. The Germans also tried to use able-bodied men from the occupied areas, particularly Belgians, of whom over 100,000 had been deported to Germany by October 1916. In Poland a German-inspired 'volunteer army' had few takers.

Table 1 *Divisions at the front*

	Allies										Total Allies	Total Central Powers	Central Powers			
	Fr	GB	R	Bl	Sb	It	Rm	Gr	Pg	US			Ger	AH	Bg	Tk
1914 August	74	20	108	6	12						220	143	94	49		
December	74	67	108	6	12						267	212	117	57		37
1915 May	81	77	112	6	12	36					324	248	149	64		38
1916 February	99	79	136	6	6	38					364	283	159	60	12	52
August	102	81	142	6	6	47	21				405	304	169	70	12	53
1917 July	116	87	288*	6	6	59	15	3	1		581	369	232	80	12	45
October	116	87	202	6	6	66	15	3	1	3**	505	369	234	78	12	45
1918 March	114	85		12	6	53		4	2	5	281	365	234	78	12	41
July	114	85		12	6	56		7		25	305	356	235	72	12	37
October	114	85		12	6	58		10		32	324	325	214	74		37
November	114	85		12	6	58		10		42	329	278	210	66		17

The Central Powers had the numerical advantage between January and October 1918.
The Allies had the numerical advantage from August 1914 to January 1918; and again in November 1918.

Key: Bl = Belgium, Sb = Serbia, Rm = Romania, Pg = Portugal, Bg = Bulgaria, Gr = Greece, GB = Great Britain, R = Russia, It = Italy, US = USA, Ger = Germany, AH = Austria-Hungary, Tk = Turkey

* At the end of 1916 seventy-six divisions had been created with three battalion regiments instead of four.
** One US division contains double the number of men to a European division.

Costs rose with every day that passed. They were immense. In France alone expenses between 1914 and 1918 exceeded receipts by 140 million gold francs. Fisk reckoned the total cost at 80 thousand million dollars of 1914, that is the combined wealth of Great Britain, Australia and New Zealand. The war of 1870 had cost Germany 7 million marks a day; the Great War cost 36 million a day in 1914, and 146 million early in 1918. These costs went far beyond capacity to pay, and were covered partly by paper, partly by borrowing. In 1913 the warring states' commerce with the United States, Argentina and Brazil left a balance, in the Americans' favour, of 15 thousand million francs. By 1918 the balance was 419 thousand million.

Churchill's words, 'Business as usual', struck a chord splendidly adapted to the British mood of 1914. Private interests would not have to submit themselves to the war effort; rather, commerce and victory would go together. England would be banker of the coalition, much as during the Napoleonic wars a century before. She would get richer in the process, and war must not be allowed to disturb commerce, which was to follow only the law of supply and demand; in 1916, when the first signs of penury appeared, government advisers announced that to throw away milk or to give it to pigs was not an unreasonable waste, and there was no case for legal sanctions against those who did this. This followed the British liberal tradition. On the continent the Jacobin tradition had gone beyond France, and, during wartime, economies would be adapted to state-intervention and the autarchic tradition. But in both England and on the continent search for profit led to similar activities, not always compatible with the public interest. Governments were more worried by pacifism.

As far as internal commerce was concerned, it was difficult to draw a distinction between legitimate business and treasonable activity. In foreign trade the Allies faced a more serious problem regarding trade with the enemy than did the Central Powers because of the blockade. Its declared and public objective was to starve out the enemy, destroy his economy, foment discontent and pacifism and deprive him of the goods needed for munitions-production. Under such circumstances any supplying, direct or indirect, of the enemy would be treason. This policy was difficult to square with 'business as usual', given that Germany before the war had been one of the British Empire's biggest clients. All commerce with the enemy was publicly forbidden, but it went on just the same. Censors surveyed it and governments tacitly assisted. Both sides felt, of course, that the commerce offered more help than hindrance. But both could not be right – though here was another problem that did not cause overmuch heart-searching.

The dimensions of this commerce in capital terms are not easy to define – historians would need to know the accounts of certain banks, such as Barclay's, that had interests in both camps. But the exchange of goods is well documented. Valuable and strategic metals went from Russia to Germany *via* Finland and Sweden. 'Leaks' from the French side were modest enough – fodder and cattle through Switzerland. The French government could well connive at this since German exports to France were much greater, involving munitions-production. As Feldman has shown, the German army required shells of the best steel, and therefore did not, after 1915, renew contracts for Thomas-steel shells. Gradually industrialists were obliged to produce Martin-steel shells, and Thomas stocks were sold through Switzerland to France and Italy. In 1916 there was a sudden rise in the demand of neutrals and of France and Italy when Great Britain stopped exporting steel. The German government needed foreign currency, and allowed industrialists to reconvert some production (back to Thomas), provided they did so at a cartellized price that would prevent any competition, and lowering of prices, between the various German industrialists selling shells abroad. Naturally enough the industrialists thereupon preferred to sell Thomas to the enemy rather than Martin to the ministry. When, on the Somme, the generals discovered for the first time that they were less well-supplied than the enemy, they demanded urgently as many shells as possible, even Thomas. Producers offered them to the ministry, but at cartel export prices, the ministry demanded a fair price, and the industrialists refused. They sold shells to the enemy, through neutral states, instead of supplying them. This did not last long, as Hindenburg in the end needed the industrialists and ordered the ministry to give them 'the price they want'. There was also some ideological exporting – Pathé in his memoirs shows how he received German film-negative up to 1917 through Americans.

British exports to Germany were also considerable, though of a different type. Neutrals maintained the fiction that they were the real purchasers of British goods, and it was difficult to refuse these and keep the neutrals friendly – an argument that quietened the conscience of exporters. The government asked neutrals to guarantee that goods bought in England would not be re-exported to Germany; thenceforth, Stockholm would simply sell to Copenhagen, or vice versa, and so to Berlin. The scale of this has been estimated by Consett, British attaché in Denmark, who was himself an indignant observer of the commerce, and who was astounded at his own superiors' indifference. His calculations are not exact, though they may be taken as a general indication of the truth; he reckoned that Holland had imported twelve times as much cocoa during the years 1914–18 as during the years 1910–14, while her exports to Germany rose virtually in the same proportion. Cotton was the same, as were fish, rubber, and other essential goods. Whereas in England and at the front there were shortages, for instance of motor-oil and oil for brakes, the same goods were going from England to Sweden, Denmark and then Germany. Cement was the same – the celebrated German block-houses came, to a large extent, from England *via* Holland, as did nickel for guns and fuel for aeroplanes.

Strategic materials were a serious matter. Most explosives had a glycerine base, and this required in manufacture a large number of tropical seeds such as copra and soya. Germany had none of these. The British Empire had been chief supplier of them before the war, as had Russia been for non-tropical fats. Consett's figures show that from 1915 onwards Denmark's imports of these doubled, exactly parallel to a graph of British sales to, and German purchases from, Denmark. The case is clear with copra, soya and copper, all of them constituting one of German industry's most dangerous bottlenecks. The Powers aimed at reconciling peacetime economic habits with war: to increase profits and win at the same time. Each state sought to exploit allies as much as enemies, while at the same time demanding all possible sacrifices from them.

Belgium displays this contradiction and shows as well the insecurity of undertakings, the weakness of small nations and the dubious behaviour of large ones with respect to them. 'Gallant little Belgium' was a favourite theme of the Allies' propaganda; the Germans also showed solicitude for the country and made themselves out to be protectors of 'the Flemish nation'. The Germans said they had entered the country only in anticipation of a French offensive there; they took Brussels and Antwerp only as a matter of military necessity. Albert I of Belgium said only that he was defending, as a matter of honour, the last little piece of his country that had escaped violation. He claimed to be neutral and faithful to treaties and wished a plague on both houses. Both sides' promises seemed treacherous, and in 1914 the Belgians felt that 'if the Germans broke their promises, so too did the Allies'. After the precipitate retreat of the French army, the Belgians had wanted to retain Antwerp, the most powerful fortress in Europe, and, if the British and French helped, Antwerp would be a serious threat to the German right. Antwerp did resist, but without Allied help on any meaningful scale, as the Allies wanted the Belgians merely to retreat and guard their own left wing. Joffre and French felt that any troops sent to defend Antwerp would merely be uselessly sacrificed, and refused to send reinforcements to the place other than troops intended to cover a Belgian retreat once the fortress was on the point of surrendering. A few weeks later the remnants of the Belgian army were forced, not without bitterness, to take up station on the Allied left. Another motive for this was to come, when Joffre and French, victorious on the Marne, suggested that the Belgian forces should be incorporated one brigade per division with the British and French – the King was in other words to dissolve his army. He replied with disdain that 'his occupied land existed only in its army'.

Henceforth, Belgian relations with the Allies were marked by mutual suspicion. The Allies accused the King of disloyalty – a reproach also levelled by the exiled government in Le Havre. Albert doubted whether the Allies would win, expected the war to end in compromise and tried to keep alive the fiction of Belgian neutrality while defending his national territory against the invader, without being associated with the Entente. His ministers, on the other hand, tried to play the Allied card resolutely. They did not expect Germany to win and reckoned the King's conduct was equivocal and that this semi-neutrality would lose for Belgium the chance of attending the peace conference and gaining some fruits of victory. They had high aspirations – peace might give them not only a large indemnity, but also Luxembourg and Dutch Flanders. With the unchanging fronts, this situation lasted until the end of 1917, hardly altered. The King several times refused to join in military operations which would have meant further destruction of the national territory, and refused to Pétain what he had refused to Joffre in 1914. Now he had better reasons to suspect his 'Allies' – Colonel House confirmed in 1916 that Britain and France were agreed to offer Germany the Belgian Congo in the event of a compromise peace. In the guise of indemnity, and as a final award for all its sufferings, 'gallant little Belgium' would merely receive what was realized from the sale of its own Congo.

The Germans also negotiated with the King. Had they signed a .separate peace with Belgium, they might have shown America and the neutrals how unfair were the accusations levelled against them.

Moreover, the Germans proclaimed how deeply they felt the 'tragic' fate of the Flemish population, and would have based their dominion on the consent of a large part of the people. Negotiations went on from November 1915 to February 1916 in Zürich, by virtue of family links between the Belgian royal house and the Wittelsbachs of Bavaria. The first difficulty was neutrality: the King 'was defending the country as a neutral, not as an Ally of the Entente'. Waxweiler admitted just the same that 'our neutrality is a fiction that we could give up'. The 'warrior-king' was in other words prepared for a *rapprochement* with Germany 'in a form that could spare Belgian susceptibilities and on condition there would be no hint of vassaldom in it'. There was even discussion of a defensive alliance between equal partners. The King wanted Germany to abandon the country. He would allow them to occupy the railways leading to France, and the fortresses of Maubeuge, Condé and Givet. Germany should defend the southern half of the country, Belgium the northern part. In return for this abandonment of neutrality and compensation for such annexations as Germany might make, Belgium might acquire territory: Waxweiler indicated the line of the Meuse north of Charleville, the Maubeuge area, Roubaix, Tourcoing and, at Dutch expense, the left bank of the Scheldt estuary. The Germans rejected this and Törring's memorandum, got together by the German foreign office, indicated more explicitly what Germany understood by 'abandonment of neutrality' – nothing short of abandonment of sovereignty. After summer 1917 the King tightened his links with the Allies, for he could see more clearly what the Kaiser intended, and could also, after American intervention, count on Germany's losing. When the Germans tried for compromise peace with Belgium, they ruled it out by the demands they made.

The Allies had accepted Belgian military assistance only conditionally, although there was urgent need of it. Statesmen, contemptuous of the lives they were sacrificing, thought of prestige; and the struggle to dominate alliances was another aspect of this 'war behind the war'. The French were disappointed at the Russian war effort: their territory had been invaded, despite the 'steam-roller' they had helped to manufacture. They remembered 1914 with gratitude, but felt they had recompensed the Russians enough in 1915 – holding down 2,300,000 soldiers in the west while the Russians held down only 1,500,000 Austrians and Germans. The Russians could answer that it was they, not the Allies, who had struck fear in the Central Powers by arriving at the gates of Hungary, and wanted war material from the Allies, particularly aircraft. One of the main officers of the French mission to Russia, Colonel Langlois, explained to his superiors that 'Russia will not herself be able to produce her monthly requirements of shell', but blandly continued, 'Still, this will not matter much, since the Russians cannot in any event match their programme regarding guns.' Arms and munitions were at the heart of the Franco-Russian dispute. The mission did, condescendingly, recommend delivery to Russia, but its real preferences lay elsewhere. Colonel Rampont wrote in autumn 1916, 'What the Russians really need is precise and concentrated work-habits. The army should adopt *our* methods, and 25,000 men trained by us should fight on the western front.' The idea was not new. Negotiations had been going on for many months regarding the sending of un-armed Russians to France. By 1916 terms of exchange had been settled. The Allies, with only slight superiority in artillery and air-craft, could not afford to be generous to Russia, and in view of the risks from U-Boats, and the seemingly prodigal misuse by Russia of the material she acquired, the Allies announced that they would meet Russian orders only in return for the sending to Marseilles or Salonica of larger Russian forces. This equation of flesh with material was all the more shocking to Russian opinion as the risks Russian troops would encounter on their way were simply left out of account. But Russia needed war material at any price and gave way.

The Anglo-Russian dispute was more serious, and also one-sided. The British were accused of getting other people to do their fighting for them, a grievance the Russians were not alone in feeling. 'The chief of the British Freemasons, Sir Asquith, has promised to arraign the crowned heads of Germany and Austria before a tribunal com-posed of parliamentary deputies and lawyers', wrote Bulatsen in the *Russki Grazhdanin*. 'For failing themselves to advance more than a yard or two, the British want us to make it up for them.' These traditional grievances were supplemented in government circles by worries as to British economic penetration, in oil and naval affairs. British investment in the Caucasus recovered and in Central Asia as well, whereas Russian financial missions had a dusty answer to requests for new loans on the London market – Bark's mission in 1916 could arrange only loans of three to six months, and if more than this, interest would be charged a per cent higher than for other clients. British policy in the Mediterranean was felt to be a rabbit-punch. As early as 1915 the British had organized the Dardanelles expedi-tion without consulting Russia. The Salonica army, the Greek card forced on Russia, and the Sykes–Picot agreements were new and serious grievances. British policy towards Turkey was, clearly, still being conducted without regard to Russia's interests; Russia was to be kept away from Constantinople and the Straits.

Suspicion between Italy and the rest stemmed from the ambiguous policy of Italy since war had been declared – despite hostilities against Austria, Italy would not declare war on Germany. A kind of 'war apart' was being waged in Albania, between Italians and Serbians, and Italy would not co-ordinate naval activity in the war against the submarine. The Italians accused their allies of not keeping promises sufficiently – the allies were guaranteeing to the south Slavs, for the future Yugoslavia, areas regarding which Italy had been given secret but firm undertakings. To the end, the Italians were against disrupting Austria-Hungary. Cadorna's military failure did dampen Italian complaints, but the problem of the Adriatic and Trieste was posed long before the final Austrian defeat.

The main allies were no kinder to each other. Russia had already been set aside during the operations against Turkey, and from the first negotiations leading up to the Sykes–Picot agreements and the Pact of London. The French and British suspected Tsarist Russia of leaning towards compromise peace. Empress Alexandra was of Hessian origin, was said to favour the Central Powers and was known to dominate the Tsar. Informed circles treated seriously the Grand Duke of Hesse's attempts to negotiate peace and the Protopopov mission to Scandinavia. There was indeed, in Russia, a group inclined to favour separate peace with the Germans – the extreme Right, the Black Hundreds. 'If the government wants Russia to live once more in order and tranquillity, it must before all else drive out "the Jew ruck",' – a term the Black Hundreds used for Duma deputies – 'conclude a separate peace with Germany and break off all relations with England.' Not many Russians thought this way, but they included court favourites, such as Rasputin, who managed to have a client, Sturmer, elected prime minister. He and his minister, Protopopov, were prevented from taking very far the negotiations they began with Germany, in view of the general hostility to a separate peace of Grand Dukes and soldiers, and in view of the liberal bourgeoisie's attachment to out-and-out war. The Tsar himself was against the idea. But the western foreign offices were alerted, and it seemed essential to treat the Russians with less disdain. Such was the object of the Petrograd conference of January 1917, during which Lord Milner, Generals Wilson and Castelnau, and Gaston Doumergue agreed to increase economic and military assistance to Russia. They were reassured as to the Tsar's good faith, but none the less left the country disturbed at its condition although believing that revolution would be put off till the war ended. During these negotiations French and Russians had concluded a secret accord on war aims, which they did not reveal to the British. Anglo-French relations, more even than Anglo-Russian ones, were tense, full of suspicion and aggression.

British diplomacy in July 1914 had revived all of a sudden the old anglophobe tradition and produced a sudden deterioration of the Entente. Fifty years later the British attitude can be more easily understood – wishing to make France hold out for peace as long as possible. Assurances given to Russia demonstrate that England meant to keep her promises, but the French felt abandoned, and maintained towards England a bitterness they counted legitimate. Further grievances had been added since – British gallivanting in August 1914, and French's near-treason in considering taking his troops home, or going south of the Somme while France was undergoing the greatest crisis in her history were not memories the French military would forget. The alliance's charm had been dissipated – despite the London accords binding each Ally not to conclude a separate peace, despite the 100,000 British dead on the Marne and elsewhere, the offensives in Artois or the Somme or Passchendaele and the million British casualties sustained by the end of 1916. The French, like the Russians, accused the British of fighting to the last drop of other people's blood, simply for their own safety. Of the half-million fighting in France, Joffre said in 1915, among other observations of the same type, 'I can't let them hold the line on their own – they'd be broken through. I can trust them only when they are held up by us.' In 1917 Pétain said the same: 'The commanders are incompetent, the troops badly-handled.' Of course the British also refused to accept the ideas of Joffre and Pétain, refusing to agree early in 1918, for instance, to the establishment of a general reserve that would have provoked the question of a single command. French resentment was kept up on one particular grievance – the British failed to accept French superiority and a secondary role for themselves. They felt, on the contrary, that France had a great deal to learn about winning wars – Waterloo, Sedan and Fashoda were, after all, the three great dates of French military history in the last century. Joffre, Foch and Mangin were accused of wasting lives – an accusation that would look better if it did not emanate from the makers of Passchendaele.

War aims also threatened the alliances' cohesion. The Entente considered these only when forced to – as was the case when Italy had to be offered her price, or when Wilson's initiatives at the end of 1916 forced secret discussions and public pronouncements from the governments. The French government was relatively modest, except as regards Alsace-Lorraine, 'the image of which suddenly rose, with the first battles of 1914, from the obscurity that had covered it even a few days before', and which was scarcely mentioned as a war aim by the soldiers who were actually doing the fighting. The French aimed to restore a historical situation, more to guarantee the country's future than to indulge in power-politics. When leading statesmen defended annexationist war aims, they thought less of aggrandizing France than of gaining compensation for territorial acquisitions that might be made by their allies. The result was not, however, all that modest. From 1915 Robert Pinot, president of the *Comité des Forges*, raised the question of the Saar, 'in view of the highly critical situation of the French coal industry, with its deficit of twenty million tons in 1913'. It would be not only compensation for wartime losses, but also a definite acquisition. Nationalists and a cohort of supporting historians – Lavisse, Sagnac, and others – demanded the left bank of the Rhine. Maurice Barrès wanted France to have 'a defensive zone against German infiltration', and the population there might choose between France and neutralized independence. The *Comité de la rive gauche du Rhin* stressed the population's affinities with Latin civilization, Barrès insisting on its Catholicism, the historian, Aulard, telling his audience how the Rhenish people had reacted to the French Revolution. Briand regarded such talk as misplaced, likely to help enemy propaganda and also socialists, whose accusations so far had been undocumented. He told the censors to 'forbid publication of articles for or against peace . . . or any that discuss conditions. There are to be no exceptions.' However, he himself continued a private discussion with Russia. Nicholas II told Paléologue, the French ambassador, 'Take Coblentz, take Mainz, take more if you want to.'

Verdun, the Brusilov offensive and Romanian intervention opened up new perspectives. Not only would the left bank of the Rhine be neutralized, but 'the German Empire and Prussian militarism' would be broken. Delcassé had discussed this earlier with Izvol'ski, in the context of German colonies and the rights of Denmark in Schleswig. He had even mentioned Hanover, for which the British might want independence. These ideas returned in 1916. Beyond this,

Joffre outlined to Poincaré his own aims: annexation of the Saar basin; formation, on the left bank of the Rhine, of three or four states 'politically independent of Germany' but tied to France by customs union; establishment of bridgeheads on the right bank of the river, opposite Strasbourg and Gemersheim; the reshaping of political Germany so as to cut down Prussia. The aim was to destroy Germany as a Great Power, even as a state. Furthermore, when Poincaré a few months later received Prince Sixtus of Bourbon-Parma to discuss, secretly, the possibilities of separate peace between France and Austria, he offered both Silesia and Bavaria, according to Lorenz, to the Dual Monarchy.

The British were not told. On the left bank of the Rhine, Briand simply referred to 'the need for security of Europe as a whole'. Doumergue and Castelnau talked more openly to the Tsar, and the left bank was in fact at the heart of these secret Franco-Russian negotiations, more so than the ostensible object of the conference, which was aid to Russia. They agreed to create autonomous states on the Rhine, neutral and independent of Germany, occupation of them being a pledge for fulfilment of the treaty. In exchange, France undertook to guarantee Russian claims to the Straits. The Russians hitherto had reckoned Constantinople as compensation for the French acquisition of Alsace-Lorraine; for the left bank of the Rhine, they demanded 'liberty of action on their western border', meaning that France should forget about Poland. Briand hesitated, but gave way on 10 March 1917. This secret treaty, concluded without British knowledge, was then swept away by the Revolution. It is not clear what pressures Briand had succumbed to for this, at a time when propaganda claimed incessantly that France was fighting for the rights of small nations. Maybe he wanted to trump the nationalists and Clemenceau; maybe he felt he must go in advance of the Tsar's wants, to forestall a separate peace, at a time when troubles had already broken out in Petrograd. But the treaty pinned down Russia and gave France a guarantee. Thus, the idea of dividing Germany gained shape, but the men behind it hid it from the British who, already, showed no willingness to guarantee recovery of Alsace-Lorraine while all the time proclaiming that restitution of Belgium was one of their war aims.

The British meant to make off with the German colonies, 'acquisition of which must be irreversible', and also intended to take much of the Turkish Empire, rich in long-coveted oil resources. The French similarly had aims in Syria, and there were secret negotiations, with which Russia, though not Italy, was associated. These culminated in the Sykes–Picot agreements, defining the three Powers' zones in the event of establishment of an Arab kingdom or federation. Palestine was to have separate status, Zionists hoping to set up a colony there. They acted towards this end in America and England, obtaining from the British government a promise made public with the Balfour Declaration at the end of 1917. In northern Turkey the Tsar should make off with the provinces of Erzerum, Trebizond and Ardahan. The Allies' disagreements became manifest at the end of 1916, when they had to answer Wilson's offer to mediate. The note of 10 January 1917, drawn up just after the Rome conference called to this effect, was a monument of ambiguity: to reconcile the secret treaties, the public promises and professions of faith, the Note outlined the war aims in the most generous terms.

Divergences between the Central Powers also affected the conduct of the war and the formulation of war aims. Here, the decisive element was the German leaders' own *Machtpolitik*, which was a deadly blow to the cohesion of alliances and in the end to Germany herself. Fritz Fischer has done the service of showing that this aggressiveness was not purely a matter of military or Pan-Germans, supposedly 'resisted' by 'sensible' elements, but was in fact supported by a wide section of public opinion, social democrats included. No doubt when the war went wrong, these ambitions were seen to be more or less unrealistic, and with defeat it was the army that remained intransigent whereas the government tried to keep its options open. But if tactics varied, objectives of 'moderates' and 'extremists' were not far apart, the intention of both being to turn Germany into a world power.

The 'September programme' shows the official aims of the German government in 1914, secret as they were. Like French statesmen, the German leaders declared their purposes to be essentially defensive: 'We must secure Germany for all time, west and east. France will have to be weakened to the degree that she can never again become a Great Power, and Russia has to be thrown far back from the German borders in the east, her power over the non-Russian peoples broken.' France was to give up the iron-ore basin of Briey, Belfort, the coast from Dunkirk to Boulogne, to raze the forts west of the Vosges, and sign a treaty which, after an indemnity had been paid, would reduce her to total dependence on Germany. Belgium was to cede Liège and Verviers, and assume vassal status; Luxembourg, increased by attachment of her Belgian part and Longwy, would be annexed.

The Netherlands would come under German control, though certain precautions might be made in view of the 'independent-mindedness of the Dutch'. *Mitteleuropa*, an economic association of Central Europe under Germany, would be set up to include Scandinavia, France, Austria-Hungary and Poland.

This programme, though only part of the German war aims, survived virtually unchanged in its essential features up to the end of the war. It matched, quite closely, the Pan-Germans' demands; they sought even Toulon. Big industry headed by Thyssen wanted the line of the Meuse, with all the departments of the Meuse and Haute-Saône. The Kaiser added a personal view that the area might be 'cleared of its population'. These war aims covered not only France but England, the navy indulging anglophobe passions by seizing as much as possible in the west so as later to face up to England, universally regarded as the main enemy. If victory against England required it, Tirpitz and the industrialist, Stinnes, were even ready for a compromise peace with other enemies. But there were other interests behind annexationism in the east, and Germany was in fact seeking a double victory. Jagow wrote, 'I cannot agree with those who want alliance with Russia, whatever the cost, only to defeat Britain . . . Russia is the weaker enemy, and to defeat the British is not so easy as these gentlemen believe. German war aims will not simply be dictated by heavy industry.' Stinnes, Krupp, Thyssen and the rest might be unanimous in seeking to reduce France to 'a territory without coal or iron, no longer our economic rival in world markets or a political danger in Europe'; but they did not stop there. The *Alldeutsche Verband* presented, through its president, Class, a programme by which Russia was to be pushed back 'to the frontiers of pre-Petrine Muscovy' by annexation of the frontier provinces, Poland, Lithuania and the Baltic. The industrialists were with this, although Thyssen would have liked the Don Basin with Odessa, the Crimea, East Galicia and the Caucasus 'for its manganese'. All this would serve the great aim of the war, 'to eliminate the insufferable supremacy exerted by Great Britain over us', for the Caucasus, Asia Minor and Persia would give a route to India and Egypt. Hugenberg had already split these areas in two: *Kulturland* to be taken over by German colonists, and *Vorland*, a bastion against Russia. There would be huge transfers of labour, each people having its task. The ethnic and economic map of Europe would be changed. The programme came up a few years later, and can be found point for point in Hitler's *Table Talk*.

Overseas ambitions were cut to the same cloth. Just before the Marne the colonial secretary, Solf, sent Bethmann Hollweg a memorandum he had drawn up for the event of peace with Belgium and France. Portugal, although neutral, would give up Angola and northern Mozambique, to link German possessions east and west. Germany in Africa would take over the Belgian Congo, French equatorial Africa to Lake Chad, all of Togo and Dahomey as well as northern Senegal and the Gambia to Timbuktu. This empire would be bounded in the north by the bend of the Niger, and its heart would be the Katanga area; Zimmermann went beyond this to include Central Africa between the Sahara and the Zambesi, along with Madagascar, the Azores, Madeira and Cape Verde. A territory like this would control British imperial sea-routes to India, South Africa and Australia. Finally, by virtue of this African empire, Latin America would be turned away from the United States. In the east, German possession of Shantung would open the way for a protectorate of China. Beyond Mesopotamia the Berlin–Baghdad axis would divide – one part *via* Persia, Afghanistan and Central Asia to China and Samoa; the other *via* Arabia and East Africa towards Santa Catarina in Brazil. These schemes left the British Empire intact – it was reckoned invincible, but the sailors, industrialists and statesmen went beyond this at times when they felt they could afford it – at the height of submarine warfare, and again during the March offensive of 1918. In Africa all Mozambique, Northern Rhodesia, Uganda and Kenya would round off what had previously been foreseen, together with the British Gambia, Bathurst, Dakar, Portuguese Guinea and a whole set of naval bases. Further east, Réunion joined Madagascar, and North Borneo came in – though control of the other islands of Indonesia would be achieved 'from within', through control of the Netherlands.

These ambitions, whether stemming from a conception of history, from generously interpreted interests or from various lobbies in Berlin, were on a different scale from those of the Allies. The various Allies, now 'satiated, and having all the living-space they want', had each had their day already; now it was Germany's turn. Men followed Ranke in believing this; and the hour of England was supposed to be over. She was now an 'old' nation; Germany, her power so swiftly ascendant, meant youth, the world's future. 'Few of us desired it, though it was at the back of all of our minds; our statesmen tried to get it by peaceful means, and our enemies were terrified at the idea; and now it stands revealed by events to us all ... Germany, through this war, will become a world power.' This was 'the German War', after Spanish, French, British ones. Germany must take her rank with the world powers: the British Empire, Russia, the United States. 'Squeezed between world powers to east and west', Germany must cut her way through, and become the 'middle empire'. Ambitions went even further, as for instance the geographer, Hettner, indicated: 'We Germans must impose on utilitarian, egocentric and frivolous peoples our own German civilization. Our civilization must spread; we are the educators of the world.'

For long it was supposed that civilians and government circles tried to define more reasonable war aims against the soldiers' extreme ones. Fritz Fischer has shown this to be wrong: Bethmann Hollweg, the Pan-Germans and most statesmen took a similar view. But the chancellor kept this secret, so as to deceive and weaken the enemy, to stimulate the national will and to anaesthetize the socialists. In any case, Hugenberg felt, 'the workers will be struck dumb with admiration if we show some fine conquests'. After the war German industry must have new resources with which to satisfy the workers' demands. But there were other reasons to conceal these aims – they would have worried Germany's allies, weakened the alliances and made victory less certain.

This was the case with Germany and Turkey. In 1914 the Turks had hoped at least to recover Cyprus, Russian Armenia and Egypt. Germany wanted Mesopotamian oil and the Hedjaz phosphates, and were indeed attempting to reorganize the world. The Turks felt their independence to be under serious threat; and the conflict was particularly clear, after Brest-Litovsk, in the Caucasus, where Pan-German met Pan-Turanian ambitions. The first collision came over the Black Sea, where the Germans arrived via the Ukraine, and by February 1918 Germans and Turks were in open conflict over Georgia, Ludendorff supporting the pro-German nationalities, the Turks trying to take the area for themselves, since it 'belonged to their sphere of influence'. The British, from the south, marched on Baku, and the two sides had to set up a *modus vivendi*, but it was shaky.

So also was the Austrian alliance. Austrian war aims were more modest than Turkish ones, leading circles even wondering if it was sensible to annex Serbia and Montenegro. Burián worried in advance at the difficulties these nationalities could cause to the Dual Monarchy, and preferred setting up satellite states, including Albania. Apart from minor frontier rectifications at Italian and Romanian expense, Austria-Hungary firmly formulated only one aim, the establishment of a separate Poland under Habsburg dominion. The Germans disliked this, and after wearisome negotiations, Poland was to be handed over to the Germans while Austria took Romania in exchange. But Germany was also obviously coveting Romanian oil, parallel with her *Mitteleuropa* plans. These plans would turn Austria into a satellite. The new emperor, Karl, looked for ways of making peace with the west, since his empire was not threatened as much by German power and *Mitteleuropa* as by rebellious nationalities. The Kaiser had tried to deal with Russia behind Austria's back; Karl would do the same with the west. Secret negotiations were undertaken by Prince Sixtus of Bourbon-Parma; they dragged on, Austria promising to help France recover Alsace-Lorraine, offering Germany Poland in exchange, and herself proposing to make a symbolic gain in Romania. But by March 1917 annexationist dreams were too great on both sides for a peace without them to be conceivable; negotiations broke down over Italy. They had been opened without German consent, and greatly strained relations between the Central Powers. They also irritated the new Russian government, not informed by Poincaré. France, though ostensibly secular and republican, had been more considerate towards the Tsar.

A few weeks later, in Karl's name, Czernin sent the Kaiser a memorandum: 'Austria's military strength is coming to an end', and with 'desperate conditions, famine, the effects of the February Revolution on the Slavs, the rebellious attitude of the workers and the minority peoples' there must be 'a conclusion of peace in the next few weeks'. The Germans lived in the hope of total victory in the east and then in the west, and refused Karl. But the letter sent to the Kaiser deserves stress: 'We cannot fail to recognize that now we face an enemy of a new type, more dangerous than the Entente – international revolution . . . Please look beyond its initial advantages to us; these threatening clouds can only be dispelled by immediately ending the war.'

Part III

The war had required an all-out effort. The mobilized soldiers' places were taken by the women, and younger classes were called up. Then came war economy, with unnumbered privations. Society was terrorized by propaganda into giving its last energies. Europe was overwhelmed, its daily life transformed, its visions of the future altered out of recognition.

Servicemen became sharply conscious of their solidarity, by virtue of common experiences – the gregariousness of the front line, the common tragedy of fighting, the brief escapes on leave. Soldiers became a new class, the class of victims: they reacted with throbbing hostility to the 'home front', profiteering businessmen or 'shirking' workers. Although this hostility left no trace in standard accounts of the war it still marked a generation of men. The conflict of civilian and military authorities has been often stressed; certainly, it affected political events of the traditional kind, and its virulence certainly stemmed from more ancient quarrels. The same resurgence of old quarrels came with the decline of *Union sacrée*: the revival of the workers' and socialist movements, dormant since 1914, came with the changed perspectives of the war, and the revolutionary ideal came alive again. Lower-class discontent, openly expressed, concealed a less open one, middle-class discontent. The economic causes were to some degree the same, but the social degradation inflicted on the lower middle classes led to their reacting in a different sense.

The antagonism of front and rear, the discontent of manual workers and the middle classes, the revival of revolutionary movements and overall resentment at war profiteers – all reflected social tension and anger. The war continued, and men asked: were operations being competently managed in view of the high losses? Was the price of victory not too high, and would compromise not be preferable? Did civilian and military leaders see that there were limits? Did not the continuation of war leave them an unjustifiably extended control over society? These questions were universally posed, and never publicly answered. But profound problems were none the less reflected in ministerial reshuffling, frequent political crises, the great events of the battlefield. Ruling classes sought to hide the truth, a form of propaganda instinctive to them in their efforts to legitimize their own authority. This, behind the masquerade of elections, was supposed to stem from competence in the public service, if not from the good old divine right. But the great leaders, despite their inborn efficiency and infallibility, seemed unable to seize victory; it was therefore essential to blame someone else. Spies were alleged to be everywhere; and if it could also be shown that the revolutionary elements were controlled by the enemy, then two enemies could be killed at a stroke, the national and the class one. This chance appeared only in 1917, with the overthrow of Tsarism, whereat ruling classes everywhere felt threatened with the tragic fate of the Russian aristocracy and bourgeoisie. Until then the *Union sacrée* atmosphere had been kept up at least in public, and leaders, both civilian and military, were given the weapon of 'official truth'. This could, on the Allied side, transform utter reverses, such as the Somme or the Chemin des Dames, into resounding victories; on the Central Powers' side, the same wand transformed the November armistice of 1918 into the wages of victory. In all countries the international solidarity of the governing classes was reflected in official truths to the effect that the Russian revolution was in fact all that the ruling classes had long desired. Despite the war, old hatreds revived, and new ones came into existence during the war: society as a whole was transformed. It was gripped by contradictions, new and old. In some countries, the new were simply added to the old; in others, the new ones were neutralized; and whether new or old ones predominated, nations were to be shaken in some degree by crises leading eventually to communism or fascism and Nazism, or indeed nowhere in particular. To start with, men merely wondered if the war could not be fought better, or they had wondered about its aims. This question soon came to the war itself, the reasons for its outbreak, the whole relationship of society and government.

Chapter 14

Tensions new and old

After 1914, the French military had rapidly taken power for themselves: 'The prefects are finished, the deputies don't matter, the generals can feed on civilian flesh' – a real *Revanche*, for which part of the professional army had been waiting since Boulanger and Dreyfus. It was now surfeited: within four weeks Poincaré himself was ignorant as to the commanders of the various armies of the Republic, and was kept in the dark by the High Command about the defeat of Charleroi and the size of losses. He was refused permission to accompany Joffre into the reconquered parts of Alsace. The military appointed judges and sub-prefects; quite early on, a circular from the High Command forbade prefects to telephone without permission, even their own ministry. A few months later Viviani learnt from his flower-seller that the High Command was going to leave Chantilly. He told the Cabinet, 'A Prime Minister can't be expected to like this.'

The caricature applied throughout Europe. The strains involved would not matter much if victory came, but with invasion and the growing death-lists, civilians and military fought it out, first on the Allied side. Russian military and bureaucrats blamed each other's blunders, the army blaming bureaucrats' lack of foresight, the bureaucrats the army's creating chaos. The Duma simply accused everyone in power, being itself removed from government. Milyukov said, 'Either the government is lying, or it is incompetent and ignorant.' The Tsarist Russian quarrel of bureaucrats and military was, by now, mere shadow-boxing; but in Italy it was a symptom of deeper problems – the Italians' own indifference to the war. Up to Caporetto there was virtually no policy regarding propaganda, and for the citizenry this was a kind of colonial war happening at the country's perimeter. Financial officials distributed credits with the parsimony shown to Libyan campaigns. Only two of the seventeen corps were fully equipped, and Cadorna could not seize the advantage he might have taken from a sudden offensive. Interventionists pushed him, and he asked for twelve further divisions. After six months' haggling he got eight, even then only on paper; and they might well not be ready for the 1916 offensive. General Staff and government were locked in conflict. At the time of Asiago, Sonnino as prime minister announced, 'A man who never tells anyone his plans or the means he employs cannot possibly be responsible for the fate of Italy.' Cadorna was summoned; in reply he sent a one-page report to the government. He had been enraged at being kept in ignorance of the negotiations leading to the Pact of London, and maybe even considered a *coup d'état*. But the army recovered, and the government dared not dismiss him. The Chamber refused a vote of confidence in the government, Left and extreme Right having voted together. The army did not emerge humbled from the test, instead feeling that the civilians should be subjected to military control and in particular should be made to consult Cadorna. The army denounced the troops' lack of ardour – caused of course by their being ordered to attack barbed wire frontally – and claimed it was the fault of Orlando, minister of the interior, for being soft on pacifism. The same happened in France later on, when Nivelle and Pétain accused Malvy of some responsibility for the mutinies.

The French case was different, however, since the country seemed truly threatened, with the enemy at the gates of Paris. The quarrel of military and politicians, initially a political one, embraced the whole nature of authority. Circumstances helped Joffre, the best of republicans, to take excessive power in 1914. In July Poincaré and Viviani had been in St Petersburg, and in their absence the government was nervous. On 25 July Messimy, minister of war, telegraphed all absent general officers to return to their garrisons; Joffre reminded him of *Annexe IIa*, which laid down what should be done in emergency. 'From then on, the minister never did anything without consulting me', he said, and his authority was successively reinforced by proclamation of a state of siege on 2 August and by proroguing of parliament the next day. Defeat indirectly had the same effect, since Joffre suggested the government should leave Paris and not make the mistake of 1870. The government prevaricated, and General Galliéni's proclamation did not add to deputies' prestige.

The Cabinet did not dare react. They had no weapons against soldiers, nor were socialist ministers behind in recommending obedience and discipline. In the Cabinet all that Millerand, the war minister, did was to ensure good relations between soldiers and civilian leaders. He prevented his colleagues from opposing the actions of the High Command, hinting that, were it not for him, the soldiers might become politically factious. Some of them were certainly not devoid of reactionary intentions: 'Clericalism has donned uniform to make war on the Republic', wrote Abel Ferry, nephew of Jules. Foch and Castelnau had well-documented clerical connections, Franchet d'Esperey well-known reactionary views. The 'republican' generals such as Sarrail were kept apart by their colleagues. But Millerand said that so long as Joffre was there, there would be no factious activity, even if the army was gradually colonizing the state, taking more and more civilian powers, using 'patriotic need' to justify any abuse of power. Joffre had no stouter champion than the minister, and he used this to cut rivals down to size – Galliéni, for one – to secure his own supremacy. There was a battle over Sarrail. In August 1914 Joffre had told him to give up Verdun, Sarrail had, rightly as it turned out, refused, and Joffre bided his time; when Sarrail failed in an operation, the chance was taken to dismiss him. He was cleverly replaced by Dubail, also a 'republican', but the government, incensed, were not deceived, and gave Sarrail command of the *Armée d'Orient* in Salonica. 'This was a turning-point,' said Ferry, 'as for the first time the Cabinet had gone against a decision of Joffre's.'

The war on Joffre was only one aspect of the parliamentary counter-offensive. This faced many difficulties, since the generals, beaten by the Germans, would take revenge on the politicians. They had dreamed for years of dealing with these, whom they identified with the 'Whore', the Republic, which they accused both of their own and of the nation's decline. War ended an intolerable situation. General Rouray recognized no deputies thereafter, arresting Jobert, a volunteer, deputy for the Yonne, on the grounds that 'under the pretext of having been, in peacetime, a deputy, he corresponds with the minister'. There was absolute incompatibility of mood and outlook between soldiers and deputies. 'Military secret' enabled the military to refuse information to the government, let alone deputies or the public. But, as Ferry told Poincaré, 'Everyone knows about offensives; place, method, day, or at least week, being well known to government, Chambers, the public, cab-drivers and the foreign press a month before they start.' But the army imposed silence just the same. The Right trembled with delight: 'France is getting better because the politicians have shut up', said Lyautey; when parliament resumed, he observed, 'It was so much better when all the talking and scribbling was stopped.'

It was material they thought about, not lives; their bloody and impossible orders went on. But the reverses of 1915, the hecatombs at the front, were finally known to the public and assessed. There was questioning and criticism. The government closed ranks with the soldiers, strengthened censorship in the name of *Union sacrée*, and muzzled journalists and deputies. Parliament, surreptitiously encouraged by some of the government, grumbled: 'Is union to mean perpetual silence?', said Chauvet. 'Are we to be heard only by saying nothing?' It was too early to make a frontal attack on the military, and attacks went against the minister, Millerand, who in his curt and obstinate way covered everything and fought it out. But in the state of affairs left by Etienne and Messimy he could not give an exact figure for guns and rifles, and this ignorance made him vulnerable – a situation singularly embarrassing for Poincaré since, unlike the Germans, he had not taken the precaution of finding out what state the army was in before going to war. Millerand was the favourite target of the parliamentary commission on military matters, and particularly of Clemenceau; and he had to give way after being 'interpellated' in public session by Accambray and 'skinned alive' by his Cabinet colleagues; he was obliged to admit to his ministry four new secretaries of state, who necessarily restricted his competence – particularly Albert Thomas at Munitions. The crisis provoked Viviani's fall and his replacement by Briand.

The efforts of the parliamentary commission on the army and the secret committees of the senate had now defined and restricted the roles of government and supreme command. Gaston Monnerville's hitherto unpublished documents show how attempts were made again and again by Paul Doumer, Clemenceau and Jeanneney to recover parliament's rights. Jeanneney said, 'The High Command's self-imposed splendid isolation, the jealous omnipotence it enjoyed, its freedom from all control, and certainly from parliamentary control, and the idolatrous atmosphere men patriotically created for it, all worked to prevent it from seeing its mistakes or from treating other people's proposals with due seriousness.' Parliamentary control had been asserted only in illusory ways. The year before Abel Ferry, sickened at the futile massacres, had invited Millerand to see the front for himself, to see how the soldiers lived. The minister was worn down by Ferry, and agreed; but he did nothing to stop the military from staging one of their traditional performances for the occasion – trenches swept, soldiers given new uniforms, and the like. A parliamentary commission later tried to see for itself, went to d'Urbal's headquarters and announced it would like to see the front line. 'The General, politely impertinent, told them they might go as far as the rear areas of the supply-lines.' After Joffre's departure on 2 December 1916 Nivelle, as 'conqueror of Douaumont', succeeded him by virtue of his different address towards deputies; he explained his plans to politicians questioning him, and ended 'military secrets'. The Nivelle episode, though ending in tragedy, was a turning-point, and his failure allowed the politicians to take their revenge, to limit the functions of Pétain, Joffre and Foch, a humiliation that was caused by Nivelle's adventuring, for which his colleagues were never to forgive him.

In 1917–18 the civilians won. But it was a Pyrrhic victory – parliamentary control came only when the French army had begun to win the war, and this made difficult any searching and dismissal of 'guilty men'. The soldiers became increasingly arrogant, and blamed the 'rear' for past defeats and mutinies: the pacifists, and Malvy, the allegedly conniving minister of the interior, being their targets. Clemenceau and the Right supported this; and the common soldiers' loyalty to the army was exploited to turn them against parliamentary or other civilian control. As Michel Baumont has said, after the war all the military chiefs – except of course Nivelle – were made out to be great heroes; the deputies and senators who had been at least as much interested in saving men's lives as the generals were discredited or forgotten.

In England Kitchener was an embarrassment, not least because he foresaw – virtually alone – that it would be a long war. His open speech was ill-suited to politician's ways. He was alleged to be more difficult to rule than India; he announced, for instance, that the French were turning war into a holocaust, that British troops should never be buried in these trenches. This was useful to the politicians, who could use Kitchener to support the 'eastern' policy, to the extent that Kitchener had against him the army commanders in France. He lost strategic control to the prime minister and the Cabinet as a whole. He was accused of responsibility for failures in Artois, by reason of not supplying shell as he should; and he was then effectively removed from control of munitions as well. The civilians successfully laid this bogey, although Kitchener formally remained in power until he was drowned while on mission to Russia.

The battle of government and military flared up again a few months later, with Haig and Robertson trying to cut Lloyd George, the new prime minister, out of strategic direction. The fact was that these two Indian army men had difficulty in imagining a plebeian's directing the affairs of the Empire. But they were tricked; at the Calais conference he agreed to put Haig under Nivelle, despite the traditional precedence disputes involved. Haig never forgave this. When Nivelle failed, Haig, despite grumbling from Lloyd George, decided to launch his own offensive. After the event he made out that his motive had been to save the French army, which at the time was gripped by the mutinies. In reality he was dreaming of dominating the field himself, of winning a truly British success in imitation of the French one at Verdun, and thereby of defeating Lloyd George. He would not be persuaded otherwise, and the Passchendaele offensive went its disastrous way, causing altogether 400,000 casualties. Lloyd George would not send further reinforcements, and Haig was thus enabled to blame the government for subsequent defeats. The lives lost in this futile quarrelling have never been computed. The quarrel was also tragic in its consequences for the Allies, for it affected the British troops' capacity to resist the German offensive of 1918. In the end Robertson was eased out through his hostility to joint command, and Haig was forced to accept Foch, and the primacy of his own government's decisions.

Government and admirals were also locked in a battle quite as serious. Early in 1915 Admiral Fisher had opposed the Dardanelles and personally attacked its main advocate, Churchill. He was then forced to resign. But when the Asquith government was reshaped, Churchill was dropped from it. There was a further crisis in the following period, with submarine-warfare. By March 1917 the Admiralty had still issued no instructions to merchant-ships, since it regarded commercial activity as none of its business. Submarines would of course be combated, but Dreadnoughts were not there to escort cargo-boats. It took Lloyd George much effort to persuade the admirals that the most important thing was not to sink submarines but to get merchantmen home safely. The admirals believed convoy impracticable, and produced many difficulties – the great number and differing speeds of merchantmen and the many different sea-routes; the fact was that they disliked employing their superb ships on humdrum tasks. But the government, supported by younger captains, organized convoys, and these triumphantly returned to Bristol and Liverpool, so the Admiralty gave way.

The story in Germany ended differently. Of course, there the generals did better, on the whole, even if there were local failures to interrupt their triumphal march – the Marne ruining Moltke, Verdun Falkenhayn. But the generals could well say that, if the war was lasting so long, it was the government's fault for not keeping out Britain and Italy. The soldiers were optimistic; their national territory was inviolate. Bethmann Hollweg thought differently – he was a natural worrier, and pessimistic in outlook. He would not publicize Germany's war aims, because it would sow discord and compromise the unity of Germans, and was then accused of cowardice, both generals and the Right accusing him of restricting the country's sword-arm. There was a trial of strength: in 1915 an initial flurry over the eastern front and then a battle over submarines. Since the failure of Verdun and the ordeal of the Somme, Bethmann Hollweg no longer believed in total victory, and Falkenhayn agreed – though this support was dangerous, as Bethmann had always disliked the power of Falkenhayn, a personal friend of the Kaiser's, and was not much put out at Falkenhayn's reverses, east and west. He was accused of invading the preserve of government, and Bethmann wanted to see, in command of the army, a general that would not 'play politician'. Hindenburg was thought to be right, and in summer 1916 the right moment came for him, when Falkenhayn obstinately stuck to his western course, neglecting both military danger and the chance of peace through victory in the east. Hindenburg was more amenable, and was also supported by Prince Rupprecht of Bavaria; the Austrians would accept his command, and his prestige, already great since Tannenberg, mounted. Brusilov and Romanian intervention destroyed Falkenhayn's position, and the clear failure at Verdun compelled him to give way to Hindenburg and Ludendorff.

But the victory was deceptive for Bethmann Hollweg, who did not realize that Hindenburg was essentially in agreement with the advocates of total war. He shared Tirpitz's views on unrestricted submarine-warfare – when Bethmann Hollweg had refused this because of promises made to America, and when Tirpitz resigned, Hindenburg and Ludendorff sympathized with him, and by October were championing the cause, 'whatever the consequences'. Bethmann Hollweg retorted that it was his business to decide, because questions of foreign policy were involved by the possibility of American intervention, but he was not supported by the *Reichstag*, many of whose elements were glad to see the 'war-chancellor' embarrassed. America did indeed declare war, and events seemed to bear out Bethmann's view; but now the Russian Revolution broke out, which gave the military a new argument for going on to a total victory, provided the nation made a last effort. Hindenburg and Ludendorff sought to mobilize the country's entire strength, whatever the cost, and extended military authority throughout Germany. Civilian life was to be regimented, which now became possible through agreements on manpower concluded between trade unions and generals. Ludendorff thought of mobilizing the youth of both sexes from the age of sixteen, who would then be sent by the army to training camps or wherever they were required. There would be neither civilians nor military left: a truly egalitarian society would emerge to take the place of the pre-war one – in Möllendorf's words, 'A nationalist-aristocratic-corporatist-socialist consciousness is to be substituted for the internationalist-democratic-parliamentary-capitalist one'. Here was a foreshadowing of the Nazi programme, a 'uniting of the fatherland', the nation marching in step, with no difference between front and rear.

In all countries, these two fought it out, though not with the same bitterness. Trench newspapers and soldiers' letters show a rising sense of grievance against the 'home front', particularly in Germany, France and Italy. *Le Ver luisant, La Fusée, Le Canard du Boyau* or any other, similarly ephemeral, publication display a remarkable feature: they never bother with victory, life in the rear or politics. They were left to others. *La Fusée* described itself as 'anti-political, anti-Boche and anti-downhearted'. Editors knew that the extreme solitude of the front, the hideousness of existence in the trenches, called for constant joking; but it leaves an echo of rancour and bitterness. As the war dragged on, with death always in the air, soldiers came to suspect that they had been subjected to some vast trickery – they were to be sacrificed, while the men in the rear, whether soldiers with safe jobs or civilians, carried on regardless, unless perhaps to express their surprise that victory was so long in coming. Ducasse, Mayer and Perreux, in several outstanding works, have described 'the spirit of the trenches', and how 'the rest' behaved: 'When the intantryman met up with cyclists, orderlies, staff-cooks and the like, they plied him with food and drink, gave him cigarettes, and made a fuss of him, to pay for their own safety.' Staff-officers were detested, 'with képis of the latest Delion fashion, Sam Brownes, canes, waxed riding-boots.

The Albert Kahn cinematographic records contain sad film of men arriving on leave at the Gare de l'Est in Paris, with crumpled caps, dirty leggings, dumb-struck at the sight of life going on regardless of war and its miseries. The front was a long way away from this life of balls, *Foire aux Jambons*, Tuesdays at the *Comédie Française*, promenades in the Bois de Boulogne. Charles Devert says, in his *Histoire d'une compagnie*:

> Saturday 22 April 1916: Paris is lovely – the crowds as before, the trees green, the boulevards sunny. I can't stop thinking of Champagne, by contrast – the houses smashed to a few bits of crumbling wall, the huge landscapes with no vegetation, save for a few pines, reduced almost to sticks, and the pieces of leprous grass growing round the shell-holes that mark the whitish and greenish earth like smallpox on a face. But here, people go about their business regardless of us – avenue de l'Opéra, boulevard des Capucines, boulevard de la Madeleine, rue Royale, place de la Concorde are all as before. The lawns are green, the flower-baskets are full of brilliantly coloured, fresh, newly opened flowers, the trees are in their first flowering of spring. It cannot be lovelier. The blue sky is dotted with silvery clouds – life is sweet, and I can see how the home front holds out so stoutly. This evening, I took the 21.50 train to Bordeaux, crowded with people off to the country for the week-end. I am consoled by the thought that, even if I end up a drying corpse on the barbed wire, this world will not be irreparably harmed.

Truffrau wrote:

> You can never believe there's a war on – the more it goes on, the better a time people have. The shops are brightly lit, there are beautiful cars, chic little women in little hats, with high boots, immaculately powdered, with muffs and little dogs, men who've dodged the war, dressed in fine-cut jackets of good cloth, fashionable breeches with leather of a yellow more highly polished than any officer's. Then you see men, dirty and helmeted, with big boots and faded caps, wandering round the boulevards.

The soldiers at the front were irritated at tales of woe from home. One wrote to his wife, 'What's all this about "front" and "rear"? It's rubbish. All the soldiers want the rear to take some of the burden. Sugar rationing, you say? It means you've at least got sugar; taxes on cinema tickets at least shows you've got cinemas to go to; coal may be rare and expensive, but at least you've a chance of keeping warm' (quoted by J. N. Jeanneney). Trench newspapers reflected the anger, bitterness, and occasional irony of this attitude: thus

Le Canard du Poilu describes the visit of some well-meaning deputy-prefect, anxious to see for himself: 'Suddenly, a shell whistled over ... we rushed to look, and what should turn up but a civilian, a sort of spectre, fresh and pink, with top-hat, frock-coat, yellow shoes. What the hell's he after, is he a spy? No, he has an oily smile all over his functionary-face, and presents himself, "I'm the deputy-prefect".' The attitudes were shown in a jingle of *La Fusée*:

> Infantryman, true Prince of Battle,
> Seize in your blood-stained hands
> Grenades, an anodyne.
> Hurl them far across the land,
> As far as you can
> To reach Lyon, Bordeaux, or Nîmes.
> For pity's sake don't miss
> The shirkers, your intended victims.

The soldiers might not doubt they were right to fight, but they were always exasperated by appeals to fight on to victory when these came from far in the rear. *Soldat Grazhdanin* said:

'Victory!' cries the crow cleaning human bones on the battle-field; but what is victory for the old mother waiting for her son to come back, or the old man guiding the plough with a trembling hand? 'Victory!' you hear from a student haranguing thousands in the public place, telling them that all misfortune comes from Germany while his father, having sold oats at sixteen roubles the pood [= 16 kg.], sits in some noisy night-club making the same talk. 'Victory!' you hear from some Allied representative touring battlefields littered with the corpses of workers. But you don't hear it from the man in the trenches. He'd say, 'take the victory-merchants to the front line, and then we'll see what they have to say'.

Whatever the case, the men in the rear were all guilty. Whether they were pacifists or jingoists, whether or not they thought about the war, whether they lived in poverty or whether they profiteered, they all had one thing in common: they were safe. When Clemenceau, speaking after the war, said of the soldiers, 'They have claims upon us all', he was only saying what millions of them felt.

Once they had been demobilized, the soldiers started idealizing their life and its virtues. They had been an example of masculine solidarity, they had been linked by a single ideal transcending religion, race, social origin; this contrasted with the social climbing, profiteering, conscription dodging, the luxuries and the delicate pleasures of life in the rear. A special 'ex-serviceman's' outlook grew up from bitterness and nostalgia; there was a common claim to the country's gratitude, an urge to get together and revive the private language of men who had gone together through tragedy. This reaction came with men's failure to adapt again to their monotonous pre-war lives. They felt wounded in their hearts, their dignity and their honour by the years they had lost, the futility of it all, the ingratitude and heartlessness of people who had not gone through it. They felt humiliated, whichever side they were on, and some of them dreamt of revenge – the nation should be regimented, taught to live and die as the soldiers had. Such were the aims of post-war associations, and the 1930s Leagues in France, formed by the spirit of the trenches. In Germany, just after defeat, Hitler unconsciously took up one of Ludendorff's themes and said, 'Germany will be saved by the anonymous front-line soldier.' Mussolini in Italy and his counterparts in France, Belgium and England took up the refrains even in victorious countries: as Hess said, 'The Third Reich comes from the trenches.' It was of course only a minority of ex-servicemen who joined the Leagues, and only a minority of their members had actually fought at all. But it was none the less an expression of the victims' resentment overall.

This class of men shared with the workers a bitter hostility to the profiteers. *Soldat Grazhdanin* inevitably turns to the kulak, selling his grain at sixteen roubles the pood. Peasant proprietors in Russia improved in prosperity with the war, as agricultural prices were pushed up by supply needs, lack of labour, and starvation conditions. But for lack of goods coming from the towns, the profits were illusory – they could not be spent. But the war did make peasants richer, and the poor ones might hope, in turn, to become proprietors, in France as elsewhere. In France the peasants were harder hit by war than anywhere else, since 52 per cent of the dead were of peasant stock, but their families profited. The war wiped out peasant debts everywhere, in Italy improving the lot even of the poorest, as is shown by the decline of squatting. Bourgeois property became peasant property, a phenomenon noted though not understood by contemporaries. They also failed to note the general decline of the middle classes, although this phenomenon appeared all over Europe, as the price rise caused by penury affected middle-class incomes. These were more vulnerable than others, and real incomes declined for white-collar workers, civil servants, landlords, annuity-holders and pensioners. They were proletarianized, and were soon joined by the army of publicists, journalists and actors reduced to unemployment and penury by the war. Kautsky and Bernstein had predicted long before that war would be fought on the savings of the little man and would turn the middle classes into a new proletariat. It also ruined small-scale industry, independent craftsmen, and subjected them to big business. This was marked in Italy, where concentration had in any case been greater, and where the small business and industry had been harder hit than elsewhere by wartime taxation. Pensioners, rentiers and petty bourgeois in general had subscribed to war-loan, lent their money to the state. They had invested their salaries and their sons in the war, and its end must bring them interest on their money, a safe old age. There could, therefore, be no peace without victory.

The working classes naturally took a different line. In August 1914 the International had been beaten by patriotism. Socialists, anarchists, militants, revolutionaries, had not kept the faith; like everyone else, they went gaily to war. Resisters, like Péricat in France or Dittmann in Germany, were almost lynched for opposing the tide of bellicosity, and the rarity of contemporary accounts of resistance shows its paucity. For Frenchman and German alike, patriotism had defeated the International – the education they had received stressed national, above class, enmity. In the July crisis the socialists had been faithful to the International up to the last moment – Jouhaux and Legien, secretaries-general of the trade unions in France and Germany, maintained close relations. When Belgium was invaded, Ramsay MacDonald and Appleton first thought of 'those poor German socialists'. But they were all swept along: men passionately welcomed the war, and socialists seemed to be living in a world apart, displaying consternation and despair. Merrheim, secretary of the Federation of Metal-Workers, wrote, 'That day – 31st July – I had a feeling it was all over. Jaurès thought war inevitable, and saw it coming with fear for the workers' future.' The night before, the precincts of *L'Humanité* were crowded by militants, the reigning opinion being that 'anti-war demonstrations are a waste of time, the International Congress won't happen'. Nothing had been done by the anarchists 'to oppose mobilization', and Jaurès's death contributed to the socialists' paralysis. The next day patriotic fever swept the country, and the central committee of the CGT unanimously rejected ideas of a general strike. Malvy, minister of the interíor, at once suspended the measures he had prepared against the anarcho-syndicalists, and told the prefects not to arrest persons named in *Carnet B*. The revolutionary leaders were freed from personal worries, and split into two groups – those who felt the defeat and tried to understand its causes, and who eventually turned to pacifism, and those who found no problem in joining the popular movement. Thus Jouhaux, who at Jaurès's funeral said, 'In the name of the workers who have gone to war, in the name of those who will go, of whom I am one', though he did not in the event go. He supported the war like the rest, and that day they voted war-credits.

After the great events of 4 August, invasion pushed the last hesitating socialists towards the *Union sacrée*: on 26 August Guesde and Sembat agreed to enter Viviani's government, followed in 1915 by Albert Thomas. The trade union leaders sat on a *Comité de secours national*, Jouhaux sitting next to the archbishop. A little later the anarchist, Sébastien Faure, was summoned to the ministry of the interior and there burst into tears – in Ferry's words, 'For fear of doing the Germans' work, he had become a warmonger.' All opposition disappeared in a month, and to justify this the four great socialist leaders Guesde, Sembat, Longuet and Vaillant sent the Bureau of the International a message, with which the Belgian Vandervelde was associated, to the effect that 'the workers have no thought of aggression, but are sure they are upholding their country's independence against German imperialism, fighting for the rights of peoples to determine their own life. They feel they have the sympathy of German socialists, that social progress must come after defence of the country.' This cut the remaining links between socialists of France and Germany, and once it became known that the German ones had voted war-credits for the Kaiser's army, there would be no question of restoring the links, despite many attempts by neutrals.

A few isolated syndicalists or anarchists, grouped around *La Voix ouvrière*, strove against the tide, and in retrospect they acquired some importance – they had contacts with the Russian émigrés who were to bring about the October Revolution, and historically they were important because they kept internationalism alive and stayed faithful to their pacifist ideals. But they were hopelessly ineffective at the time. The first people involved, according to a little work of Martov's, not yet published, on 'La crise de la démocratie en France', were Louise Saumonneau, of the socialist women, and Nicod, who together wrote a circular against the official party line. On the unions' side, the first leading figure to oppose the war was Charles Merrheim, who tried to bring together the socialist and trade union opposition movements, with Monatte's group, which sought to prevent the foundation of an exclusively anarcho-syndicalist International excluding socialists. Rosmer soon came in, but opposition was tiny. Romain Rolland's declaration against the war in the *Journal de Genève* of 22 September 1914 gave it a disproportionate effect, but his inspiration was neither socialist nor Internationalist. 'Au-dessus de la mêlée' was simply 'a cry for bleeding humanity'. 'It exaggerated the opposition of France to the war.'

There was *Union sacrée* in Germany as well, the *Burgfriede*. To start with, socialists and union-leaders had blamed the Austrian government: *Vorwärts*, the semi-official newspaper of the Social Democrats, wrote, 'Not a drop of German blood for Vienna.' But when Russia threatened, the war became one of defence against the Slavs, even for socialism against autocracy; on 31 July there was no protest from *Vorwärts* when mobilization was ordered and peace-meetings were forbidden; and when the party met to discuss war-credits, 'The mood was such', in Bernstein's words, 'that we hardly mentioned Austria, only France and Russia, who were thought to have needlessly provoked war over a Balkan quarrel.' Only a few deputies, out of principle, would refuse credits, but they, including Karl Liebknecht, still proclaimed the need for discipline in voting, so their attitude had no effect. On the contrary, it was the left-winger, Haase, who set out the party's reasons for joining the *Burgfriede* and voting war-credits. The government was much surprised, to the extent even of being liberal towards the opposition. It and the trade union leaders came together to discuss the economic and social changes required by war.

The workers' leaders in both countries thus took much the same attitude. Jules Guesde justified this in January 1918:

Class-collaboration in politics and government in peacetime is the worst kind of trickery, on the social level, because it preserves capitalist *society*, the destruction of which is essential for the freedom of labour and humanity as a whole; but in wartime, on the national level, it becomes just as much a duty for socialists, because it defends the *nation*, against aggressive war, and thus maintains the indispensable framework for socialist activity today and the first condition for internationalism tomorrow.

The 'civil truce' was marked in France and Germany by socialist participation in government or integration of the trade union apparatus with the state.

There was not the same unanimity in England or Russia. In England the most pacific became the most warlike as soon as the German threat was clear, and the country's interests touched by the attack on Antwerp. But some socialists would not join the throng – MacDonald, Snowden and most of the British socialist party recognized that the government could well go to war over Belgium, but it was no part of a socialist's duty to approve government acts, and in any case the causes of the war were more complex than the July crisis alone had shown. Asquith suggested to MacDonald, leader of the party, that he should join the government coalition; he refused – 'I don't want any part in this business.' The movement was supported by 15 per cent of industries, which went on strike on 8 August, just after the passing of the Defence of the Realm Act – more than in any other country. Newspapers such as the Glasgow *Pioneer* and *Forward* went on attacking Grey, and broke with government socialists like Henderson or jingoists like Hyndman who preached his minority cause in his weekly, *Justice*. In September the Union of Democratic Control was set up to achieve popular control of foreign policy and to denounce secret agreements. It aimed at a large audience, and was soon claiming 500,000 adherents.

A minority in Russia was still more radically opposed to civil truce, since in Russia the revolutionary militants and the working class were less integrated with society than in the west. Still, the Tsar called up fifteen million men. A million deserters had been thought likely, but there were in fact only a few thousands. Russians thought the cause was just, and honoured the promise given to 'the little brothers' of Serbia. Besides, alliance with the west left room for a hope that, after the war, Russian institutions would be altered on western lines. Plekhanov himself, 'father of Russian social-democracy', gave full priority to war against Germany and expected revolutionaries to suspend the war on the Tsar so as not to disrupt this war effort.

But not all opposition was silenced. Some of the émigrés, Lenin, Martov and Trotsky, at once denounced 'imperialist war' and blamed both sides for it. But whereas the rest merely demanded immediate peace, Lenin from September 1914 demanded 'a transformation of imperialist war into civil war'. The absolute evil was Tsarism, and military victory could only consolidate it; therefore revolutionaries must work for their own country's defeat, a tactic valid, by

Lenin's reckoning, not only for Russia. But defeatism – *porazhenstvo* – had not much effect; some of the Bolshevik émigrés in France even joined the French army, and listened far more easily to Plekhanov than to Trotsky and the *Nashe Slovo* men. There was similar patriotic contagion in Russia. Social democrats might vote against war-credits in the Duma, the *trudoviki* might even walk out, but they still declared they would help defence, and only the Bolsheviks' opposition was absolute. It was still ineffective – when Goremykin deported the five Bolshevik deputies to Siberia, there was hardly a protest, and only a few factories struck in response to Bolshevik appeals. The war seemed to have ended revolution.

The Second International was certainly shown bankrupt, despite Serbian and Russian socialists' opposition and despite the odd reservation made by isolated socialists in the west. Various justifications were made for this behaviour on the militants' part, and Annie Kriegel has suggested, for France, a schematic analysis of these, which has much value for Europe as a whole:

1. Theoretical justification drawn from the nature of the war:
(a) There is no question of the country's being guilty; the war is a legitimate one of defence, permitted and even required by socialist doctrine;
(b) The working class has as much interest in victory as the bourgeoisie; the class war does not mean adding to capitalist exploitation a further exploitation by enemy capitalism;
(c) The war is not just an imperialist one; it aims to liberate national territory invaded by the enemy.

2. Justification based on socialist-international considerations:
(a) The powerlessness of the International leaves no other way;
(b) The enemy country's socialists having voted war-credits, the International ideal can only triumph by defeat of the enemy;
(c) All socialist parties in the warring countries have joined in *Union sacrée*.

3. Justification based on particularly national considerations:
(a) Parts of the national territory have been, in the past, unjustly taken from the nation;
(b) An enemy victory would threaten liberty and the chances of establishing socialism, for which national existence is essential;
(c) Only one's own national spirit can give humanity the regenerative values to be expected from socialism.

It was even declared, by adherents of *Union sacrée*, that socialism would emerge from the war, though this had nothing in common with the arguments of Lenin or Rosa Luxemburg. Martov showed the path of intellectual development taken by Hyndman in Britain, Hervé in France – he would have added Mussolini in Italy a year later – and stated:

They began by stressing their own socialist aims, but then the working class saw how vain this was, and expected patriotism in its leaders; they then went fully to the patriotic labour line. Hervé reckons class-socialism is finished, and feels that, as in Germany, there will be 'a socialism of thinking people'. Jouhaux thinks that an era of class-collaboration has begun, and Rosenthal, in *Le Populaire*, has started working out programmes for it.

This, in Germany, was to go far. Trade unions were fully recognized and came to negotiate on equal terms with the employers and the state.

Not everyone was convinced by these 'successes'; in all countries, opposers of the war came fumblingly together. They did not intend, like Lenin, the defeat of their own countries, but they suspected the nature of the war, and rejected any idea that it was purely defensive; they opposed attempts to legitimize the war from a class-angle. But without mass support they were largely ineffective, and would have been even if they had been able to revive the International. Still, the existence of some nucleus, some revolutionary theory was a help, since it gave discontent some significance in ideological terms and exploited it for the cause of socialism, internationalism, and the Revolution.

But the General Staff of revolution had been set up before troops showed willingness to turn up. All it could do was to set out concepts that the later movements would adopt. Via the neutrals, particularly Italy, Holland and Scandinavia, links between the future revolutionaries were restored, and there was a reassembling of those who felt this was an imperialist war, that the International must be revived to stop the war. At Lugano and Copenhagen appeals to this effect were launched. They had no effect, the French and Belgians rejecting the very notion of attending a meeting where the Germans would be represented. The Allied socialists, conferring in London, invited neither the Serbians nor the Russians, Menshevik or Bolshevik, because they opposed the war; and the Central Powers' socialists, conferring in Vienna, likewise excluded neutrals or enemy.

The first conference gathering militants of both sides was that of the socialist women, in Berne. It had been convoked following a

Russian initiative, inspired by Elizabeth Petrova (Inessa Armand), Nadezhda Krupskaya and others of Bolshevik tendency, and organized by Clara Zetkin. She would have liked to invite only the left wing, without distinction of nationality, but the Berne meeting contained less extremist elements since 'you can't easily distinguish right and left among the women . . . and since many refused to come if only the left were present'. German socialists turned up, unauthorized; there were no Austrian delegates, four British ones, the Frenchwoman, Louise Saumonneau, and several Russians and Poles; the Belgians, however, were not given passports by their government. At Berne resolutions rejected both *Union sacrée* and defeatism; they reflected the British and Dutch pacifist 'do-goodery' more than they reflected the organizers' intentions. But the Bolsheviks subscribed to this rather than disrupt things.

There was also a conference of young Socialists in Berne, including Russians, Germans and neutrals, but it, too, did not stem from the International, whose organizers still adhered merely to the hopes expressed at Lugano. At the insistence of the Italian, Margari, and the Swiss, Grimm, this hope came to fruition, despite the obstruction of most members and offices in the various countries. Thirty-eight delegates met secretly at Zimmerwald in September 1915, and this had only a limited representational value, since they represented only the left wing; they were not even a remnant of the International, since the meeting was not initiated officially by its agencies. Invitations were issued not only to people of left-wing views, but also to moderates such as Haase, Troelstra and Branting. The conference was expected to limit its activity to appeals to the workers to act for peace, and not to found a new International. There were, from the beginning, three main currents. A majority of some twenty members wanted the conference to be a great demonstration for peace, avoiding an open breach with 'social-patriots' and the International. This was supported by the Frenchmen, Merrheim and Bourderon, respectively of the Metal-Workers and the Copper-Workers, the latter being a member of the socialist party, but not attending on that account. This group included most of the Germans, among them Ledebour, the Mensheviks, Martov and Axelrod, and some Italians and Poles. A further group of eight to ten delegates, including Lenin, Zinoviev, Radek, and the Swiss, Platten, did not accept these views, as too moderate; they demanded denunciation of *Union sacrée*, a breach with 'social-patriotism' and a transformation of the war into civil war. Between these groups was a further one, including Roland Horst, Grimm, Trotsky and Balabanova. The majority was thus a right-wing one, although itself of course on the left of each of the socialist movements represented. But the Left agreed to sign a common manifesto, the Zimmerwald Manifesto, which was to have a great echo in the socialist and syndicalist world.

THE ZIMMERWALD MANIFESTO

WORKERS OF EUROPE!

The war has lasted for more than a year. Millions of corpses lie upon the battlefields; millions of men have been crippled for life. Europe has become a gigantic human slaughter-house. All science, the work of many generations, is devoted to destruction. The most savage barbarity is celebrating its triumph over everything that was previously the pride of mankind.

Whatever may be the truth about the immediate responsibility for the outbreak of the war, one thing is certain: the war that has occasioned this chaos is the outcome of Imperialism, of the endeavours of the Capitalist classes of every nation to satisfy their greed for profit by the exploitation of human labour and of the treasures of Nature.

Those nations which are economically backward or politically feeble are threatened with subjugation by the great Powers, which are attempting by blood and iron to change the map of the world in accordance with their exploiting interests. Whole peoples and countries, such as Belgium, Poland, the Balkan States, and Armenia, either as units or in sections, are menaced by annexation as booty in the bargaining for compensations.

As the war proceeds its real driving forces become apparent in all their baseness. Piece by piece the veil which has hidden the meaning of this world catastrophe from the understanding of the peoples is falling down. In every country the Capitalists who forge the gold of war profits from the blood of the people are declaring that the war is for national defence, democracy, and the liberation of oppressed nationalities. THEY LIE!

In reality they are actually burying on the fields of devastation the liberties of their own peoples, together with the independence of other nations. New fetters, new chains, new burdens are being brought into existence, and the workers of all countries, of the victorious as well as of the vanquished, will have to bear them. To raise civilization to a higher level was the aim announced at the beginning of the war: misery and privation, unemployment and want, underfeeding and disease are the actual results. For decades and decades to come the cost of the war will devour the strength of the peoples, imperil the work of social reform and hamper every step on the path of progress.

Intellectual and moral desolation, economic disaster, political reaction – such are the blessings of this horrible struggle between the nations.

Thus does the war unveil the naked form of modern Capitalism, which has become irreconcilable, not only with the interests of the working masses, not only with the circumstances of historic development, but even with the first conditions of human communal existence.

The ruling forces of Capitalist society, in whose hands were the destinies of the nations, the monarchical and the Republican Governments, secret diplomacy, the vast employers' organizations, the middle-class parties, the Capitalist Press, the Church – all these forces must bear the full weight of responsibility for this war, which has been produced by the social order nourishing them and protecting them and which is being carried on for the sake of their interests.

Workers!

Exploited, deprived of your rights, despised – you were recognized as brothers and comrades at the outbreak of the war before you were summoned to march to the shambles, to death. And now, when militarism has crippled, lacerated, degraded, and destroyed you, the rulers are demanding from you the abandonment of your interests, of your aims, of your ideals – in a word, slavish submission to the 'national truce'. You are prevented from expressing your views, your feelings, your pain; you are not allowed to put forth your demands and to fight for them. The press is muzzled, political rights and liberties are trampled upon – thus is military dictatorship ruling today with the iron hand.

We cannot, we dare not, any longer remain inactive in the presence of a state of things that is menacing the whole future of Europe and of mankind. For many decades the Socialist working class has carried on the struggle against militarism. With growing anxiety its representatives at their national and international conferences have devoted themselves to the war peril, the outcome of an Imperialism which was becoming more and more menacing. At Stuttgart, Copenhagen, and Bâsle the International Socialist Congresses indicated the path that the workers should follow.

But we Socialist Parties and working-class organizations which had taken part in determining this path have since the outbreak of war disregarded the obligations that followed therefrom. Their representatives have invited the workers to suspend the working-class struggle, the only possible and effective means of working-class emancipation. They have voted the ruling classes the credits for carrying on the war. They have put themselves at the disposal of their Governments for the most varied services. They have tried through their press and their envoys to win over the neutrals to the Governmental policies of their respective countries. They have given to their Government Socialist Ministers as hostages for the observance of the national truce, and thus have taken on themselves the responsibility for this war, its aims, its methods. And just as Socialist Parties failed separately, so did the most responsible representative of the Socialists of all countries fail: the International Socialist Bureau.

These facts constitute one of the reasons why the international working-class movement, even where sections of it did not fall a victim to the national panic of the first period of the war, or where it rose above it, has failed, even now, in the second year of the butchering of nations, to take up simultaneously in all countries an active struggle for peace.

In this intolerable situation we have met together, we representatives of Socialist parties, of Trade Unions, or of minorities of them, we Germans, French, Italians, Russians, Poles, Letts, Roumanians, Bulgarians, Swedes, Norwegians, Dutch, and Swiss, we who are standing on the ground, not of national solidarity with the exploiting class, but of the international solidarity of the workers and the working-class struggle. We have met together in order to join anew the broken ties of international relations and to summon the working class to reorganize and begin the struggle for peace.

This struggle is also the struggle for liberty, for Brotherhood of nations, for Socialism. The task is to take up this fight for peace – for a peace without annexations or war indemnities. Such a peace is only possible when every thought of violating the rights and liberties of the nations is condemned. There must be no enforced incorporation either of wholly or partly occupied countries. No annexations, either open or masked, no forced economic union, made still more intolerable by the suppression of political rights. The right of nations to select their own government must be the immovable fundamental principle of international relations.

Organized Workers!

Since the outbreak of the war you have put your energies, your courage, your steadfastness at the service of the ruling classes. Now the task is to enter the lists for your own cause, for the sacred aims of Socialism, for the salvation of the oppressed nations and the enslaved classes, by means of the irreconcilable working-class struggle.

It is the task and duty of the Socialists of the belligerent countries to begin this struggle with all their power. It is the task and duty of the Socialists of the neutral countries to support their brothers by all effective means in this fight against bloody barbarity.

Never in the history of the world has there been a more urgent, a more noble, a more sublime task, the fulfilment of which must be our common work. No sacrifice is too great, no burden too heavy, to attain this end: the establishment of peace between the nations.

Working men and women! Mothers and fathers! Widows and orphans! Wounded and crippled! To all who are suffering from the war or in consequence of the war, we cry out, over the frontiers, over the smoking battlefields, over the devastated cities and hamlets.

'*Workers of all countries unite!*'

In the name of the International Socialist Conference:

For the German Delegation: GEORG LEDEBOUR, ADOLPH HOFFMAN [ADOLF HOFFMANN]

For the French Delegation: A. BOURDERON, A. MERRHEIM

For the Italian Delegation: G. E. MODIGLIANI, COSTANTINO LAZZARI

For the Russian Delegation: N. LENIN, PAUL AXELROD, M. BOBROFF [BOBROV]

For the Polish Delegation: ST. LAPINSKI, A. WARSKI, CZ. [JAKÓB] HANECKI

For the Inter-Balkan Socialist Federation: (For the Rouman-

ian Delegation) C. RACOVSKI [RAKOVSKY]; (For the
Bulgarian Delegation) WASSIL KOLAROW [VASIL
KOLAROV]
For the Swedish and Norwegian Delegation: Z. HÖGLUND,
TURE NERMAN
For the Dutch Delegation: H. ROLAND-HOLST
For the Swiss Delegation: ROBERT GRIMM

The working classes, wooed by the ruling classes, by the 'social-patriots' and the pacifist internationalists, reacted differently according to country, depending on their relationship with the state, the extent of industrialization and the leaders' attitudes. The workers' position was ambiguous, though they were an essential element of wartime society. Politically conscious workers had succeeded long before in giving their class a revolutionary aim, persuading it that it alone was qualified to create the new society to which all the oppressed aspired. Workers lived in hopes of 'the final struggle'. But war had cut across this; in Russia, particularly, men felt that war had subjected them all the more to their old masters. Their distress and disarray were all the greater since public opinion sympathized only with the soldiers, 'who were giving their lives for the country'. More than ever, the workers felt they were 'the damned of the earth'. Moreover, ruling classes could always favourably compare the workers' situation – better the assembly line than the trenches. They were blackmailed with conscription to break their will to resist. In England the tribunals sent increasing numbers of workers to prison even before conscription was formally brought in – 15 arrests in August 1915, 772 in July 1916, the usual justification being failure to pay fines. In France, says Henry Maunoury:

An elegant way was found by the war ministry to remove some of the more fractious syndicalists from political affairs, although they had previously been exempted on medical grounds or sent back from the front. Under the pretext of mass recombing, these men were sent for re-examination by doctors who had been suitably 'influénced', and they were all conscripted.
Colonel Goubert, head of the Second Section, suggested that the most hot-headed should be sent to the Sahara – particularly a certain R. – since there the shaping of roads coincided with the shaping of character, and not a few would fail to return.

This last was probably not put into effect, but the doctors' affair caused much protest in university circles.

The daily existence of the workers remained precarious. For the worst-off of them, the Russians, life simply meant not dying: twelve hours a day at the Korsovka station in the far north, eleven and a half for children in Petrograd, and for all a miserable wage. Film has preserved these tragic adolescents, crawling in mines with a chain round their ankles, drawing a cart of ore. Insecurity grew with the war – in Germany accidents in work rose from 102,332 in 1914 to 112,257 in 1918, in the chemical industries and mines alone. In England fatal accidents at work rose by 35 per cent in the same period, although of course conditions had been improving considerably for some time, particularly in the west, and especially for workers in war industries. Calculated as a percentage, the rise of real wages after 1915 made statisticians and economists tremble; politicians and union leaders were satisfied with this, and failed to see that alienation is not a matter of percentages. Besides, with the price rise, workers could see that the improvements were often illusory, and the gap between them and the rest of society was not bridged – their condition as workers was not changed.

The working class, at first helped by the campaign for full employment, was in fact handicapped by the influx of new types of worker, prisoners-of-war, foreigners, and particularly women and adolescents. Employment of prisoners was laid down by international conventions that were by and large respected, although the Germans did begin a kind of forced labour for Belgians who were deported in thousands to the Ruhr. In Russia there was 'special' treatment for some Slav prisoners. They were distributed among landowners, who thus acquired a labour force costing nothing, at the expense of thousands of the rural poor. In France there was also xenophobia and general discontent from the influx of foreign labour, but the greatest pressure on wages came from women and adolescents. Out of 1,580,000 employed in French defence industries, 362,879 were women – nearly a quarter. Forty per cent of industrial labourers in Rouen were women; it is tempting to wonder if Joffre realized what he was saying in his remark, 'If the women in war factories stopped for twenty minutes, we should lose the war.' In Germany their number rose from 1,405,621 to 2,138,000 during the war, and in the big factories by seven times. This was also true of Britain; and in the United States there were two and a half times as many women workers in 1918 as in 1917. Along with this, the number of miners aged under sixteen rose seven times in Germany, the number of metalworkers under sixteen four times. It was the same in Russia.

The women and adolescents, with fathers and husbands at the front, receiving either a tiny pension or none at all, had been forced to work by necessity, and accepted shameful wages – 30 to 50 per cent of a man's wages in Russia, and hardly more elsewhere. 'Down with war wages' was a universal cry, first from the unskilled workers, and then since most workers' real wages were stagnating, from others, especially 'the labour aristocracy'. It was only in the privileged munitions factories that wages were not effectively declining, usually at the skilled workers' expense. These had legitimate complaints – in England the average skilled wage declined relative to the unskilled one. In 1914 a skilled mechanic earned 171 per cent of the wages of an unskilled man, and this declined to 130 per cent in 1919. This was true, also, of railways and naval construction. By the end of 1916 price inflation made money wage-increases illusory, though many families were living better than before because they had two pay-packets coming in. But injustice, restriction, constraints of all kinds weighed on them, and there was a revival of militancy.

All types of workers were involved, each with their own motives. Curiously enough, the roles of old and young workers were changed – women and adolescents could not understand why their elders put up with so much. It was the women workers who got the revolution in Petrograd going with the huge processions of March 1917; they were soon followed by workers of large factories, for the most part young workers who had been won round to Bolshevik ideas. In France also the war led to a drop in the age of revolutionary personnel: to thirty-five years, two months. Ten years later, of 246 cases documented, the average was thirty. In 1911 there had been twenty-one leading militants under twenty-five, and forty-one in 1921. This was particularly marked in the provinces, where the average age dropped by eight years. The new workers, at first a handicap to the movement, thus ended by stimulating it, even if the various workers' interests were antagonistic. In the end the discontents came together.

The price rise was a first impulse to militancy. It was hardly perceptible in the first eighteen months of war, but galloped ahead in 1916, and by 1917 the indices were reaching 350, 400, even 600. We do not have the information for a complete picture of European price movements, though the figures do record the shattering decline of purchasing power in Russia in 1917, and the serious deterioration of conditions in Italy and Austria, where government incompetence was added to scarcity. With 1914 prices as the base, wages in

England were 118 in 1917, and food prices 170; in France 130 and 174; in Italy 138 and 184. In Germany clothing and shoes rose six times.

There was a further stimulus to militancy in the emergence of profiteers, the 'sharks'. Governments demanded equal sacrifice from all; but daily life, the emergence of *nouveaux riches*, showed this to be nonsense. Soldiers on leave and workers agreed on this, sharing bitterness against 'the merchants of death' and other suppliers, the legion of retailers, wholesalers and the rest of the parasites. In April 1917 it was revealed in the Chamber that a company with capital of 125,000 francs had made profits of two million francs in a year, and financial columns in London or Zürich recorded many similar feats. There was an extraordinary revival of industry in Magdeburg, which before 1914 had been in seemingly inevitable decline; in leather and chemicals, the war brought regularly increasing profits, and dividends which rose in two years from 20 per cent to 37·7 per cent and from 19 per cent to 31 per cent. The big bosses in Germany had a true flowering in 1917, when Hindenburg let them have what they wanted 'for the sake of production'. In six months declared profits rose to ten thousand million marks. In Britain and America war profiteering was even more fantastic: Anglo-Persian oil rose from a deficit of £26,700 in 1914 to profits of £85,000 in 1916, £344,100 in 1917 and £1,090,200 in 1918. Rubber gave profits that rose forty times between 1914 and 1918. Yet these were comparatively recent industries, with a relatively modest turnover; in chemicals and metals it was on a different scale: in three years, the Washington Iron and Steel's profits rose from £184 million to £485 million, those of Henry Briggs & Sons from £81 million to £184 million. Vickers, Krupp and Zakharoff vastly extended their empires. In the United States Anaconda Copper's profits rose between 1915 and 1916 from 9 to 51 million dollars, Bethlehem Steel's from 9 to 43 million, and General Motors' from just under 4,000 million dollars in 1914 to nearly 11,000 million in 1917.

Labour leaders, denouncing profiteers and upholding wage-claims, criticized more the way the war was being fought than the fact that it was being fought; they denounced the government's economic policy rather than its policy overall. Maybe the rank and file reacted differently – Severine recounts that in December 1915, when a Paris deputy spoke on the price rise, three thousand socialists and trade union members shouted at him to talk instead about peace. Militancy had been stifled by *Union sacrée*, but it could be revived by the length of the war, the difficulties of daily life, or traditional suspicion of government. These factors were more important in France than Zimmerwaldian ideas, which had a weak echo. Early in 1916 there began a *Comité pour la reprise des relations internationales*, which affected the advanced Left, but opposition to *Union sacrée* was still limited. A minority might demand withdrawal of socialists from the government and revival of the International, but there was no question of a split, party unity being a categorical imperative, and in any case the minority itself was considerably to the right of Zimmerwald. Labour leaders were at their ease with the 'bourgeois' – 'Guesde competed in chauvinism with Poincaré.' To mark an agreement with the bosses, Jouhaux attended a dinner of the *Union des industriels et commerçants*. Many workers were doing well out of *Union sacrée*, the nation was still invaded, and so pacifism 'encountered a triple censorship – the state, the party and union, and the public'. Strikes, insignificant up to autumn 1916, were purely concerned with wages. Thus, after the second Zimmerwaldian conference held in Kienthal, the resolutions were printed in only ten thousand copies, whereas for Germany over a million were distributed.

It was true that in Germany the working-class leaders collaborated more closely with the government than elsewhere – no socialist was minister, but deputies often took attitudes that shocked men. The *Leipziger Zeitung* calculated that a good half-dozen of these 'proletarian representatives' could easily have been put into a middle-class group, another fifteen could be called 'imperialist', and the same number again could be classed 'imperialist for the duration'. There were 'realists' as well, who stuck to the 'majority'. Men such as Ebert and Scheidemann were in the centre, but the latter did in fact officially visit the front in occupied Belgium. Once the Russian danger was shown to be mythical, and with annexationist war aims being publicly discussed, such visits were barely compatible with socialist principles.

It was above all the leaders of the trade unions who gave the most loyal support to civil and military authorities once they had been assured they would no longer be molested and would be regarded as legitimate bargaining partners. The war ministry and the unions began a subtle game by which the unions' power increased and the state was protected from any too strong expression of militancy. Feldman has described how the unions became agencies of the state, denouncing 'agitators' hostile to the agreements concluded with ruling classes and government. They even sought help from the class enemy to stamp out the independent, 'yellow' unions. Having been allotted their share of executing the auxiliary service laws, the unions were linked with bosses and bureaucrats to direct labour. Workers risked losing the right to change jobs, and had to submit to the Manpower Office. They could change jobs for higher wages, but only with a favourable report from their union. Their interests were thus protected, only they had lost liberty to their own representatives. This was not at once appreciated, because the unions portrayed as a concession wrung with difficulty from the bosses the workers' right to participate in decisions affecting them, a line taken also over concession in wages. The more extreme social democrats were offended, accusing the 'majority' and men of Legien's stamp of betraying the revolution. Karl Liebknecht refused, in protest, to vote war-credits in March 1915; a deputy of the Right demanded his exile, and Legien went beyond this to threaten his own resignation from the party if this was not done. Split was ineluctable: a 'minority', Zimmerwaldian in inspiration, was made up of the Independents – Ledebour, Haase, Kautsky, Bernstein, although the last two were not, properly speaking, Zimmerwaldians. Liebknecht, Rühle and Luxemburg did, on the other hand, adopt the Zimmerwaldian line, and soon became the *Spartakus* group. Socialism in Germany meant too much – the ideas of Zimmerwald, the Liebknecht–Luxemburg tactics, and the practice of trade unions co-operating with the government. Here was more than a schism: it was two different conceptions of state and society, an antagonism that events were fully to display.

In summer 1918 the bosses began to appreciate that Germany was being led to disaster. Discreetly, the bankers and industrialists demanded that the Kaiser should abdicate, thus abandoning the crown before army, *Reichstag* or majority socialists did. They also made up to the unions, and there was an agreement to limit catastrophe, on 9 October 1918, between Legien and Stinnes. They feared revolution more than defeat, and the formation of soviets of the Russian type. The industrialists' attitude is understandable, the unions' less so – but, having become a cog of the old régime, they feared that revolution would lose them the power they had acquired with such difficulty in the war years; and there was no doubt that soviets would place in government men much more extreme than the union leaders. Early in November Legien sent an ultimatum to the first workers' soviets: if they tried to outflank the unions on the left, the unions would cease functioning, and the bosses 'would decree a lockout with all its frightful consequences'. Stinnes, thenceforth, was going to win: even on 8 November he did not concede the forty-eight hour week or the principle of collective bargaining, and even reserved freedom to deal with breakaway unions. But agreement was concluded and did preserve some of the advantages won in wartime. The unions shielded the bosses, in return for bosses' recognizing union authority over the working men. In the same way, Ebert, the social democratic leader, became arbiter of the situation politically. The pacific birth of democracy was threatened by soviets and the Russian example; Legien had discussed things with Stinnes, and now Ebert concluded agreement with Groener, the general 'whose wartime collaboration is remembered with pleasure'. The army agreed to support the Republic, provided it kept order against the extreme Left.

Men who, from both sides, regarded this alliance as immoral later became the twin opposition movements of Weimar – Nazis on the right, Spartakists on the left. For years, the young had looked with common contempt on bosses and unions, accomplices in deceiving the workers – the bosses for profit, the unions for power. There was an epilogue when Hitler came to power. Hitherto, both sets of extremists had denounced the 'infamous collusion', and both sought to take power by coup – Spartakists in 1919, extreme Right in 1920. It failed then, but effectively succeeded in 1923, when Hitler learnt to proceed by legal methods, and thus be sure of keeping socialists and communists apart.

In England, as elsewhere in the west, a section of the union and party leadership had adopted class collaboration – Arthur Henderson's Cabinet seat symbolized this – but from 1915 this encountered an obstacle unique in British history, conscription. The question had been better understood by Asquith and Lloyd George than by Poincaré, Briand, Joffre or even Kitchener – 'This was an industrial war, and it would be won not on Polish or Belgian battlefields but in French and British factories.' Conscription had not been introduced, and, later, there was much exemption from it, with the unions having a right of supervision which they used and abused much as in Germany. But 'dilution' was a problem, since men replaced by women and youths might be sent to the front; and the skilled workers were violent in protest, despite the opposition of government, bosses and unions in concert, the union leaders being no doubt delighted at the swelling of their numbers, through those for whom they found employment.

There was a revolt of the base, through the shop stewards and factory committees that would not leave the unions all decisions regarding strikes and returns to work. They had been active before the war, and the causes of the great strikes in 1915 and 1916 in Wales or on the Clyde lay in pre-war issues. The miners did not object to the war or to national unity, and 45 per cent of them volunteered for the army. But they knew that coal had risen in price, and profits along with it, and when the bosses refused a minimum wage promised years before, to give rises of between 5 per cent and 20 per cent depending on region, they protested. They decided not to strike, being sure of their cause and being anxious to maintain output. They appealed to the government. Asquith pronounced in favour of minor changes, not even on a national scale. The miners felt this to be unjust, and struck. They were challenged by a government invoking national defence and the Munitions of War Act. National unity lost its charm, and the conflict of worker and bosses became a rebellion against the state itself, which henceforth would not enjoy the same trust. The problem of the war itself came up in natural consequence, since the workers had experienced, in practical reality, what pacifists had always said about the character of the war. The union leaders had been equivocal over the miners' strike and over 'dilution'; the rank and file denied them authority to which their own leaders now pretended; henceforth a large section of the working class was sceptical about their government's war, as is shown by the increasing strike movement. Newspapers such as *The Call*, *Forward* and *The Pioneer* were openly pacifist, and had allies in parliament, where the Independent Labour Party took similar ideas. The highly oppositional Union of Democratic Control had recruited many sympathisers by the end of 1916 and was particularly active after the Russian Revolution.

Italy was not the same: up to 1917 left-wing interventionism was more active than working-class opposition, despite the fact that the socialist party itself had adopted the Zimmerwald line as its official position. Some of these ideas were included in *Avanti!*, the editors of which sent the censors a faked copy. But, if the war was not very popular, neither was defeatism, and besides, the pacifists were subject to a repressive apparatus that, in Italy, was peculiarly harsh. The labour code was militarized, and leaving a job equated with desertion. Party propaganda had to lower its tone and adopted Lazzari's 'ne aderire, ne sabotare'. So long as war weariness was not a mass phenomenon, any other attitude would have been mere adventurism. Italy had entered the war late, and even by the end of 1916, after Asiago, discontent and weariness were not much evident.

In Russia this brought down the régime. Strikes had begun again, to an outstanding degree, as scarcity, collapsing purchasing power and repression caused discontent to rise. The people were weary, though the workers hesitated to declare their pacifism, since it would offend patriotic sentiment and the Duma. Strikes were undertaken as much with political as with economic ends, by a kind of return to the pre-war revolutionary tradition. Lenin, who felt that he was thereby being proved right, remained uncompromising, writing on 23 August 1915 to Shlyapnikov, 'Military defeats will hasten the fall of Tsarism and encourage the revolutionary workers of Russia and elsewhere to unite. Our victory will immeasurably strengthen the cause in Germany; with Tsarism beaten, we shall suggest a democratic peace to all the warring countries, and if they refuse we'll begin revolutionary war.' In 1916 Lenin, who was about to publish *Imperialism, the Highest Stage of Capitalism*, reckoned that revolution would come in a weakly developed country first, rather than in countries where capitalism was strongest – the war had upset the terms of Marxism, the explosion being now more probable in Russia than elsewhere. Lenin also thought that minority nationalisms would contribute, and encouraged them.

These sectional quarrels split a working class otherwise unanimous in its hatred of the régime, and although militants could swear their undying detestation of the autocracy, the quarrelling made them ineffectual, as no one could suppose that the mere multiplication of slogans, even mutually contradictory ones, could cause the revolution. But a police report of early 1917 shows the feelings, the war weariness and the impossible conditions of the working class:

> The proletariat of the capital is on the edge of despair – it is generally believed that the slightest explosion, however trivial its pretext, will lead to uncontrollable riots, with tens of thousands of victims. The preconditions for this are there, for the masses' economic condition, in spite of large wage increases, is close to that of distress . . . Even if wages have risen 100 per cent, the cost of living has risen 300 per cent. The inability to buy goods, the frustrations of queuing, the rising death-rate owing to poor living conditions, and the cold and damp produced by lack of coal . . . have all created a situation where most of the workers are ready to embark on all the savage excesses of a food riot.

The contagion passed from rear to front, from the line battalions to the depot. Soldiers, already infuriated by officers whom they judged responsible for the hecatombs of 1915, blamed the *baryn* for everything. Their letters are full of invective against their leaders, and there was overall talk of a 'settling of accounts' once the war was over, or perhaps even before.

Table 2   *Movement of strikes*

	1913	1914	1915	1916	1917	1918
Russia	2,404*	3,534	928	1,410	1,938	
	887,096	1,337,458	539,528	1,086,384		
Great Britain	1,459	972	672	532	730	1,165
	664,000	447,000	448,000	276,000	872,000	1,116,000
France	1,073	690	98	314	697	499
	220,000	162,000	9,000	41,000	294,000	176,000
Germany	2,127	1,115	137	240	561	531
	266,000	61,000	14,000	129,000	667,000	392,000
Italy:						
industry	810	782	539	516	443	303
	385,000	173,000	132,000	121,000	164,000	158,000
countryside	97	123	69	61	29	10
	80,000	44,000	48,000	15,000	6,000	700

* The first figure indicates the number of strikes, the second the number of strikers.

Table 3   *Percentage of strikers in relation to the number of factory workers*

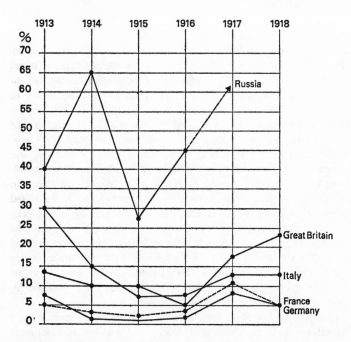

The increase in 1917 was apparent in all countries. In Russia it began in 1916.

The pattern of strike action in France and Germany is more apparent in this method of calculation than in that used for Table 2. It shows equally the strength of the movement in Great Britain and Italy.

With regard to the year 1914, it should be borne in mind that the war started during the second half of the year: the fall between July 1914 and October 1916 is not as pronounced on the graph as it would be on a graph showing monthly variations.

Chapter 15

Crises of war

The states were now being shaken by one crisis after another – the changing fortunes of war, quarrels over war aims, new types of social tension, revival of old quarrels. Worn economies threatened to collapse, social structures to tear apart, old forms of authority to disintegrate. No one foresaw that the war would cause great revolutions, and in time régimes such as the communists or fascists, but there were men who appreciated that this 'European civil war' would threaten the hegemony of old Europe, the foundations and values of western society: Giolitti in Italy, Joseph Caillaux in France, Lord Lansdowne in England, Prince Max of Baden in Germany. In the climate of hysterical patriotism their reward was to be called defeatist, as for instance Caillaux, who was accused by his enemies, Poincaré and Clemenceau, of more than he actually said, since he was always prudently reserved. But at bottom no one much cared for Caillaux's 'European' notions; he was known as an advocate before the war of Franco-German friendship. He gave over his *Bonnet rouge* to an agent, Almereyda, who was then attacked by Clemenceau and the *Action Française*.

In Italy, by contrast, 'neutralism' had threefold support – from the extreme Left, the Giolittian majority and the Church. Their aims were different – some wanting to have peace to stop revolution, others peace to start revolution – but they came together to weaken the war effort. In England a memorandum presented by Lansdowne, father of the *Entente Cordiale*, at the end of 1916 showed how war weariness was gaining in influential circles. Lloyd George and Bonar Law reacted against this attitude, which Asquith himself shared to some extent, and, like Clemenceau, they demanded more dynamic government and a total subordination of private interests to the demands of national defence. The formation of Lloyd George's War Cabinet, which excluded Asquith, demonstrated a new type of more highly concentrated and personalized rule.

In Russia the Tsar had taken over command of the army after the defeat of 1915. This decision, like the maintenance of the elderly

Goremykin and the subsequent appointment of Sturmer, a friend of Rasputin and a supposed Germanophile, provoked universal opposition, even from conservatives. At the end of 1916 the *starets* fell victim to a palace conspiracy, and a wider one, involving Duma deputies, generals, and some grand dukes, was aimed at the Tsar himself, since his political blunderings would be fatal to monarchy itself; the country must be saved, the revolution from below forestalled.

In France ministerial changes reflected changes of the military and political background. In 1915 Viviani and Delcassé had been forced by Accambray's interpellation and Bulgarian intervention to give way to Briand. A year later Joffre's replacement by Nivelle was accompanied by a ministerial change in Briand's government; and Briand was soon to have on his hands a parliament that had tasted victory over the High Command and meant to control the government, while the country at large saw a resurgence of strikes and of the socialist opposition. By the end of 1916 socialists' participation in bourgeois governments was approved by only 1,637 votes to 1,372 – and this might mean the end of *Union sacrée*. To keep an opening to the left, the intelligent and flexible Briand decided to leave the government to the elderly Ribot, a moderate, gifted with acuity and finesse, strong and calm by nature, hating demagoguery and hypocrisy – which earned him, from Clemenceau and Poincaré, accusations of weakness. But he and Painlevé removed Nivelle after the Chemin des Dames defeat; and he then covered Pétain, for a policy of moderation, and Pétain managed to limit the greatest of all crises that Europe saw in the war before the October Revolution – the French mutinies.

These came in April 1917. Frenchmen refused to fight and maltreated their officers. The movement spread, most units being affected, some even wanting to march on Paris, overthrow the government and proclaim peace. But Pétain managed to hold the movement, retaining control of much of the army; the government entrusted him, after dismissing Nivelle, with 'restoring morale' and organizing the repression. Order was restored in a few weeks, but there are two mysteries – why the movement took over so much of the army, and what it cost to check the movement. In 1917–18 censors, for obvious reasons, forbade mention of the affair – national morale and 'security' were at risk. But as regards both causes and suppression of the mutiny, men made peremptory assertions that could not, for lack of evidence, be challenged. Thanks to Guy Pedroncini, it is now possible to do so.

Some of the military chiefs said it was the 'bad eggs' who refused to fight – 'the bravest and most resourceful had been killed off . . . and there were, in the infantry, many men who, having already recovered from sickness and wounds, were not anxious to risk their skins again'. Most generals – about four-fifths of them – reckoned 'the movement seems to come increasingly from secret organizations in the rear, whose decisions are communicated to the front through men returning from leave'. Franchet d'Esperey was probably the most ardent champion of such interpretation, writing on 4 June 1917 to Pétain: 'The situation is clear. There is an overall organization based on Paris, at German instigation, which aims to abandon France to the enemy. The government must strike.' The organization was of course pacifist, socialist, anarchist, revolutionaries of all types; the men were said to be acting together, and even enjoying contacts with the ministry of the interior itself.

This was GHQ truth, and requires examination. Pacifism did in fact reach the front, often through teachers. But Pedroncini shows that it was not such regiments that were particularly affected by the mass disobedience. Analysis of the mutinies in timing and in place can solve the problem of cause:

First of all, the essential area was between Soissons and Auberive, where mutiny was most serious and frequent – this was the sector of the April–May offensive. West of Soissons, there was a zone virtually unaffected by mutiny: the front here had been quiet throughout, seeing action only on one day, 13 April, when Humbert's III Army attacked. Finally, from Auberive to the Swiss border there was a thin chain of incidents, the Verdun area being the thickest part. If the front is divided in three, we can see that it was the offensive, whether because it had failed after obviously sloppy preparation, or because soldiers feared it would go on being useless, that determined the region of mutiny. At first, Pétain's appointment changed nothing, as the attacks went on. Men waited to see them ended. Once they could see that a new way of fighting was being thought up, mutinies lost their vigour, and did so before there were any executions. Certainly, particular and local causes worked here and there, still; but as a whole the movement had been broken. When Pétain planned his Verdun attack, there was some agitation among the units concerned – no doubt war weariness was there, but the mutinies were above all a refusal to accept a certain way of fighting. This is borne out by the spread of mutinies in terms of region.

This has little connection with the military leaders' own diagnosis. The documents themselves showed that it was the generals who had been wrong: all the more reason for them to be silent. Painlevé subsequently set up an enquiry into the circumstances of the preparation and launching of the April offensive, and Nivelle was dismissed. He had blundered, and the official history made him a scapegoat, which was hardly fair, for the Chemin des Dames was one of many failures, each one of which had been announced as a certain prelude to victory. It was the accumulation of these, the generals' own unconcern, and the egoism of the rear that explain the soldiers' despair and the mutinies they staged after the Chemin des Dames. The soldiers themselves left accounts which Jeanneney preserved for later generations: 'We wouldn't march, though not because we wanted the Revolution that would be bound to happen if we went on that way. All we wanted was to call the government's attention to us, make it see that we are men, and not beasts for the slaughterhouse.' Men shouted, 'Down with the War', sang the *Internationale*; but they did their duty just the same; they only refused to be used as cannon-fodder for the careers of 'red-tabs'.

Pedroncini puts the number of mutineers at thirty to forty thousand, excluding incidents at stations, which were numerous but were not explicit acts of mutiny. The scope of punishment is not easy to assess. In 1920 *Le Progrès civique* reckoned 2,700, an estimate accepted by the historian, Mathiez, and others. In 1934 *Le Crapouillot* said that in the war 1,637 soldiers had been shot, 528 in 1917. Galtier-Boissière said, 'Some writers none the less assert that the number of regular executions, excluding summary justice on the field, ran to 2,500.' Recently it has been claimed that war tribunals pronounced 38,315 sentences in 1917; Chastenet, by contrast, thinks there were 150 death sentences, of which twenty-three were carried out. There was also, allegedly, 'decimation' – Jean Giono, who stresses it in one of his works, answered an enquiry of Pedroncini's by saying that, although he had never witnessed it, he had heard it had been used. It is in fact quite easy to see how the legend arose – the selection of mutineers to go before tribunals had often been done by drawing lots. This did not mean that they were all shot, or that the drawing of lots had been deliberately organized by commanders. Summary execution would have been impossible in the climate of the times, and with the solidarity of the men – any officer attempting it would have been lynched. But it is worth remembering the possibility that illegalities were committed – unrepentant soldiers being set impossible tasks, or perhaps included in a punishment unit.

Commanders did use astonishing methods. Joffre during the Charleroi retreat ordered rounding-up and execution of all fugitives; Pétain, in November 1914, had a *chasseur* executed 'as an example', and Joffre approved. Civilian authorities reacted to the severity and arbitrariness of 'military justice', but not until January 1915 did the President of the Republic acquire a right of consultation before carrying-out of executions. By then some fifty soldiers had already been shot. By 1917 military justice functioned more or less regularly. Following the mutinies, 3,427 sentences were decreed, 10 per cent of the mutineers; of these 554 were condemned to death, and 49 actually executed. This is lower than the anti-militarist tradition would have it, although it is still large enough, the more so as the men who were really responsible, those who had blundered into the offensive and still advised its continuation despite the fact that success was not at all likely, were not themselves molested or sentenced in any way. Throughout, Pétain's role seems clear – he wanted a repression at once limited and merciless. More than his colleagues, he understood the real causes of the mutinies, for they simply confirmed what he had always argued against Joffre or Nivelle. When, on 19 May 1917, he decided to give up costly offensives, this was simply what the men had demanded as a prelude to restoration of discipline. The mutinies were not a refusal of war, only of a way of waging it: Pétain understood. He was not an all-out advocate of defence, but he allowed men to think this, and never lost the popularity this gained him.

The government was more shaken by the mutinies than even by the Chemin des Dames, and associated them with the increasing strikes and the growing pacifism. The Russian example showed how civilian demonstrations, much less serious at the outset, had degenerated as soldiers joined workers to overthrow the régime. First they had abolished old forms of discipline, and governments feared that this would be followed by a separate peace.

In Russia, by mid-February, the Petrograd authorities were introducing a system of ration cards. The public, on hearing of this, formed larger and larger queues at the bakers, butchers and grocers, waiting for them to open. They were emptied in a few hours, and a few pulled down their iron shutters. There were riots and shop-fronts were broken down. The following days saw the same with riots coming after long hours of waiting, in temperatures of twenty degrees (centigrade) below zero, when the crowds heard the fateful 'Nyetu' (nothing left). The Petrograd governor's prohibition notwithstanding, both legal and illegal parties mobilized the workers to demonstrate throughout the city, and there was soon a crowd of all the discontented people, crying, 'Bread!', 'Down with the Tsar!', 'Stop the War!' The crowds were joyful enough and won over the Cossacks who were supposed to maintain order. Demonstrators became revolutionaries on the day the soldiers, enraged by their officers' orders to fire, mutinied, joined the marchers and went with them to the seat of the Duma, the Tauride Palace. The Duma deputies were worried and frightened, not knowing whether this concourse had come to protect them or to attack. 'The deputies were excited and preoccupied, clung morally to each other and felt that something dreadful was happening, which threatened even those who fought the Tsar. It was the Mob.' Kerenski, disobeying his colleagues, rushed out to greet the soldiers, and by this initiative saved the alliance of people and Duma. Soon there would be no legal authority in the capital, as the ministers fled and the entire army rallied to the revolution. That day a group of militants released from the Kresty prison arrived in the Duma, spoke of forming a Soviet and asked Kerenski and Chkeidze, a Menshevik leader, to mediate with the Duma and arrange for them to meet in the Tauride Palace. Thereby, a revolutionary group set itself up as headquarters of the revolution, under the name of Soviet. With Chkeidze and Kerenski as presidents, the group contained a majority of moderate socialists; Molotov and Shlyapnikov were the only Bolsheviks in the central committee, which had about thirty members. The Duma was worried at formation of a Soviet, and turned itself into a 'Committee for the Restoration of Order and Co-ordination of Government', the title of which revealed its programme. The rebellious soldiery, having promulgated *Prikaz I*, refused to obey their officers and said they would only obey the Soviet. The Duma Committee began negotiations with the Soviet with a view to setting up a provisional government. After much discussion, the Soviet accepted this in principle, 'provided there is a government programme we can agree to'.

They approved the choice of Prince L'vov as head of the provisional government, with Guchkov as war minister, Milyukov as minister for foreign affairs. To give the Cabinet a revolutionary colouring, Chkeidze and Kerenski were added, at Duma insistence.

Chkeidze refused, but Kerenski accepted, going over the heads of
the Soviet's central committee by appealing to a plenary session and
fixing, in effect, a plebiscite for himself. Two great unknowns dominated the attitude of the Tsar and that of the military leaders. No
one knew on 1 March, after five days of shooting, what these would be.
Alexeyev, assured that the provisional government did not propose
to set up a Republic, suggested petitioning the Tsar, and, having
understood that to save Michael, Nicholas would have to go, he
invited the army commanders to send the Tsar telegrams recommending abdication, 'so as to safeguard the independence of the country
and the future of the dynasty'. Apart from Evert, the generals
replied at once, 'respectfully applying revolvers to the temples of
their adored sovereign'. Nicholas II, having displayed throughout
an extraordinary passivity, made no attempt to resist, and left his
empire like a cavalry captain leaving his squadron. He did however
note in his diary, 'I am leaving Pskov, sickened at what I have seen.
On every side, treason, cowardice, skull-duggery.' He was put under
house-arrest, and assassinated by Red soldiers in 1918, who feared
that Kolchak's Whites would soon deliver him. The ferment now
returned to Petrograd, which had wind of a scheme to replace
Nicholas by Michael; the city rose again. Kerenski and Prince L'vov
went to see Michael and asked him, in turn, to abdicate. Milyukov
wished him to resist this, but he too, without hesitation, agreed.

The success of the revolution had been as surprising as its outbreak. The generals, like the grand dukes and other notables,
accepted it, and in the provinces the old régime disappeared at a
stroke. The population, without waiting for instructions, installed
new authorities at once, and in the space of a few days there was not
a single town from Minsk to Vladivostok that failed to set up its
own revolutionary administration, soviet or committee. By 17
March 1917, forty-nine towns had already set up soviets, by 22
March, seventy-seven; and to these must be added the soviets of
peasants and soldiers, revolutionary committees of all kinds. There
was thus 'dual power' in the new régime, the government, which tried
to keep up the state and administration, and the Petrograd Soviet,
which contested power, and with which the provincial soviets were
federated. The political parties sought to influence the Soviet until
such time as they could control it. But it was public opinion that
counted, for the moment, pressing its demands vociferously on
government, soviets and parties. The future of the February Revolution depended on how these responded.

The government members had always wanted for Russia a régime of the parliamentary, western type. When they took over in February they did not propose to overthrow the economic and social order, but rather to renovate the state and win the war, leaving to a constituent assembly the task of structural reform. But they disagreed as regards methods. Guchkov and Milyukov regarded any concession to socialists as a prelude to catastrophe, and wanted to join battle with the Soviet. Kerenski, by contrast, felt that the Soviet could be made to disappear by inviting its leaders into the government.

After Tsarism had collapsed, the peoples of Russia expressed their hopes for a better world. The traditional claims of workers and peasants were naturally opposed by the propertied classes, who pleaded the needs of war to maintain the established order, while the workers, peasants and soldiers perfectly understood what they meant. But they, in their turn, might agree as to reform and immediate improvement and be determined to enforce them, but were divided by the war, and would raise the subject only circumspectly because 'many of them had no sympathy at all with the slogan, "Stop the War!" '. This cry came out, fleetingly, as meetings ended. But the chemical workers of the artillery arsenals shouted, 'War until victory', and so did workers of the electrical factories on the northern front; the army of railwaymen was very patriotic. The problem was not the same in the army. The soldiers had revolted against their officers' behaviour – this was the significance of *Prikaz I*, which did not spell 'the death of the army' as Russian and Allied generals asserted, but merely the death of one idea of discipline. The text of this order ran through Russia, despite the generals' efforts to stop it. It was so close to what the soldiers wanted that, everywhere it arrived, it had immediate effect. General Ruzski reported one of his generals, Dragomirov, as saying, 'Each time I gave an order, the soldiers said, "No, you can't do that". One of them kept looking at some piece of printed paper he held, and repeated, "No, that's not on". When I asked him to see the paper, they wouldn't let me.' The soldiers boldly interpreted it, and dismissed some of the officers; the reasons given by the fifth section of 1st infantry regiment display some of the grievances they felt – officers used coarse language, struck the men, were unjust, abused their powers, ordered excessive punishment. Hence the violence offered to officers when the troops saw that they were not going to change. The officers always preached the need for discipline, and there was 'a gulf between them and the men'. 'The officers vainly sought to explain the facts, but were not listened to.' The soldiers were human beings; they wanted better lives, wanted the state to remember the price of their sacrifice, for their families were impoverished and often without sustenance. The 15th rifle regiment set out many claims, expressing the aspirations of soldiers of all countries: (1) increase of pay; (2) increase of allowances paid to soldiers' families, with a guarantee against loss of capacity to work, this being essential to allow the soldiers to feel secure as to their families and to devote all their energies to the war; (3) guarantees to men who might lose their capacity to work because of the war; (4) elections of certain types of officer; (5) improvement, particularly in medical matters, of soldiers' conditions; (6) suppression of saluting and presenting of arms; (7) political matters should be open to discussion in the army – though the officers' committee opposes this – because prohibition would be a return to Tsarism. The second point shows that, however natural the soldiers' aspirations were, they gave way to patriotism, and there are many accounts of Bolshevik militants' being opposed when they raised the problem in soldiers' assemblies. The soldiers wanted 'to be worthy of the responsibilities which the revolution has imposed'; it was 'a question of honour between ourselves and the old officers'. The officers' 'monopoly of patriotism' was broken. The soldiers did demand an end to the war, and asked the government to begin negotiations, but they did not say how, and did not want a peace harmful to the country. But the officers' attitude forced them to revise their own. It was even counter-productive, since the soldiers were forced to the point of re-examining the war itself, its supposedly defensive character, since they felt the officers would use it to revive the old régime, which the soldiers ardently wanted to be destroyed for ever. The soldiers and NCOs of the Kiev garrison said firmly, 'The officers have not understood what our revolution means.'

Chapter 16

Revolutionary peace, compromise peace, victorious peace

Up to the Russian Revolution the rightness or otherwise of the war and its aims had been a matter for governments. There was opposition, particularly in Germany, but it aimed mainly at the way the war was fought or the aims of the government, and in any case the questioning had little effect since the ruling classes kept the population well in hand through propaganda, control of the press, and censorship. True opposition was still tiny. With the fall of Tsarism, all this changed. In Petrograd power fell to a government that could exist only in so far as it satisfied public opinion. Opinion was naturally divided, but now all problems of the country's future could be discussed without hindrance. Lenin, arriving in Petrograd, said Russia was the freest country ever to exist.

Of all problems the greatest was the war. Opinion and the Soviet approved the formula, 'peace without annexations and contributions', and expected their government to adopt it; and thenceforth the war and its aims were contested, not just by powerless oppositions, but by one of the warring states, by a government talking the language of authority. The Petrograd Soviet, speaking for revolutionary Russia, launched a peace appeal on 27 March 1917 to the peoples at war, and this opened the question of peace. As yet no one knew whether it would be the revolutionary peace demanded by internationalists, or the victorious peace sought by governments, or the compromise peace sought by some conciliatory spirits.

After February the Russian bourgeoisie had by instinct assumed some of the airs of a ruling class. The bourgeoisie, supported by most of the intellectuals, university men and the like, who had been terrorized by February, wanted to achieve its own goals, which for the most part were opposite to those of the proletariat. The war must be pursued to a victorious peace, and the workers' own democratic principles could be used to justify leaving serious reform to a future constituent assembly, since an assembly could hardly be convoked in wartime; this meant leaving reforms until peace returned. The middle classes were anxious to take over and regenerate the Russian economy to maintain the war effort. They at once clashed with workers demanding the eight-hour day, as they did also over wages and factory committees. The bourgeoisie was full of illusions as to its own strength, and did not understand what the Revolution meant or where the real power lay. Only the officers were more short-sighted. The government thus had to control conflicting claims. It wanted to restore the army, and this would be possible by continuation of the war; the government was heartened by the support it received from petty-bourgeois, railwaymen, artisans and some peasants. It feared more than it needed the counter-revolutionary threat, and believed it was acting wisely in opposing extreme claims. The ruling class and the High Command were dissatisfied, and did not much help the new government; thereby they pushed the lower classes into fury, and were themselves swept away.

Only a small minority of Bolsheviks and Anarchists had foreseen this. They received, early in April, the support of Lenin, returning from exile; his *April Theses* demanded peace, unrelenting opposition to the provisional government, transfer of power to the soviets. After April the 'Lenin Party' stood as the only organized enemy of the February régime. This régime, however, failed to satisfy the workers; by dint of constantly repeating that the war would prevent any change or reform, it merely gave peasants, workers and soldiers a wild desire to stop the war. But Milyukov, far from trying for general peace, acted as if Russia had overthrown her Tsar merely in order to prosecute the war more efficiently, and thought that the government would be able to link the country more solidly to the western democracies and thus consolidate the social order threatened in February. Hostilities should go on: the enemy – and indeed the Revolution – would be exhausted. Constantinople would be given as a dowry to the New Russia, and in the meantime the revolutionaries could be divided and the army set against the workers by a constant brandishing of the German danger. On 18 April he sent the Powers a long-awaited Note, stressing quite unexpectedly the strength that the Revolution had lent to the defence of the principles for which Russia *and her Allies* were fighting. He emphasized the government's loyalty to undertakings already made. There was no word of the hopes of 'Russian democracy' for 'a peace without annexations or contributions'; on the contrary, he talked entirely of 'guarantees' and 'sanctions' that the Allies might require in order to make peace last.

This Note infuriated democrats. It provoked the Bolsheviks into organizing a riot against the government, and the Soviet leaders into allowing the riot to go on. The Menshevik leaders managed to control things and agreed to enter the government to secure victory for the Soviet's policy. Milyukov left it, predicting its impotence, a view also taken by the Bolsheviks. They, to prevent any resumption of hostilities, opened a fraternization campaign – simple little gestures, along the front, that were a kind of stuttering revolution. Russians took the initiative, but Germans, with a strong interest, encouraged them. The Soviet at once condemned this, and the Bolshevik leader, Frunze, who had gone to the front to organize fraternization, recanted. Here was clear proof that the Soviet remained the unchallenged guide of the Revolution. A few weeks later Kerenski's tour of the front displayed this again. Speaking for the new government and the Soviet, he revived the army's patriotic spirit, which Milyukov's manoeuvrings had nearly extinguished.

To restore its offensive capacity, Kerenski saluted it, in his person, in the name of the Revolution. He would explain the war to the soldiers, and would, if necessary, take on any of the thousands of hecklers. Under the sceptical eyes of officers and Bolshevik soldiers he would thrust into an arena, into the gaze of the thousands of soldier-'aficionados' who had gathered to see his exploits. He gained the nickname, 'Convincer-in-chief'. The sight was indeed remarkable, and some of the incidents deserve to make up an anthology. First, in the capital before his departure, Kerenski displayed, to a congress of delegates of the front, outstanding oratorical skill:

> Comrades – for ten years you suffered in silence. You knew
> what it was to obey the orders of a hated system. You would
> fire on the people when the government told you to. What are
> you doing now? Have you lost your courage? Is Free Russia
> to become a nation of revolting slaves? [Agitation throughout
> the assembly] Comrades; I won't hide the truth, I can't hide.
> If only I'd died two months back, I'd have died with a happy
> dream, a dream that a new life had begun, for eternity, in this
> country. People would respect each other, would not need
> whips and canes.

On the eve of the offensive of 29 June 1917 the Russian army had recovered from its condition of the period following the April crisis. It agreed to make a last effort, to trust its leaders and obey them in this last offensive that would be a prelude to peace. The soldiers trusted Kerenski because the government and the Soviet, linked since April, had now asserted they would conclude a peace without annexations or contributions. There was to be no question of sticking to Tsarist treaties, and this might involve a Russian régime, renouncing Constantinople, in forcing the Allies to give up their annexationist aims as well. Alsace-Lorraine was at the centre of this. In the Soviet a majority felt the inhabitants must be consulted, because 'in half a century life has changed so much in Alsace-Lorraine, and therewith the inclination of the population', the very reason that French 'patriotic labour' advanced to refuse any referendum. The Left was uncompromising – it was 'the obstinacy of the French bourgeoisie in trying to recover Alsace-Lorraine that is causing the war to go on, and threatening Europe and Alsace itself with ruin'. The Bolshevik, Kamenev, added, 'A peace based on peoples' rights will not sanction the Great Powers' taking colonies, and as a first step, the troops must evacuate Alsace-Lorraine, Belgium, Poland, Serbia, Macedonia, Salonica, Persia, Ireland, Egypt, Bosnia and the rest, so as to give the oppressed peoples their freedom to define their own boundaries.' For Russia 'this means giving up Finland, Poland, Turkestan, the Ukraine', and he concluded, 'Peace on such lines cannot be set up by capitalist governments, but must be imposed by the proletarian masses on the imperialist bourgeoisie.'

The new Russian foreign policy was thought out by Tseretelli, a Menshevik leader, who believed that American intervention and the Russian Revolution would check the Great Powers' appetites. Russian renunciation of Constantinople would set the example. The Soviet should promote the peace programme to be adopted by government and parties alike. The government should be made to approach the Allies, for them to proclaim their adherence to the declaration of 3 May, and the presence of Zimmerwaldians in the Cabinet would guarantee the success of this in Russia. But there was general suspicion, both of Allies and of Central Powers, so Russian democrats must support the action of socialists in the belligerent countries, and assist in the restoration of the International, in which Tseretelli had 'a messianic faith'. There should be, in Stockholm, a conference of all socialist parties to discuss a peace that they could then impose on their governments. This was easy in Russia, but the work must also be done elsewhere. The struggle would therefore be waged on two levels, that of inter-government relations, and that of socialist–government relations in each country.

This was based on several calculations. It was thought that in the various countries the socialist Left would be able to push the majority of their party into dragging their governments' policies to the Left. Tseretelli, for his part, would exploit Wilson's utterances in support of a revision of war aims. The annexationists, thus disavowed by Stockholm, Washington and Petrograd, would be obliged to give way, and both sides would gradually come to adopt the Soviet position. This was a mistaken calculation of the effects of revolution in Russia on wartime Europe. On the Central Powers' side, some observers regarded the Revolution as 'a crisis of war' – the bourgeoisie had taken over, and Russia would now fight unrelentingly; and the attitude of the government and the High Command showed that such was their interpretation, at least in part. German divisions on the Russian front did not change in number in April, but rose from seventy-two to seventy-five in May and seventy-eight in June.

Others, in increasing number, felt that the Russian people, starving and war-weary, had been on the point of rising for bread, peace and liberty. The war-mongering liberals had merely joined the movement to lead it and swing it towards war again. The declaration of 27 March lent point to this argument. Henceforth, to exploit the will to peace of a section of Russian opinion, the Central Powers refrained from launching any great offensive in the east, since this could be a catalyst for patriotic sentiment. A passive stance would allow disintegration to do its work. Furthermore, the German government could give all facilities to Russian 'pacifists' seeking to travel from their Swiss exile to Russia, and Lenin, Martov and their Zimmerwaldian friends obtained a transit-visa in the record time of thirteen days. Scheidemann and Czernin also responded to the appeal of 27 March, and the Central Powers gave their 'majority' socialists full powers to deal with Russian democracy. They used Parvus (Helphand), who had formerly been associated with the socialist Left in Russia, though he had subsequently gone over to 'social-patriotism'. The German socialists also intervened through a Dane, Borgberg, who had gone to Petrograd in mid-April to organize the socialist conference, and who gave the Russians the peace-terms proposed by German 'majority' socialists. This journey and these measures marked the opening of the Stockholm campaign.

In the west revolution had a varied welcome. Socialists and liberals were pleased at the Tsar's fall, though conservatives were not. At first they tried to make out that the Tsar had assented to a change of government, and became very uneasy with the Soviet appeal of 27 March. Governments tried to put a good face on things, but even when it became clear that only the 'maximalists' were pacifist, and not the whole Soviet, there was not much rejoicing, although the press stressed the difference between Lenin, who was cast as a German agent, and the Soviet, which was humoured. The Allies saluted the new régime as if there were no cause for alarm. Nivelle demanded from Alexeyev an offensive, and said that the 'comedy' of the Revolution must stop. When the Soviet appealed 'to the world', Allied governments 'intervened' with Prince L'vov, through their own socialists, who insisted that there must be victory over the common enemy. Two missions left for Petrograd – an 'extraordinary' one, of the two socialist ministers, Thomas and Henderson, and a delegation, charged with saluting the Revolution in the name of western socialism, including Marcel Cachin, Marius Moutet, Sanders and others. Both missions were meant to revive Russia's will to win.

After the traditional ceremonies, the Allied socialists at once felt the suspicion surrounding them; in the Soviet they encountered 'a Siberian frost'. 'They looked like agents of Shylock come to demand from the Russian Revolution their pound of cannon-fodder', wrote Sukhanov. Their representational credentials were severely examined and they learnt that the Soviet had asked the British and French governments to allow Zimmerwaldians to go to Stockholm. They were forced to give assurances regarding India, Ireland and Morocco. They said they accepted the Soviet's peace formula; but there was no common ground on Alsace-Lorraine. The Russians wanted the population to be consulted before its fate was decided, and the French, though agreeing, made difficulties, saying that it was France, the aggrieved party in 1871, who should supervise the referendum, whereas the Soviet wanted to leave this to some international body. The Russians were also opposed to the defeated side's making cash payments, for the responsibility for the war was universal, and every state should take its share in compensating the victims of it.

The Russians none the less rejected any notion of separate peace, and the Allied socialists soon got over the poor welcome. They made excellent personal connections with the Soviet, and were able, as desired, 'to stiffen the soldiers'. They were even converted to the Soviet ideal, being gradually overcome by the extraordinary spectacle and the intoxication of a successful revolution. They had arrived as shame-faced advocates, worrying for their governments, and they left as priests of the new faith. But their governments' answer to the Russian Notes was disconcerting. While recognizing the justice of the Russians' democratic principles, even agreeing to revise war aims after new negotiations, they made reservations to such a degree that *Rabochaya Gazeta* could say, 'The Allies want to put old wine into new bottles.' Wilson's reply, in particular, was distressing. He was obviously against the Russian schemes, and publicly stated that peace without victory would simply strengthen German imperialism, which he felt now wanted a compromise peace. *Izvestiya*, the Soviet newspaper, attacked this, describing it as 'foggy and somnolescent'. It concluded, 'This is not a language to use towards Russian democracy.' Chernov said, 'This note is a settling of accounts between Wilson the peace-maker and Wilson the war-leader.'

'The ground crumbled under the feet of my successor, Tereshchenko', wrote Milyukov. Like Lenin, he was right. The Left, henceforth, felt that Russia might as well declare herself 'freed of all undertakings'. In the view of the leaders of new Russia, their policy of revolutionary peace could only succeed through an international conference at Stockholm. Delegates from all warring countries would assemble and find a formula they could then dictate to their governments. But the governments did not have to worry. The different elements of the socialist movement could not agree even on procedure, and the conference never took place. Negotiations were of course opened, even between militant socialists of both sides, with Tseretelli and the Mensheviks constantly offering their impartial services. But even in Russia the policy was attacked, from the Right and also from Lenin and the Zimmerwaldian Left, who feared that 'the Stockholm peace' would save the world bourgeoisie from revolution. Allied socialists in particular feared the reaction of their own public, which had been inflamed by propaganda for victory. In England it was not the government but the dockers' union that stopped MacDonald from going to Stockholm. Even before Wilson and then Ribot refused passports for Stockholm delegates, the spell had been broken, the initial impetus lost. The conference had died in men's minds and hearts and was dead before it had been born.

Revolutionary peace had failed, and thus left advocates of compromise facing advocates of victory. Compromise was gaining ground in Germany, though it remained ineffectual since what German leaders called compromise was merely an arrangement by which not all war aims would be met. With the Russian Revolution a new situation was created as socialism advanced. Deteriorating conditions, rising discontent and increasing strikes caused a new climate, which brought in a revival of political quarrels. After the Soviet's appeal, the social democrats had vigorously demanded peace without annexations or contributions. Later, following *Prikaz I* and other news from Russia, there were naval mutinies. These had their origins in the failure of submarine-warfare and the maltreatment of sailors, but the political stand was inspired by Russian developments. The military at once accused the socialists, and in Kiel it was indeed the Independents who were managing things.

The majority socialists were frightened. They feared that their control of opposition would vanish, and demanded from Bethmann Hollweg an equalization of the Prussian franchise, with an immediate statement in favour of peace without annexations. Bethmann produced some anodyne phrases for the first, and would not budge on the second. He did write to Hindenburg that the chances of compromise peace were now good – submarines had not fulfilled men's hopes, America had intervened, and the people, their hopes thwarted, might publicly show their rage. To reject now all talk of peace could have 'incalculable consequences'. Bethmann was supported by Czernin, but not by the generals. They were already indignant at the verbal concessions made over the Prussian franchise, and gave a negative answer to the 'pacifist' proposals, despite the fact that these still implied continuing control of Belgium, Poland and the rest. If morale was running down, they said, it was the civilians' fault 'for not inspiring the nation'. Hindenburg wrote to the Kaiser attacking Bethmann, and raised the question of his successor. When in the *Reichstag* Erzberger rallied the Catholic *Zentrum* to the majority socialists' line, Bethmann tried to make his peace with this new majority. But it in turn refused, as it meant to dissociate itself from the chancellor. Bethmann, disavowed by army and opposition alike, offered to resign on 12 July.

On 19 July the Erzberger–Scheidemann resolution was adopted by a majority in the *Reichstag*. It was an extraordinary repudiation of the Imperial government's policy, but was also devoid of consequences. Power henceforth belonged to the generals, who controlled the new chancellor, Michaelis. Separate-peace ideas also collapsed in Austria-Hungary. The young Emperor Karl had several times shown his willingness to compromise, so as to be able to devote all his energies to solving the nationality problem. But the overtures he had made, through Prince Sixtus of Bourbon-Parma, to Poincaré had led nowhere, although he had said he would give up claims on Poland, and would have ceded Galicia to Germany if she could swallow the 'humiliation' of returning Alsace-Lorraine to France.

Negotiations collapsed over the question of Italy: Karl would not agree to give up territory both in Poland and the Tyrol, and in any case neither Poincaré nor Ribot, it seems, ever dared to make proper use of the offer. Karl could no longer take the initiative, and was, like his ministers, reduced to repeating, wherever possible, 'Austria-Hungary is exhausted.'

In France advocates of compromise had different motives. Caillaux had 'European' notions, and did not share pacifist, internationalist ones. Like Giolitti in Italy, he feared that war might soon cause revolution, and concentrated on France, seeing that in the long run the decline of the demographic curve would weaken the country in its economic and moral struggle with other nations. France had also been forced by her geographical position to take the brunt of the war, and would therefore be weakened more than her allies or enemies, and her real losses would increase the longer the war lasted. For these reasons he had advocated compromise peace since 1915, though he underestimated very greatly the annexationist intentions of Germany. Formerly he had advocated Franco-German friendship, but he had other motives – he could see that the conservatives, having profited from the war to seize real power, would find ways of keeping it at all costs. He suspected the Right and *Action Française* of meaning to subject the country to the torture of a long war so as to kill off the Republic. His arguments, whether justified or not, enraged the elements in France that claimed a monopoly of patriotism. Caillaux was aloof and sarcastic, not a party man; isolated, he was vulnerable. Léon Daudet and the *Action Française* attacked him vigorously, accusing him of covering shady deals, of hiding gold abroad and the like. Speaking in Mamers, Caillaux was forced to declare that he would never 'consent to a peace that failed to give a pure and simple reintegration of Alsace-Lorraine into the French family'. Then he set up a 'Ligue républicaine', but it included only secondary figures such as Accambray and Pierre Laval. He did enjoy support from some left-wing newspapers, from *Le Canard Enchaîné* to *Le Journal du Peuple*, but the alliance was defensive, and the socialists, intoxicated by Stockholm, always stressed that their support for Caillaux did not 'affect their disagreement with his peace policy', which they described as 'bourgeois'.

The summer of 1917 severely shook the confidence of ruling classes, with mutinies and strikes reviving and the Russian Revolution taking effect. Rulers artificially connected these events, wrongly alleging that the mutinies had been started by 'pacifism', that

Bolshevism and Zimmerwald had been 'inspired by Germany'. An uprising of Russian troops fighting in the west added to the confusion. This was not their war, and many of them wanted to go home. Painlevé feared their influence at the front, and indeed, the High Command, to prevent any German attack on Russian sectors, had had the troops split up throughout the front, so that they were able to propagate revolution everywhere. The ambassador, Izvol'ski, and General Bobrikov, were preoccupied with the 'deterioration of relations with our French ally', and agreed that the troops should be transferred to the camp of La Courtine, near Limoges. There they revolted, much surprised at their treatment at the hands of republican France. Bobrikov requested French help, and Poincaré agreed, on condition that 'every care is taken to avoid any bloody engagement, because it would be exploited by our enemies'. A few weeks later the Russians at La Courtine gave in, and were deported to Mers-el-Kébir. But 'in view of their influence on the Arabs', the French generals sent them on to Laghouat.

The socialists were still in a euphoric mood, campaigning still for Stockholm. Their conscience as patriots was untroubled, as democratic Russia, while pursuing peace, was still effectively at war. As strikes were on the increase – even in munitions factories, where wages were better – they supposed that parliament and country would have to follow them. The Right and Clemenceau continually accused Malvy, whose weakness towards pacifists was made out to be the cause of declining morale, for compounding the gravest crisis France had known since 1914. The generals took up this refrain. In February 1917 Nivelle had complained to Painlevé of 'the Army's being infested with pamphlets, it is a veritable epidemic' – tracts and pamphlets produced by the *Libertaire* or the *Comité pour la reprise des relations internationales*, for which conscripts took out subscriptions and supported strikers with their pennies. At Bourges 'they have even dared to form a Union'. After the mutinies, Pétain sent another report to Painlevé: far from accusing the generals, his colleagues, of blundering into the April offensive, he attacked 'agents provocateurs', pacifists, and demanded strong action against socialist propaganda. No permission should be given for men to attend the Stockholm conference. He accused the Paris press of fomenting demoralization, demanded a purging of railway-station personnel, measures against conscripts in the factories who agitated, and in general supported the themes of *L'Echo de Paris*, *Action Française* or Clemenceau's newspaper.

Ribot bent before this, and refused passports for Stockholm. He had ignored the visit of Soviet representatives, who had come to Paris as 'peace-pilgrims'. The advantage was exploited by Clemenceau, whom 1870 had marked indelibly, and who was inspired to revenge and a victorious peace. On 22 July, in a public session of the senate, he resumed the attack on Malvy, and indirectly aimed at Caillaux and all advocates of a compromise peace. Ribot withdrew, leaving a place for Painlevé. But despite Thomas's efforts, the socialists would not participate in the government because they had been refused passports. The way was thereby opened to Clemenceau, in effect, and he incarnated the Jacobin spirit of resolute war, while denouncing the profiteers.

In the end, he imposed himself on us all, [wrote Ribot] through the popularity he had won in the army and the country by his ardent attacks on Caillaux and Malvy. The Chamber always saw him come with trepidation, but accepted him because of the socialists' unrelenting hostility to him. They had been convinced that no one would dare appoint a government headed by this former prime minister whose name evoked bitter battles with the workers [the Draveil strike for instance] and in withdrawing from the *Union sacrée* they actually opened the way for him. They had misapprehensions about their own strength and the country's sentiments, and it was they who contributed most to give power to the man they regarded as their worst enemy.

Clemenceau began, 'We present ourselves in the single aim of total war. My policy has one aim: to maintain the morale of the French people in this, the worst crisis of its history . . . My foreign policy and my home policy are the same. At home I wage war. Abroad, I wage war . . . I shall go on waging war.' Once in power, he became a hanging judge, took up the case assembled by Léon Daudet in the *Action Française* and sought permission to start proceedings against Caillaux. He had absorbed the lesson of the Dreyfus case, and, though formerly a friend of Zola's, put Caillaux in prison although there was not even a forgery to support the accusation of treason. Parliament grumbled but let him have his way; it only objected to military justice's having a monopoly in the business. A few socialists protested, but Clemenceau knew he could rely on the party's right wing, led by Alexandre Varenne, and now tending towards schism. For Clemenceau the socialist peace was already finished with,

whereas the Caillaux peace, supported by Briand, could be revived.

Repression had proceeded apace once Malvy gave up the ministry
of the interior. Zimmerwaldians, such as Hélène Brion, and anarchists
were arrested, and their newspapers suppressed. Clandestine pamphlets took up the refrain and according to the monthly report of the
administrative police attached to the ministry of the interior, they
had never been so numerous as in the first months of 1918. The tract,
Poilus et civils, nos frères, which tended towards pacifism, was found
in twenty Paris girls' schools; an appeal for peace launched from
Nice was distributed in twenty-three large towns; at Issoudun, in
February alone, seventy-one pacifist tracts were confiscated. Strikes,
though insignificant compared with Britain or Italy, increased regardless of the situation at the front and the bombardment of Paris by
'Big Bertha'. They were not affected by the defeats of the spring,
and even tended to increase, the average rising from thirty to forty
strikes a month, to a peak of fifty-four in August. They were not
purely economic in motive but were stimulated by a climate of
political agitation and militancy, although the climate was not such
as to prevent two-thirds of the strikes from being settled at once as
soon as wage claims were met. Only a small minority of workers were
affected and there was little effect on production of munitions. In any
case, Germany had the same problem, and America could, for France,
cover any gaps. But partisans of an immediate peace continued, sug-
gesting 'an international general strike' against the war, although
they could see the 'passivity' of people, their lack of logic, particularly
in Paris 'where the striking workers make patriotic speeches'.

The opening of negotiations at Brest-Litovsk pulled the Russians
off their pedestal, and reduced the credibility of their revolutionary
ideal. The French government concealed the fact that the new
Russian régime, before opening these negotiations, had invited all the
warring states to join them. Much play was made of the feelings that
Russian 'treachery' would provoke at the front and in the rear. The
treaty itself, in the spring, destroyed the position of the compro-
misers, and only victory now seemed desirable. Clemenceau could
'force France into victory'; his determination stemmed from the
depths of French national consciousness, and he defeated the now
vacillating advocates of a compromise peace.

Italy was the same, though the generals' blunders and the crisis
of morale had led to disaster at Caporetto. This was the only country
whose parliament opposed the war, though it had little effect

because the extremists had mob-support. This had shown how representative government lacked strength, and it strengthened the anti-parliamentarians, who dreamt of overthrowing the monarchy and of installing a national revolutionary régime – power to come not from parliament but from 'Patriotic Associations', ministries to be filled with experts, not politicians. The *Fasci* were driven on by their challenge to liberalism and defeat only heightened the challenge. But early in 1917 interventionism still had many enemies. The workers' discontent, provoked by scarcities and by inflation of prices, fuelled a Left opposition. The difficulties of everyday life were particularly serious because, as in Russia, the economy had been excessively squeezed by the war effort. For lack of British coal the already inadequate railways were working only to 50 per cent capacity. Textile factories were turning out only 40 to 50 per cent of their pre-war production. More than half of the peasants had been called up, and agricultural output was unstable – there was a bread shortage several times in the big cities. Many strikes broke out over wage claims, and pacifist demonstrations as well – the 1 May celebrations showed the scale of them in 1917. In supposedly 'interventionist' Milan there were over a thousand arrests; in the towns and country-side of the south women were particularly active, crying 'Stop the war!' 'Give us back our men.' *Avanti!* was suppressed in eleven provinces, but Zimmerwaldian propaganda was constantly dis-seminated. When Turati, a frequent speaker, addressed a meeting in Milan, the crowd yelled, 'Shut up and get down to the job.' These demonstrations reached their height in summer 1917 in Turin, just after the visit of Soviet delegates. Nowhere in Europe was their reception so enthusiastic: the same slogans had been repeated in Milan, but in Turin they were truly part of a revolutionary mood. The strikes here were reminiscent, in many ways, of those in Petro-grad in February. Women and youths had a vital part in them, trying to fraternize with the *carabinieri* and shouting, 'Don't fire at your brothers.' But the movement was limited to Turin and was badly led. It came to nothing, for those who had begun it had never bothered about the problem of power. Once the general strike had been proclaimed and its leaders arrested, they put up barricades and molested the citizenry. The way was open to repression, resulting in fifty dead, 800 wounded and over 1,500 arrests.

The Left had scarcely any link with the countryside. This was not true of the Church, which was also worried about interventionism: the Pope now had another reason for opposing the war. He described it as 'a useless massacre' in unequivocal terms. Benedict XV tried to overcome his own pro-Austrian leanings early in 1917, and offered to mediate; his action was made public on 15 August, and alarmed all the governments. The action provoked one of the diplomatic flurries that the war occasionally witnessed and confirmed the German view that Great Britain was still the chief enemy: there would be no question of abandoning Belgium which was Great Britain's first condition for peace. The affair also showed that the Pope, the British and the Americans would not insist on Alsace-Lorraine or the Trentino as a pre-condition for negotiations. The Pope wanted a peace based 'not on violence but on reason'; Pierre Renouvin has said, 'His own inclination certainly pushed him to try to end the massacre, but the interests of the Church were still more urgent – the war had broken his flock's solidarity, and weakened the Catholic Church as an international organization . . . If it went on, things could become still more serious . . . The Church could not take second place to the Stockholm socialists.' The peace proposed by the Internationalists certainly had little in common with that proposed by the Pope. It would have been imposed on governments, whereas the Pope's would have saved them from revolution. But these two campaigns complemented each other: the interior, indoctrinated by priest or militant, expressed its feelings to soldiers who were already weary of spending years away from home. The effect was foreseeable; in Genzano province there is a quantitative link between the socialist Left's activity and the length of the sick-list. In Sicily, where it was only the Church that counted (though of course sustained by an age-old tradition of insubordination), there were 20,000 deserters. In the countryside there was even an inclination towards *jacquerie*: 'Let's skin the bosses.' Turati rightly said, 'They mean us as well.' In 1917 there were 48,282 mutineers and 56,268 deserters: the numbers rose all the time. From May to October alone there were 24,000 new mutineers or deserters.

The front-soldiers also displayed discontent. They protested against the harshness of the war and their generals' inhumanity. In II Army the generals forced soldiers not at the front to undertake back-breaking labour 'to make them want to go back to the front'. The arrogance and indifference to lives of the officers recall the Russian navy. There were mutinies in Ravenna in the spring of 1917 and cries of 'Give us bread', 'Leave'. Forty-eight men were shot, as were 38 in mutinies at Catanzaro. More and more soldiers were executed – 66 in 1915, 167 in 1916, 359 in 1917. In September

1917 there was no counting the number of times soldiers refused to march, according to *La Sentinelle* of La Chaux-des-Fonds; and the generals worried, because they knew they depended on the Russian front to take the pressure off them – and Kerenski's armies, thrust onto the defensive by the fall of Riga and the developing revolution, would be unable to do in 1917 what they had done in 1916. The transfer of Austrian troops against Italy would be fatal, yet no one knew how to prevent it. When the Central Powers launched their offensive on the Isonzo, on 23 October, they had only trivial numerical advantages – 44 divisions, 7 of them German, against 41, and 4,126 guns against 3,564. Cadorna manoeuvred wrongly, Capello disobeyed and a reverse turned into calamity. The front was broken through and a retreat was carried out in confusion. Italian troops had been surprised, were demoralized in advance and broke up, some 200,000 of them surrendering without fighting. Whole divisions fell into the hands of the Central Powers, who took 293,000 prisoners. Fugitives reached as far back as the Abruzzi. As in France in June 1940, when men also went to war in despair and were prey to a common propaganda of the Right and the pacifist Left, the Italians could not seemingly recover.

The Caporetto defeat, though it was stopped on the Piave, contained a social element. The refusal to obey and to fight was a kind of revolutionary muttering. Mario Isenghi stressed this, quoting a forgotten observation of Malaparte's: 'Later on . . . the defeated lost interest in Caporetto, or were ashamed of it. The fear of seeming to be cowards or traitors to the country impelled them to deny this finest of gestures, this most courageous of actions in a cowardly life.' Caporetto and the October Revolution were a turning-point in Italian politics. The invasion revived national feeling, created a kind of *Union sacrée* which even Giolitti joined. The economy was militarized, interventionist groups and the *Fasci* decked themselves out as forces of order, and only the Leninist Left was left out. Lazzari and Serrati, editor of *Avanti!*, were arrested, and the socialist party dismantled. A gap between reformists and revolutionaries, who had before then been isolated, grew; neither of them noted the rising influence of the *Fasci*.

Part IV

1917 had been marked by the triumph of revolution in Russia. In other countries governments had been able to forestall the pacifist contagion and to restore patriotic fervour. In that year the intervention of America, China, Brazil and others gave the war global dimensions. The peoples of Asia and Africa brandished the Fourteen Points and asserted vigorously their right to independence, proclaiming the genius native to their own civilizations which, after all, had never caused a holocaust like this. But it was also characteristic of 1917 that new weapons and techniques failed – unrestricted submarine-warfare, tanks, new methods of 'breaking through' in offensives. Each side had won successes, though not decisive ones. Early in 1918 the will to win was intact, but leaders had fewer delusions as to their chances.

Suddenly, in autumn 1918, the Central Powers were to give in, although merely a year before they had Caporetto, the Russian peace and the surrender of Romania and seemed stronger than ever before. This apparent enigma lay at the origin of a carefully nourished myth, that the Germans had not been defeated when their government asked for armistice. They had been 'stabbed in the back'. Socialists were made out to be responsible for this, having stirred up trouble in the rear so as to take power in a weakened, defeated Germany. A new era began in Germany, and soon in other countries as well: on both sides the army and some of the ex-servicemen identified themselves with the nation. They accused politicians and civilians of betraying the national cause whereas they, the soldiers, had had to die for it. There was a further great change. The Allies' victory and the subsequent peace came as a result of America's sudden intervention in the affairs of a crushed and diminished Europe. The Bolsheviks' success also meant the creation of a new society. The separate peace of Brest-Litovsk, and the call to world revolution, outlawed socialist Russia among the nations of the *ancien régime*. Ruling classes, threatened alike, put up a common front, overcame their divergent national interests and agreed on a need to fight the

Soviet régime, its admirers and allies. This was to define fifty years of political life, a transformation that began in the war, when the Bolsheviks had to face the linked hostility of Allies and Central Powers, despite their own hostilities in the west. Just as revolutionaries everywhere, following the Soviet appeal, fixed their gaze on 'the great light in the east', the war turned into intervention, a new crusade.

Chapter 17

Between war and crusade

The Stockholm conference had been still-born. This, and still more the failure of Kerenski's offensive, caused new discontent. Fundamental reform was slow in coming, and since people knew that the war took precedence over everything else, they were in a hurry to deal with that problem. But its solution, unlike other questions, was not only a national matter: allies and enemies would have to be convinced of the need to make a neutral peace. This seemed impossible. Some men blamed Germany; the Bolsheviks said this was not true, as bourgeois ministers were also responsible, in all countries. They, like the Tsar, must be overthrown. Besides, it was bourgeois ministers who did nothing for reform and who, in Russia, were still condemning the workers and peasants to poverty.

But by autumn 1917 society had been transformed, and Russians no longer recognized the authority of the social system they had inherited: an industrialist, forced to attend a meeting and then beaten up, said, 'The world is upside-down.' In the joint committees set up in the summer, factory committees told their old masters what the workers' rights were. The same committee policed the plant and occupied the management offices. In the countryside soviets undertook the partitioning of land, and in little towns the people's committees took over small shops and sold requisitioned goods to the countryside. Long before October the proletariat had taken over dictatorial powers, the embryo of a new political and social order. The Kornilov *Putsch* revealed that the danger of counter-revolution was real: Kerenski, the Bolsheviks and the Soviet came together temporarily to defeat it, although Kerenski and the Soviet executive committee, imprisoned in their own policies of conciliation, wanted to spare the defeated Right. This alienated them from opinion, for the people were against any use of their desire for civil peace as a way of pardoning counter-revolutionaries. The Bolsheviks, in the September elections, had a triumphal success.

In the days preceding October no one, and certainly not the Bolsheviks, thought that Lenin's party alone would be able to take power, and take it for ever. The Bolsheviks sounded a Jacobin note to bind themselves together against the reactionaries, the government and the Germans, who were made out to be 'accomplices'. Men grouped defensively about the Bolshevized soviets, as previously they had grouped around the threatened commune. The October uprising was at once a move to defend the Revolution against parties that threatened it, and an offensive in itself, to launch Soviet power and a new phase of revolution. When Lenin started it, he did not suppose that revolution would come only in one country, and he did not suppose that this revolution, limited to Russia, could be properly socialist. He did not of course propose to extend the Revolution to Europe at this moment; he only meant that a revolution in isolation could not survive. The takeover in Russia, a democratic peace to end the war, and a proletarian revolution in Europe were for him inseparable stages of revolution.

Thus it was not the aim of Lenin and Trotsky on 8 November, when they proposed peace to *all* the belligerents, to safeguard their links with the Allies: 'The offer was meant to lead inevitably to a rising of the proletariat against any government that opposed it.' Peace became a weapon, one necessary, as Arthur Ransome said, to install the social revolution. Lenin observed, 'If the unlikely happens, then none of the states will accept an armistice, and we shall be able to call the war just, and defensive. Russia will become the ally of the world's proletariat, of all the oppressed of the globe.' The Soviet government would be the heart of the world revolution. The decree of peace was a simple appeal to governments and peoples. Lenin knew that France, Germany, England and Italy would never agree to a neutral peace, but he hoped to enlist America and perhaps Austria-Hungary, and thus set in motion an interlocking machinery. He did not enunciate the principles of a socialist peace, but rather one based on the right of self-determination. He did not say capitalism had 'caused the war', nor that socialism was 'the only remedy for war'. He used Wilson's own language and was perfectly understood by Wilson, who on 8 January answered with his Fourteen Points, stressing the democracies' willingness to base peace on the right of self-determination, the abolition of secret diplomacy, the complete freedom of the seas, the evacuation of Belgium, the reconstitution of Poland, the return to France of Alsace-Lorraine and the formation of a League of Nations. But this apparent agreement on terms concealed a fundamental contrast of aim. The Allied ambassadors and the Russian representatives abroad both sensed it strongly. There was nothing in common between the ideas of Lenin and of Wilson. But the game had not been entirely lost in Russia. The provisional government might not exist, but Kaledin's Whites, who had risen in November, might soon be masters of the country.

The Bolsheviks faced a great contradiction. To preserve themselves and the Revolution they would have to conclude the peace demanded by the peasants, workers and soldiers. But the Allies would not negotiate; therefore the Bolsheviks would have to make a separate peace with the Central Powers. This would strengthen German imperialism and destroy the chances of revolution in Germany, an essential base for the future socialist Europe. On 23 November Lenin and Trotsky requested an armistice, and at the same time published the secret treaties with the Allies, which was at once a way of justifying their action and countering Allied threats to support Kaledin. The British and French became increasingly hostile, and the Bolsheviks on 7 December launched an appeal to the oriental peoples, inviting India, Egypt and all colonial peoples to shake off the imperialist yoke. Bolshevism was now taken seriously in London, and the Foreign Office gave orders to prevent any circulation of this document. But it could not be kept secret; and Tilak, in Cambridge, addressed speeches Bolshevik in inspiration to the Indian students there. Joffe, Kamenev and Trotsky felt that revolution, through fraternization and diplomatic gaining of time, would soon win in Germany, and thus negate the German army's 'victory'.

The Germans suspected that they were being duped. When they learnt that the Ukraine had risen against Bolshevik rule, the military demanded suspension of negotiations, and meanwhile the Central Powers signed a treaty with the Kiev *Rada* that was intended to make the Ukraine the Central Powers' granary. By early February the Bolsheviks were in a less favourable situation than in early December, as the great strikes in Vienna, Berlin and Budapest had already ended, the Ukraine was breaking free of Moscow, and in Finland Mannerheim had raised the banner of independence. Trotsky had declared that he would not conclude an annexationist peace and declared that the war was over. The Germans, taken aback at this – which was caused by the Bolsheviks' inability to get their soldiers to fight – broke off relations and on 8 February attacked, meeting almost no resistance. Hoffman noted, 'This is the strangest war I've ever seen.' Hitherto, Lenin had left the work to his friends and had told them only not to go to war again, even revolutionary war. Now he demanded signature immediately, on whatever terms. These were harsh enough – the Red Army to leave the Ukraine, the Russians to make peace with the *Rada*, and give up all claims to the Baltic states. In view of this, Joffe and Trotsky had considered appealing to the Allies since they, having landed troops at Archangel, might be regarded as 'objective' associates now that Germany threatened to destroy Russia. Bukharin still felt that peace with Germany would only strengthen imperialism and would dig the grave of world revolution and exclaimed, 'You're turning the party into a pile of shit.' But Lenin, supported by Zinoviev, Sverdlov and Stalin, won. Sokolnikov signed the treaty on 3 March and it was ratified by the soviets by 784 votes to 261.

Alexeyev, in November 1917, had raised the south against the October Revolution. His troops, under Denikin, were to find unexpected support from the Czech legion, a force recruited from Czech prisoners from the Austrian army. These were crossing Siberia to go home, but clashed with local soviets. The White government in Samara was able to use them. The Allies considered playing this card since the Whites, if they won, would resume the war and restore the second front. Allied troops were landed on the Murman coast, at first to block the German advance, and stop Finnish nationalists from cutting the Petrograd–Murmansk line, and, very soon, to give the Whites increasingly open support. 'Bolshevism is a plague', said Gauvain in the *Journal des Débats*, 'and if we don't fight it, Germany will . . . It will seem to be her natural mission.' She must be forestalled; and intervention was supported by many influential people, such as Colonel Knox and General Janin, heads of the Allied Military Missions to Russia, which was the heart of interventionism. Before Brest-Litovsk, the Allies had already struck counter-revolutionary notes, although up to 11 November their chief motivation lay in defeating Germany. The Bolsheviks too looked at German demands, the secession of the Ukraine and Finland, the menace of Russia's total disintegration, and considered collaborating with the Allies rather than with the Germans. The Allies also appreciated that the most anti-Bolshevik elements in Russia were also the elements that had hoped for some understanding with the Kaiser's Germany before the Tsar fell. One way and another, it might be vital for the Allies not to support Lenin's opponents too far. In any case, via the links of Trotsky with Sadoul and Thomas in France, and those of Trotsky with Bruce Lockhart and Henderson in England, parliamentary circles were overestimating the chance of Germany's going Bolshevik. But when, in Rosa Luxemburg's expression, 'the persistent immobility of this corpse of a proletariat' in Germany forced the Russian revolutionaries to make their peace with German imperialism – as the only power in the country – and with the corpse-like attitude of the German proletariat thereafter, German imperialism exploited the Russian Revolution for its own ends, and the Allies could legitimize the battle they meant to join against the fortress of the international proletariat.

But in any event they had not waited for Brest-Litovsk; they were already helping elements hostile to the Bolsheviks. Despite socialist opposition, they had assisted Kornilov against Kerenski, and recanted just before October in the expectation that Kerenski would have to join up with the military. After the Bolshevik victory, the King of Romania suggested that the Allies should link up with Kaledin's Cossacks and then try to extend the link through the Kuban to the British advancing from Mesopotamia. Balfour and Churchill wanted to recognize the White government, and help to Kaledin was decided upon despite reservations from Lloyd George and Wilson, because the other opposition movements, 'even in coalition are no more than a bunch of chattering theoreticians'. The British government was leading the dance, since it measured more accurately than others the extent of the danger to capitalism. But German imperialism had not yet been overthrown, and Lloyd George appreciated the difficulties of treating at the same time with Petrograd Bolsheviks against Finns and Germans, and with Novocherkassk Whites, to avoid their linking up with Germany. Both before and after Brest-Litovsk, both parties were engaged in a double game; Bolsheviks, not knowing which was the greater danger, Allies or Germans, and keeping links with both; Central Powers at the same game, signing with Lenin at Brest-Litovsk and supporting anti-Bolshevik movements in Georgia, the Ukraine and Finland.

The open intervention of Japan, in sending troops to support the Whites and enforce recompense in the maritime province, forced Germans and Bolsheviks together. It was of course clear that the American landings that followed had been made to check Japanese ambitions, but overall the Allied military intervention there was increasingly dangerous for the Bolsheviks. The Germans' failure in their spring offensive confirmed this view. On 3 June 1918, the Allied war council decided that each country was to send 4,000 to 5,000 men, 'to sustain the Czechs and support the Whites'. The Bolsheviks then appealed to Germany, herself urgently requiring to transfer troops to the west, and agreement was reached towards the

Part IV

end of August. By one of the clauses, 'The Soviets will henceforth refrain from all propaganda in the states of the Central Powers.' Long before Stalin, the Bolsheviks were thus ready to sacrifice the European revolution to the need to save their own régime.

Maurice Barrès, in his *Cahiers* for 12 October 1918, recorded a set of remarks from the *Kreuzzeitung*, the great Rhenish newspaper: 'The struggle against Bolshevism must force the three Allied powers and their enemies together. A strong Germany will resist Bolshevism, whereas, if she succumbed to it, the worst kind of revolution would annihilate Europe. The Entente must surely see this.' These arguments had a receptive response, at least as far as Foch was concerned. The Allies were now hopeful as to the outcome of the war, and intervened openly in Russian affairs; it was not now the creation of a second front, or the 'protection' of Russia that worried them, and the political character of intervention became clear. From October a clear distinction was being drawn between the struggle against the Central Powers and the struggle against Bolshevism, which hitherto had been lumped together. In Britain and France the argument of investments was used to justify what was being done by governments, and even the Whites were worried about the ill-defined reasons and ambitions involved. Wilson was not even informed of the Clemenceau plan, which had been inspired by the generals and passively accepted by the British. On 23 October 1918 Clemenceau described it to Pichon:

Bolshevism has become a force to be reckoned with. It threatens us through the Red Army, which is to be brought up to a million men in strength, and there are dreams of setting up soviet régimes first throughout the old Russian territories and then in the rest of Europe. This new and monstrous form of imperialism will threaten Europe all the more fearsome as it comes precisely at the end of the war, which will inevitably provoke, in all countries, a serious economic and social crisis . . . The Allies must therefore cause the soviets to collapse. This will not be achieved by carrying the war to Russia, but rather through economic encirclement of Bolshevism . . . occupation by Allied troops from Romania, Odessa and the rest, of the Crimean and Ukrainian corn belts and the Donets coal-basin, which will be vital pledges for the payment of the 26,000,000,000 we have lent Russia, and which the Bolsheviks have repudiated . . . the armies of the Balkans, British armies in Turkey will, after the Turks have given in, furnish the few divisions needed to establish, around Bolshevism, not only a *cordon sanitaire* to isolate it and kill it by starvation, but also the nuclei of friendly forces around which the healthy elements of Russia will be able to organize, and bring about the renovation of their country under the aegis of the Entente.

The Great War had turned into a crusade.

On 15 October 1918 a company of the 21st battalion of colonial infantry unloaded at Archangel and refused to fight the Bolsheviks when the first rumour of an armistice came through, from the western front. These sparks multiplied, and caused governments more worry than the anti-war agitation carried on at home. Some groups in France and particularly in Great Britain sought to alert the public against the violation being perpetrated by Allied governments against the motherland of revolution. They had few listeners for the moment: at the socialist conference of July 1918 1,172 votes approved intervention and only 1,544 condemned it. Even then, as Annie Kriegel says, people could well vote against intervention, because Russia no longer mattered much for a French victory. But on both sides there were now men who regarded their first task as being to uphold the motherland of revolution. Their elders had not been able to stop war, and they could, by contrast, strive to save socialism. On the other hand, many men now put defence of the social order above defence of the country against 'the hereditary enemy', on both sides the social being dissociated from the national. Patriotic sentiment no longer absorbed, as in 1914, the social struggle. The war had come as a revelation, a detonator that blew up one element of the old system of authority. Before the signature of peace treaties – which themselves contained the seeds of a new war – the Great War was already pregnant with the civil conflict which, to this day, divides society.

Chapter 18

The illusions of victory

Early in 1918 the British and French worried about the moral and physical health of their armies. By early 1918, the war seemed to have done best for the Central Powers. The Italian army had been badly defeated at Caporetto, and Bolshevik Russia had given up the fight; Romania, in consequence, had been forced to declare an armistice. On the other side, the Allies had hardly a success to their credit. They had managed to check the submarine-menace; but their offensives on land had failed. They no longer hoped for a quick victory and now counted only on 'the tanks and the Americans'. Since the summer, the French and British armies' capacity for offensive warfare had been in doubt; the initiative now lay with the Central Powers. The western front remained the vital one, and the Allies feared that Germany would be able to transfer all her troops from the east before the Americans arrived in mass. The German army, to win, must first win this race against time.

In France itself Pétain's defensive ideas had been challenged by Foch, who meant to replace him. Pétain told Poincaré, 'If the coming battle lasts more than a month, I shall not have enough men to reconstitute the divisions engaged and to make the counter-offensive that will be needed to relieve the front attacked.' In his fourth directive, of 22 December 1917, Pétain showed that he could not resist and break up German attacks unless he waged the battle on rear positions instead of on the front line, a tactic he successfully used in June and July 1918, but one that Clemenceau condemned as cowardly. He had become the apostle of out-and-out resistance, and would not sanction any withdrawal from first positions. The two Allies agreed only against Pershing, who refused to let his Americans be incorporated into Allied units. With difficulty, he was able to take over a sector of the Lorraine front, and a vain quarrel over competence held up for several months any mass utilization of American forces – no doubt with many useless deaths in consequence.

The Central Powers were more vulnerable than they appeared. Germany's economic situation had improved but the year opened under poor auspices. The harvest of 1917 had been terrible, the potato ration was reduced to seven pounds a week, the meat ration to 250 grammes, the fat ration to under 100 grammes. Scarcity did stimulate invention: for lack of cotton, cloth was made out of paper and nettle-fibre, and fifty million pairs of shoes had wooden soles. But there was discontent and an increasing number of strikes, which reached a peak in January, though forceful government intervention led to a resumption of work. Cessation of hostilities in the east allowed the Central Powers to divide their effort more sensibly. Still, since the Treaty of Bucharest, there had been much difficulty with a Bulgaria indignant at not acquiring the Dobrudja, and the Austrian and Turkish alliances were also less sure. Hindenburg could also see that there was little hope of rapidly transferring troops from east to west: in spring 1918 there were still nearly a million German soldiers in Finland, Russia and Romania. It was even felt imprudent to transfer any more, since some of the divisions had been won over to revolutionary ideas and might contaminate the others; and in early 1918, when the Germans decided to strike their great blow in the west, conditions were less favourable to them than a few months before. They hoped to get a quick finish and also knew that this offensive was their last chance, that, for victory, a few weeks alone would matter. The first scattering of pamphlets over Germany, the regular bombardment of Paris by *Tauben*, the *Gothas* and 'Big Bertha' – a huge gun concealed in the Compiègne forests – kept up this war of nerves. Worry was greater than before, as if both sides sensed that the decisive ordeal was coming.

Ludendorff decided to launch a series of attacks on the British, whom Passchendaele had particularly affected, and to make the main effort at the join of the French and British sectors. He knew that Haig and Pétain were in disagreement, and it was far from certain that the French would help out. On 21 March he made the first attack, near Saint-Quentin, with 6,000 guns supporting attack by sixty-five divisions. The British could not sustain a shock on this scale, and were broken through. Ludendorff could 'push the two sides of the door apart'. As he had foreseen, Pétain at first preferred to keep his army intact so as to parry a second attack, which he could see coming, and made difficulties before sending Fayolle's troops to help Haig. The British thought they could not hold Amiens, and prepared for a general retreat to the Channel ports. In the south the Germans took Noyon, and in Paris things looked critical, with arrangements being made for the government to retire to Tours.

Clemenceau at once summoned an inter-Allied conference at Doullens, and Foch managed to recreate there an atmosphere of Entente. His ardour was in striking contrast to the gloom of Haig and Pétain; 'I shall fight in front of Amiens, I shall fight in Amiens itself, and I shall fight behind Amiens.' The Allies gave him powers to co-ordinate their actions in the west, and Foch immediately took reinforcements from the French front. They arrived in time to close the Germans' breach. On 9 April Ludendorff struck again – this time at the extreme northern end of the Anglo-Portuguese front, so that it would be more difficult for the French to intervene. He wanted to isolate the Belgian army and part of the British, and throw them into the sea. But the thirty-six divisions of Prince Rupprecht could not break through, despite violent battles around Kemmel Hill between 25 and 28 April.

On 27 May Ludendorff attacked the French on the Chemin des Dames in Champagne, at the other extremity of the front. This was intended to be a diversionary operation, designed to allow a resumption of attempts to destroy the British front. The French had had to extend their lines since March, and they had been further thinned by despatch of reinforcements to Picardy and Flanders. The Germans were much surprised at bringing off a great victory – in forty-eight hours they breached the front between the twin strong points of Soissons and Reims. On 30 May they reached the Marne, and Pétain in turn planned a great retreat. But Ludendorff gave up his original plan, and decided to push ahead; the dykes held, and on 11 June he had to break off the offensive. This had been a clear success – an advance of up to sixty kilometres, occupation of an area equivalent to a French department, Amiens and Reims threatened. But it was not decisive, and Mangin even managed a minor offensive success. Emotions ran high in Paris when it was realized that the Germans were once more in Noyon. The Chamber summoned Clemenceau to explain, and the 'Tiger' turned. Deputies hoped to lay him low, but he saved Pétain and Foch, and concluded with the phrase, 'Let the living now complete the magnificent work of the Dead.'

Ludendorff made a final attempt on 15 July 1918 – the *Friedenssturm*, in Champagne, but the French had been forewarned through prisoners. They repeated Hindenburg's withdrawal manoeuvre of 1917 and stopped the Germans on second lines prepared in advance. The Gouraud–Mangin counter-offensive, carefully prepared from the forest of Villers-Cotterêts and supported by tanks and aircraft – these last receiving their first massive use on the battlefield – forced the Germans into a general retreat, and this, the second battle of the Marne, was a turning-point of the war. Foch, who was named first commander-in-chief and then Marshal of France, now applied his own plans for an offensive, despite the reservations of Haig and Pétain, who stressed the enormous losses. Neither side imagined that this would be, in fact, the last offensive, that the war would soon be over. Clemenceau and Foch sketched out plans for 1919, expecting to procure the collapse of Austria-Hungary, where Slav deserters were already forming bands, the Green Army; the two also hoped to help the Whites and restore a second front. Now all the fronts were to begin movement successively – Palestine, Salonica, and the western front from Flanders to Lorraine, where already the American troops were massing. Italy had made great efforts at Monte Grappa, and it was agreed that her offensive should begin only in October.

On 8 August, with over thirty divisions, the British and French attacked in the region of Amiens. The British, under Rawlinson, made the chief attack, and, owing to surprise, fog and tanks, it was the first great breakthrough since 1914. Ludendorff called it 'the black day of the German army', and there was a new phenomenon: thousands of Germans surrendered virtually without fighting. After a pause, the Allies attacked again on 20 August, and Ludendorff had to order a general retreat to the Siegfried Line, from Saint-Vaast to La Fère. He already had in view a further position, far to the rear, from Guise to Rethel. The Americans then attacked Lorraine, and liquidated the Saint-Mihiel salient in four days. The French, Belgians and British then resumed the offensive near Cambrai, and Ludendorff offered his resignation. By mid-September the entire western front was in movement, and the offensives in support, in the 'side-shows', could now be launched.

The first great victories came on the Palestine front where Allenby triumphed, almost without fighting, at the battle of Megiddo, the Turkish Sedan (19 September 1918). The Turkish army soon surrendered. From Mesopotamia another column violated Persian territory to reach Baku, to wrench it from the Germans and Turks, to seize the oil-wells and prevent the Bolsheviks from taking over. An Armenian Legion was set up under British auspices, to fight the Turks and Soviets. The Italians started their offensive on the Adige on 25 September and a month later brought about the victory of Vittorio Veneto. On 26 September, after a pause marked by new quarrelling between French and American generals, Pershing launched another offensive in the Argonne, Gouraud one in Champagne, Haig one in Flanders. The British and Canadians broke through and gained the greatest success, liberating Cambrai and Lille. In the Balkans Franchet d'Esperey, who could now count on Greek support, crossed the Moglena massif, took Gradsko, Prilep and Usküb from the Bulgarians, while Jouinot's cavalry advanced on Nish. The Austrians could not send the necessary reinforcements in time, and King Ferdinand decided to give in, on 26 September. The French failed to invite their Allies, and signed the subsequent armistice on their own, and the British did likewise with the Turks. King Ferdinand had been enraged at the clauses of the Bucharest Treaty, and was worried at the sympathies Bolshevism had aroused in Bulgaria. His army disintegrated, its commanders either fleeing or, as in Yekov's case, reporting sick, and Ferdinand abdicated in his son's favour so as to save the throne. In this way Briand was proved right: the dawn of victory rose in the east.

The German generals had for some time been talking of ending hostilities, for they did not want the Allies to find out the true state of the Imperial army, still less to have the army incapable of resuming action. To save the army, if not the régime, negotiations would be opened while still only 100 kilometres from Paris. Ludendorff had asserted this, and repeated it in private, though a few weeks before he had dismissed Kühlmann for saying much the same in the *Reichstag*. After the second battle of the Marne, Hindenburg and Ludendorff came to accept that their fate would indeed be, at best, a neutral peace, though they hoped to keep what they had gained at Brest-Litovsk. After 8 August, defeat became certain, and Ludendorff offered to resign. This was refused him. With the Americans' reduction of the Saint-Mihiel salient – in four days, where the French, for lack of resources, had failed before – and, particularly, with the British successes near Cambrai, nerves broke in the German High Command. Defeatism reached it, and it demanded the immediate conclusion of an armistice, and the despatch of a peace-note to President Wilson.

On 28 September the German public learnt that Bulgaria was surrendering, that Damascus had fallen, and that the chancellor, Hertling, had been dismissed. Prince Max of Baden, who was known for liberal and pacific ideas, was called to succeed him, but refused to take office unless the social democrats took power as well, since otherwise the United States might refuse to deal with a government they could claim to be unrepresentative. All this mattered little to the military, who were irked at the delay, and who were still talking as masters, as if indeed they had won the war. Prince Max and the politicians were dumped into power. The generals read them a report that proved how imminent was catastrophe. Ebert went white as a sheet, Scheidemann and Prince Max were thunderstruck. Graf von Waldow, a Prussian minister, said, 'It only remains to blow our brains out', and von dem Bussche's account did not exaggerate things. Prince Max hesitated to open negotiations in these conditions, but the Kaiser told him, 'We didn't call you in to make difficulties for the generals.'

The socialists had accepted Cabinet places to stop the war and save Germany from disaster. When Wilson answered – without consulting the Allies – it seemed he was demanding above all else a transformation of German institutions. It was because the army refused this and Ludendorff resigned with such a flurry, that the myth was born that the civilians had 'betrayed' the country. Public opinion, which was ignorant of the true facts of the military situation, was convinced. When a new German offer arrived, Wilson and his allies responded with a direct challenge to unseat the Kaiser. Already the Habsburg Empire was falling apart. A popular movement in Prague acclaimed the Czechoslovak Republic on 29 October, and at the same time Count Károlyi proclaimed the birth of independent Hungary, the Slovene national council also proclaiming the formation of Yugoslavia. In its turn, the German-Austrian national council, following the armistice of the Villa Giusti, proclaimed its own state.

But if Emperor Karl renounced 'all participation in the affairs of state', the Kaiser would not admit that he was the only remaining obstacle to an armistice, and imagined that Wilson and the German people would be satisfied if he changed the nature of the régime, and let Prince Max proclaim reforms. On 24 October Noske opposed this in a comment on Wilson's third Note, though he did it in a roundabout way: the majority social democrats, who were now a party of government, believed that they should treat the dynastic question with circumspection. This was not true of Independents or Spartakists, who wanted abdication 'at this time, when all crowns are rolling in the dust'. The 'national' Germans went even further than the 'socialist' ones, and on 24 October the *Frankfurter Zeitung* asserted that an honourable peace would come only after abdication. But the Kaiser meant 'to stick by the army', and Prince Max did not dare stop him, for he preferred the abdication to be voluntary, which would 'save the unity of the country'. Hindenburg and Groener, who had replaced Ludendorff, were with the Kaiser, and felt that abdication 'would mean the end of the army'. They accused the government of letting the press talk wildly and of responsibility for the general disarray. Only Drews, minister of the interior, dared to tell these generals the truth. 'Who was it that kept telling us by telephone to arrange an armistice? Who wanted us to send a Note to Wilson, and wanted us to form this government?'

The socialists were masters of the game. Once in power, they waited for Prince Max to obtain abdication from the Kaiser, threatening to leave the government, hinting that revolution would then break out, and declaring that they would not be responsible for the consequences. Prince Max was caught between his loyalty to the Hohenzollerns and the duties of his office, and he did not know whether to act or to resign. He tried to convince the Kaiser, who, far from offering to abdicate, simply cut short any discussion. It was now a trial of skill. Early in November the Germans were hoping to conclude an armistice as soon as possible, before the Allies saw the extent of their victory, and before German territory was violated. The army retired only step by step, and was able to prevent any collapse of the front. But the Allies had no delusions now about victory; they hesitated before agreeing. Foch and Clemenceau could see dangers in any over-hasty conclusion of armistice, but, like Haig, they feared that things could still go wrong. Their troops were exhausted and they could now hope for good conditions. They did not want to sacrifice lives for nothing. But Pershing was anxious to associate American troops more closely with the victory and was much opposed to any premature armistice. Poincaré agreed with this because he imagined that the negotiations might hamstring the French army.

On 3 November there was a mutiny in Kiel, where the sailors refused to sail out and fight a last battle 'for honour's sake'. The Americans had demanded an immediate end to submarine-warfare, and Admiral Hipper wanted to engage in a final battle with the Home Fleet. The sailors mutinied and decided otherwise: some of them were arrested and carried off to Kiel, while the mutineers organized demonstrations, sang the *Internationale* and announced they would overthrow the régime. A soviet was established and in a few days, despite the intervention of Noske, revolution swept Germany. A system of councils emerged from Strasbourg to Munich and Leipzig; but this, the *Rätzbewegung*, was not like Russian soviets, because it came more from soldiers than workers, although of course some workers did join in, under Independent or Spartakist leadership. With Noske at Kiel, Ebert, Scheidemann and other leaders of the social democrats or trade unions tried to neutralize the revolution. But their authority could be restored only if the Kaiser immediately abdicated, as the spirit of the January strikes was already reviving and the working class going over to Independents and Spartakists. Revolution was in the air. On 9 November Prince Max of Baden resigned and handed over to Ebert, and both of them – Crown Prince of Baden and former saddler – forced the Kaiser's hand by announcing that he had abdicated. The Kaiser in Spa said he would restore his authority as King of Prussia, but in fact fled to Holland. It was to be a socialist government, not his, that paid the price of defeat.

On 11 November 1918 the Germans accepted the Allies' armistice terms – evacuation of occupied territory, including that taken since Brest-Litovsk – repatriation of prisoners, delivery of 5,000 guns, 30,000 machine-guns, evacuation of the left bank of the Rhine by the German army, prevention of any transfer of population from the evacuated territories, prohibition of destruction of railways or roads, restoration of devastated areas (mines and water supplies), restitution of 5,000 locomotives and 15,000 wagons, right of requisition in occupied territory for the Allies, restitution of objects stolen in wartime, surrender of the war fleet. The British and Americans thought these were too harsh, and so they were when compared with Wilson's first proposals. But they were light enough relative to the devastation the war had caused on French soil and the Allies' relatively higher loss of lives. Reparations were to follow, although it was already clear that the British and Americans did not want a peace of revenge that would in turn provoke a spirit of revenge in Germany. The Americans even opposed French troops' entering Alsace-Lorraine and agreed with the British that occupation of the Rhine bridges was 'useless and excessive'. These foretastes of Allied disunity already revealed the disappointments France would have to endure after the war. However, if, after 1919, it would be the 'Anglo-Saxons' who had the capacity to assert their own policies, this was not true of November 1918. The French could still get what they wanted.

It has often been said that fear of Bolshevism made the Allies spare the German people. Foch certainly had this idea, and German statesmen played with it. Left-wing circles in France heard of this, but there is no evidence that it greatly influenced the government – hence indeed the debate, fifty years later. Poincaré did feel that harsher clauses should have been enforced, but Foch and Weygand assured him that their military objectives had been achieved. By an error of judgment that today seems astonishing they felt that the terms were enough to put Germany 'at the mercy of the victors'. Beforehand they, no more than Poincaré, did not see that it might be right to make the enemy feel the full reality of defeat by carrying the war into Germany. In November 1918 they had no scheme for destroying Germany's industrial potential or controlling the German economy. The military had concluded an armistice 'between soldiers'. Europe and the nature of war had entered an industrial era, and they were ignorant of it. They were medieval knights who had wandered into the modern age – it is significant that, having used motor-cars to get about for the whole of the war, they insisted on taking part in victory parades on horseback and believed that a nation disarmed was a nation conquered.

Once the armistice was signed the Allies discovered instead of a cowed people, a nation roused to fury. Since 1914 the Germans had been preserving their own country, and on the armistice, they still occupied three-quarters of Belgium, Metz and Briey. For over four years the Imperial army had occupied enemy territory and destroyed its economic capacity. They had lost a battle, but apart from a few people in front or rear, there was no feeling that the war had been lost. Public acclamations revealed this in an overjoyed Berlin, when the troops paraded after the armistice. Ebert greeted them as soldiers 'returning undefeated from a glorious combat', thus consecrating a myth on which Nazi propaganda was to feed.

At Versailles Germany lost Alsace-Lorraine, Posnania, Eupen and Malmédy and her overseas territories. The victors gave a dubious promise to hold plebiscites in the Saar and Silesia. The German army was reduced to 100,000 men, the fleet confiscated, and in article 231 of the treaty there was a verdict to the effect that she had caused the war and must therefore make reparation. Germans accused their leaders of accepting this treasonable peace. Occupation of the left bank of the Rhine for fifteen years as a pledge of fulfilment was the last straw in this national rage and, fuelled by nationalist propaganda, a revanchist myth, the 'stab-in-the-back' legend, was born. The victors' dishonesty added to this, for, claiming to fight for the self-determination of peoples, they had applied it only in their own favour. The Sudeten Germans were 'attributed' to Czechoslovakia and the Magyars of Transylvania to Romania. The Allies simply assumed that this anger was a sign of defeat and did not appreciate that they were losing the peace at the moment they won the war. Apart from losing a province or two Germany had remained intact and had suffered no material damage in the war. Her economic potential was still immense, and the reparations demanded at Versailles limited neither her growth nor her freedom of manoeuvre. Whereas France had been bruised, bled white and partly destroyed, and spent much of her energies simply in reconstituting her economy, Germany had only to reconvert hers.

France and Britain had been ruined by the war effort, by foreign purchasing, and had lost their prosperity of 1914 with their credit abroad collapsing and turning into debt. They no longer enjoyed investments in Russia or Turkey, their financial base was weakened, and they lost the advantage it had given them against Germany before the war. The United States could rightly be considered the only victor of the war, since their territory was intact, and they became creditors of all the other belligerents.

On the strategic levels too England and France were losing. British markets in Asia went to Japan and British rule was contested by coloured peoples from Calcutta to the Middle East. In the French case it was forgotten that the Germans' *Drang nach Osten* had formerly been limited by the redoubtable obstacles of Austria-Hungary and Russia. But Russia had lost her western lands and was thrown back to the east in the name of a crusade against Bolshevism, and at the same time the Treaty of Saint-Germain substituted a set of little states for the Habsburg Monarchy. This situation would soon facilitate the creation of *Mitteleuropa*, since the Danubian and Balkan states could easily be swallowed up by Germany, the more so as Germans now recognized that the French ruling class was liable to forget the 'national' enemy to concentrate against the 'social' one. Besides, when they reduced the former Habsburg metropolis to the proportions of a dwarf, the Allies were virtually offering Austria to Germany as a gift, for Austria, humiliated by her fall from grace, with her former subjects now enjoying that grace, preferred to disappear altogether into the *Reich*. From early November 1918 the Austrian parliament demanded 'attachment to the German *Reich*'.

There was general rejoicing on 11 November. This war had ended war; Paris, London and New York celebrated the armistice, and armies of diplomats gathered in Versailles, and later Saint-Germain, Neuilly and Sèvres to found the League of Nations and to sign treaties that were supposed to secure peace for centuries. The victorious governments expected to dominate events. They underestimated

Italian discontent at the partial sacrifice of their 'interests' to Yugoslavia, and the rage of the Germans. They forgot the disorders of the
Balkans and Ireland and the fire that smouldered in Asia and the
Arab world. Their main fear was the revolutionary contagion
expressed in Béla Kun's success, and they tried to contain it, by any
means.

Soldiers went home, destroyed homes were restored and men
returned to civil life and its private joys and woes. Then they began
to wonder. Once the excitement had passed, they had to face the
problem of their own past and future. Having forgotten the delusions
of the first years of the war, survivors could see that they had been
actors in a drama without precedent. Many wondered if they had
been right and pondered over the general meaning of the conflict.
Recent immigrants, minorities, Jews and others had been transformed through their baptism of fire into citizens, virtually uncon-
tested. But what had war brought the rest? When they returned
home and forgot the jubilation with which men greeted the end of the
nightmare, they had to undergo all the ordeal of reconversion. The
government was good at flattering them and honouring them in all
manner of ceremonies which welded them to the governmental
order. But governments did not give them the rights they had expected from the nation. Demobilization was badly organized and they
were often reduced to unemployment, even beggarhood. This lack of
effective concern on the part of governments and the rear for the fate
of these unfortunates was made all the harsher by its contrast with
the promises and speeches. Old wounds, hardly closed, were re-
opened – the bitter memory of leave in wartime, consciousness of
injustice, resentment of workers who had dodged their duty, resentment of the rear and the deputies. In reaction the solidarity of the
trenches seemed to be idyllic, where social classes and privileges were
unknown, and this other myth grew, to be illustrated in films and
novels for the next twenty years. The post-war period had its own
problems, particularly the workers who perpetuated the revolutionary tradition of the previous century. The protesting unemployed
ex-servicemen who paraded through London, caps on their heads,
could swing either way – to Labour or to Mosley's Fascist 'troops'.
They felt, in England as elsewhere, that they alone were patriots
since they alone had made the patriotic sacrifice. They could not of
course dissociate themselves easily from politicians who continued
to glorify them, and in most countries they elected in 1919 the same
representatives as before. They mostly wished the Reds to hell, along

with Dadaists and the surrealist *avant-garde*, who announced that the ex-servicemen had all been fooled, simple puppets pulled by Capital and arms manufacturers. Soldiers felt humiliated by this, and in reaction they closed their ranks and, to legitimize their own sacrifice, became nationalists. In some cases they revived an idea, formerly expressed by a few military leaders, of regimenting the whole nation and teaching it duty *manu militari*.

The chief ex-servicemen's associations, *Croix de Feu* or *Stahlhelm*, bitterly hated the rear, the 'shirking' workers and the profiteers, the politicians who were losing the peace, the trade unions 'who had the cheek to demand more leisure while they, the soldiers, were risking their lives twenty-four hours a day' for the country. There was also resentment against women who had also profiteered in their way from war because the men's departure made their emancipation possible. As Henry said, most of them avoided the danger of remaining spinsters either by marrying foreigners who were not conscripted, or by marrying men four or five years younger than the men they would have married had the war not carried them off. There was less difference in age between husband and wife and the balance of the married couple after 1918 was not as in 1914. The traditional family dissolved, much as patriotism was sundered by the success of revolution and a crusade against Red Russia. The moral imperative of work was weakened also; and it is not coincidental that, when the ex-servicemen took power in France in 1940 they adopted the slogan, 'Family, Work, Country'.

Previously states and ruling classes had had to fear only revolts from below. These were still a threat, a more serious one than before, because the success of revolution in Russia gave the revolutionaries of all countries an example and a base; these men were heralds of a cause which came from the east. But there were discontents too of a different type – emanating from the men whom the war had ruined, the rentiers and the petty-bourgeois in particular, men who incorporated the renovating ideals of the socialist tradition, the cult of the earth, the taste of violence that had grown in the mud of the trenches. Imitating the Italian *Fascisti*, they sang the praises of a revolt that would revive in style the martial rites to which men were still attached. 'Renovating and yet conserving', anti-socialist but also against international Capital, this movement was presented as a struggle for civilization in a new form. Its violent triumph in Italy, its success in Germany and Central Europe, fascinated some of the rulers and part of the middle classes, and those whose social stature had declined in the war and the post-war period, the young, the ex-servicemen obsessed with the Red peril.

But the rulers readily imagined that this uneasy atmosphere, the disunities of the victors, the difficulties of applying Versailles and the crises emerging from economic and social reconstruction, were all simply crises of transition and that capitalist society would be able to overcome them just as it would discredit socialism. The Tango, the Charleston took the place of martial music, military parades and *La Madelon*. Technological progress and its peaceful application made for new diversions which, together with the spectacles of sport, films, the music-hall, holidays, would give society the escape it required. This met the appetites of Frenchmen, Germans and British who were glad, after their nightmare, to come alive again. As early as 1920 more people turned up in Paris at the *Mi-Carême* celebrations than at the commemoration of victory. In Germany and Italy – and soon in the Soviet Union – gymnastic displays of gigantic dimensions were already revealing the menacing aspirations of 'a new order'. The 'War to end War' had ended in a Brave New World.

Table 4 The balance sheet

	Number mobilized between 1914-18 millions	Dead millions	Wounded millions	Dead and wounded of those mobilized %	Net effect on population * millions
France	8·41	1·35	3·5	60	– c. 1·2
Great Britain	8	0·95	2	37	– c. 0·8
Italy	5·25	0·5	?	—	
U.S.A.	4	0·1	?	—	
Russia	—	2·3	?	—	
Germany	13	1·6	4	41	– c. 0·9
Austria-Hungary	9	1·45	2	38	
Turkey	—	0·4	?	—	

* Calculated by taking the excess over the normal death rate, and adding it to the decrease in the total of live births.

Note: These figures cannot be considered definitive, but there is a substantial measure of agreement on them among various authorities (except the last column). Correlations and comparisons between them are useful indicators of the effect of the war.

France lost through the war: 700,000 houses and 20,000 factories destroyed, together with 50,000 km. of roads and railways made unusable; 3 million hectares of land were devastated; the production of cereals dropped by 40 per cent, industrial production by 50 per cent.

Select bibliography

General

According to Dedijer, more than 3,000 works have appeared on the events at Sarajevo. This gives some indication of the enormous literature of the Great War. The Bibliothèque de Documentation Internationale Contemporaine at Paris has collected more than 50,000 titles on the war; to these can be added newspapers, review articles, archival materials – printed or manuscript – films etc.

There is an excellent select bibliography in Pierre Renouvin's important work, *La Crise européenne et la Première Guerre Mondiale*, Paris, 1962, 4th ed., 779 pp. (highly recommended, together with Pierre Renouvin's other works).

Two other books may be highly recommended: Fritz Fischer, *Griff nach der Weltmacht, die Kriegszielpolitik des Kaiserlichen Deutschland 1914–18*, Düsseldorf, 1961, 902 pp. (a shortened version appeared in English as *Germany's Aims in the First World War*, London, 1967, 652 pp.); J. Mayer, A. Ducasse and G. Perreux, *Vie et mort des Français*, Paris, 1959, 510 pp. (Other works by Mayer and Ducasse are also useful.)

Chapters 1–6

In addition to those works previously cited, the following are useful.

ANDERSON, E. and P., *Political Institutions and Social Change in Continental Europe in the Nineteenth Century*, Berkeley, California, 1968, 461 pp.

CLARKE, I. F., 'Forecasts on warfare in fiction', in *Comparative Studies in Society and History*, 1967, I.

CONTAMINE, H., *La Revanche*, Paris, 1957, 280 pp.

DEDIJER, V., *The Road to Sarajevo*, London, 1967, 550 pp.

GEISS, I., *July 1914: Selected Documents*, London, 1967, 400 pp.

GIRARDET, R., *La Société militaire en France*, Paris, 1960, 328 pp.

HAUPT, G., *Le Congrès manqué*, Paris, 1965, 300 pp.

MORAZE, C., *Les Bourgeois conquérants*, Paris, 1957, 491 pp.

STONE, N., 'Army and society in the Habsburg monarchy 1900–1914', in *Past and Present*, 33, April 1966.

STERNBERG, F., *Le conflit du siècle*, Paris, 1957.

VIGEZZI, B., *L'Italia di fronte alla prima guerra mondiale, I. Italia neutrale*, R. Ricciardi, Milano-Napoli, 1966, 1007 pp.

Chapters 7–13

To the works cited above should be added:

BIDOU, H., *Histoire de la Grande Guerre*, Paris, 1939, 696 pp.

BROOKS, ROBIN, 'Domestic violence and America's wars', in *The History of Violence in America*, by H. D. Graham, T. R. Gurr and S. Herbers, New York, 1969, 821 pp.

CRU, N., *Témoins*, Paris, 1929, 727 pp.

DUROSELLE, J. B., *De Wilson à Roosevelt*, Paris, 1960, 493 pp.

FELDMAN, G., *Army, Industry, and Labor in Germany: 1914–18*, Princeton, 1968, 572 pp.

HURWITZ, S. J., *State Intervention in Great Britain*, Columbia, N.Y., 1949, 321 pp.

LASSWELL, H. D., *Propaganda Techniques in the World War*, New York, 1938, 233 pp.

PARIS, R., *Histoire du fascisme en Italie* (1), Paris, 1962.

PERICARD, J., *Verdun*, Paris, 1933, 534 pp.

PETERSON, H. C. and FITE, G. G., *Opponents of War, 1917–1918*, Madison, Wisconsin, 1957.

PAXSON, F., *America at War*, Boston, 1939, 2 vols.

RATINAUD, J., *La Course à la mer*, Paris, 1967, 365 pp.

RENOUVIN, P., *Les Crises du XXe siècle*, Paris, 1957, 2 vols.

SCHERER, A., and GRUNEWALD, J., *L'Allemagne et les problèmes de la paix*, Paris, 1962 (documents published by the authors).

There is a useful up-to-date bibliography in HERZFELD, H., *Der erste Weltkrieg*, Munich, 1968, 371 pp.

Chapters 14–18

In addition to the works cited above, the following are useful. Most important are:

KRIEGEL, A., *Aux origines du communisme français*, Paris, 1964, 2 vols.

MAYER, A., *Politics and Diplomacy of Peacemaking, Containment, and Counter-revolution at Versailles*, New York, 1967, 920 pp.

I have also used:

CARR, E., *The Bolshevik Revolution*, London, 1950–3, 3 vols.

DELMAS, J., *L'Etat-Major français et le front oriental* (November 1917–November 1918), 3rd cycle, Sorbonne, Paris, 1965.

FAY, V., FERRO, M., BROUE, P., KRIEGEL, A., DE CLEMENTI, TYCH, F., NAGY, B., STEINER, H., and SCHARF, J., *La Révolution d'Octobre et le mouvement ouvrier européen*, Paris, 1968, 229 pp.

FERRO, M., *La révolution de 1917* (1), Paris, 1967, 606 pp. Translated in full into English as *The Russian Revolution of February 1917*, London, 1972.

GUERIN, D., *Fascisme et grand capital*, Paris, 1936, 269 pp.

ISNENGHI, M., *I vinti di Caporetto*, Marsilio, Padua, 1967, 270 pp.

KARLINER, M., *Rabocheye dvizheniye v Anglii v gody 1914–1918*, Moscow, 1961, 487 pp.

KIROVA, K., *Revolyutsionnoye dvizheniye v Italii. 1914–18*, Moscow, 1962, 432 pp.

LUTZ, R. H., *The Fall of the German Empire*, Stanford, 1932, 2 vols.

PEDRONCINI, G., *Les Mutineries de 1917*, Paris, 1967, 325 pp.

ULLMAN, R. H., *Intervention and the War*, Princeton, 1961, 345 pp.

Revue d'Histoire moderne et contemporaine, January–March 1968, a special number on 1917.

Journal of Contemporary History, 4, 1968, an issue entitled 'From war to peace'.

I have also used the Klotz Archives (BDIC) and several sources in the military archives at Vincennes.

Index

Index

Index

Index

Index

MacDonald, Ramsay, 158, 161, 195
Malvy, Minister, 148, 151, 158-9, 198-200 *passim*
Mangin, General, 127, 137, 216
Mann, Thomas, 113
Mannerheim, C. G. E., 209
Margari, 164
Marne, battles of, 52-5, 57-8, 77, 95, 152, 216-17
Martov, 159, 161, 163, 164, 193
Marx, Karl, 35
Masaryk, T. G., 16
Massis, Henri, 13
Maud'huy, General de, 63
Maunoury, Henry, 53-4, 169
Maurras, Charles, 13, 14
Max, Prince (Baden), 180, 218-21 *passim*
Mayer, J., 154
Megiddo, 217
Mensheviks, 191-2, 195
Merrheim, A., 158, 164, 168
Merrheim, Charles, 160
Mesopotamia, 67
Messimy, Minister, 148
Metz-Thionville fortifications, 31
Meyer, A. O., 122
Meyer, Jacques, 92
Mexico, 114-15
Michael, Prince, 186
Michaelis, Chancellor, 196
Michel, Bernard, 99
Micheler, 83
Middle classes, 145, 157-8, 189-90
Middle East campaigns, 65-7, 103-5
Military disputes with politicians, 147-54
Millerand, A., 87, 148-50
Milyukov, P. N., 147, 185, 187, 190-1, 195
Minenwerfer, 87
Mines, 110
Minorities, 10-11, 15, 46, 98-103, 161
Mitteleuropa, 141, 144, 223
Modigliani, G. E., 168
Möllendorf, W. J. H. von, 154
Molotov, Y. M., 185
Moltke, H., 31-3, 43-4, 49-55 *passim*, 152
Monatte, 164
Monnerville, Gaston, 150
Monro, General, 66
Monte Grappa, 217
Montenegro, 72

Morand, Paul, 128
Morocco, 105, 127-8
Moslem world, Germany and, 23
Moutet, Marius, 194
Mulhouse, 49
Müller-Meiningen, Ernst, 124
Munitions, 55, 58, 78, 118, 131, 135
Mussolini, Benito, 68, 69, 157, 163
Mutinies, 83, 181-4, 185, 187-8, 196-198 *passim*, 202-3, 213, 220
Mysticism, 5

Naegelaen, Raymond, 89
Namur, 49
Nationalism, 12-16, 38, 46, 138, 225
Nationality movements, 10, 16, 46, 98-104
Naumann, Friedrich, 102
Naval: rivalry, 20, 27-8; warfare, 106, 108, 109-11, 125
Nazism, 154, 175
Nenni, Pietro, 69
Nerman, Ture, 169
Netherlands, 132
Neutral trade, 106-10, 130-2
Newspapers: non-political, 5; trench, 154-6
Nicaragua, 111
Nicholas, Grand Duke, 57
Nicholas II, Tsar, 45, 122, 138, 180-1, 186
Nicod, 159
Nivelle, General, 78, 81-3, 148, 151, 152, 181, 183, 184, 194, 198
Nixon, Sir J., 67
Nobility, 3-4
Noske, 220-1
Novoe Vremya, 5
Noyon, 216
Nuremberg, 44

Oriani, Alfredo, 24
Orlando, V. E., 148
Ostend, 111

Pacifists, 9, 14, 38, 75, 113-16, 148, 158-9, 176, 182, 198, 200-1; *see also* Peace movement
Painlevé, Paul, 82-3, 181, 183, 198-9
Paléologue, M. G., 43, 45, 60
Palestine, 140, 217
Pan-German League, 15
Pan-Slavism, 16, 17, 46
Pan-Turanianism, 103-4, 143

236

Index

Index

Index

Trench: newspapers, 154–6; warfare, 47, 62–5, 70, 77, 86–93
Treves, Claudio, 69
Triple Alliance, 23–4
Tripolitania, 23–4, 104
Troelstra, P. J., 164
Trotsky, L. D., 161–2, 165, 208–10 *passim*
Tschirschky, Ambassador, 40
Tseretelli, 192–3, 195
Tuchman, Barbara, 32
Turati, 201, 202
Turkestan revolt, 103
Turkey: Allied aims, 139–40; armistice, 218; attacks on, 65–6, 100–1, 217; German colonization, 23; war aims, 143
Typhus, 71, 72, 121
Tyrol, 72–3

Ukraine, 209–11 *passim*
Unemployment, 158
Union of Democratic Control, 161, 176
Union sacrée, 145–6, 159–60, 162, 164, 172–3, 199
United Kingdom, *see* England
United States of America: conscription, 115, 116; European immigrants, 6; intervention in war, 100, 106, 110–17 *passim*, 119, 121, 124–125, 153, 205, 217. 220; neutral trade, 106, 107, 113–14, 130; pacifism, 113–16; Sedition Act 1916, 116; troops in action, 217, 218

Vaillant, E., 34, 159
Vandervelde, E., 159
Varenne, Alexander, 199
Venizelos, E., 65, 66, 71
Verdun, 54–6, 72, 74–8, 91, 93, 94, 152–3
Versailles Treaty, 222–3
Victor Emmanuel, King, 68, 69
Vigezzi, 68
Villa Giusti, 219
Villers-Cotterêts, 95, 216
Vimy ridge, 64, 83
Vittorio Veneto, 217
Viviani, R., 150, 181
Vliegen, 37

Vorwärts, 160

Wages, 171–2, 177
Waldow, Graf von, 219
Wallonia, 103
War: aims, 19–20, 24–5, 28, 43–4, 68, 98, 127, 133–4, 136–44, 191–3; civil, 9; costs of, 130, 223; declaration of, 21, 39–46; duration forecasts, 27–9 *passim*, 31, 46, 51; glorification of, 13; guilt, 45; patriotic, 9–18; preventive, 33; to end war, 8; total, 113, 118–21, 153, 199; trench, 47, 62–5, 70, 77, 86–93; weariness, 75–6, 79, 177, 180, 182, 193; world, 118, 205; *see also* Causes of war
Warski, A., 168
Wassmuss, 104
Waxweiler, 134
Weapons, 83–4, 87–8, 92–6, 110, 205, 216–17
Wells, H. G., 27
Weygand, General, 222
White Russians, 209–12, 217
Wilhelm II, Kaiser, 21, 40–3 *passim*, 122, 141, 174, 219–21 *passim*
Wilson, President, 98, 100, 113–15 *passim*, 117, 138, 140, 193, 195, 208–9, 211, 212, 219
Women in wartime, 170–1, 225
Working class, 169–79; enthusiasm for war, 3, 7; social aspirations, 8; *see also* Discontent, popular
World revolution call, 208–9
World War, 118, 205

Yanushkevitch, Grand Duke, 60
Young Socialists' conferences, 164
Ypres, 56, 63
Yuan Chi-Kai, 117
Yugoslavia, 98, 100, 136, 219

Zeebrugge, 111
Zeppelins, 94
Zetkin, Clara, 164
Zhilinsky, 57
Zimmermann, A., 114–15, 142
Zimmerwald Manifesto, 164–9, 173–4, 192, 198
Zinoviev, G. E., 164, 210